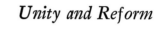

Unity and Reform

Statue of Cardinal Nicholas de Cusa in His Titular Church in Rome

UNITY
AND REFORM

Selected Writings of

NICHOLAS DE CUSA

Edited by

JOHN PATRICK DOLAN

UNIVERSITY OF NOTRE DAME PRESS

PREFACE

It would be a "praesumptio periculosa" to attempt in a few pages
an evaluation of the writings of Nicholas of Cusa. Like the century in which he lived, much remains to be investigated. The
breakup of Western Christian unity that followed so soon after
his tireless efforts to preserve it, has led many to believe that his
was entirely an age of disquiet, of decadence, an era that witnessed the anti-climax of all previous intellectual development.
Even more widespread is the conviction that there was then, or
is today, a basic contemporary philosophy. Then, as now, continual cross-relations between various schools of thought were
producing a variety of hybrids. The fifteenth century was, like
our own, rich and variegated in intellectual productivity and Cusa
towers above most of those who contributed to its richness.

Few great thinkers have enjoyed fame in their own lifetime,
even fewer have exerted a great influence on the problems of
their own age. Philosophy by its very nature must transcend the
here and now. Yet to many, the thought of Cusa has a certain
"nowness" that reaches beyond mere fascination or vogue. The
very structure and depth of his thinking makes it challenging. His
writings are more to be ruminated than merely read, or better
yet, they are more to be meditated upon.

It is the purpose of these selections to afford the ordinary reader
this opportunity. A critical analysis, a more penetrating appraisal

we leave to the specialists. Regardless of the often conflicting judgments of his critics, it must be borne in mind that his guiding principle is not conformity to a system but rather compatibility with the content of faith. For Cusa the ultimate realities of human and cosmic existence fall within the object of revelation and involve the world as known by science as well as philosophy. His quest for the ultimate operates always between the poles of the mind's ceaseless search for ultimate truth and God's revelation of its essential elements.

Himself a humanist, a scholar, a scientist and mathematician, as well as a churchman, Cusa is a personal synthesis of the disparate elements of his time, a concrete instance of diversity in unity and unity in diversity. His relevance to our own century is only too evident; his spirit is a pattern, his failure a warning.

JOHN P. DOLAN
Notre Dame, Indiana

ACKNOWLEDGMENTS

Sincere thanks are extended the publishers concerned for permission to reprint selections from the books *Of Learned Ignorance* and *The Vision of God*. The publisher of the former book is Routledge & Kegan Paul, Ltd., London, and it was issued in 1954. The Frederick Ungar Co. of New York published *The Vision of God* in 1960. The American rights to this book are held by E. P. Dutton Co., New York.

All other translations are the editor's own and are from the Paris edition of Cusa's *Opera*, ed. Jacques Lefèvre d'Etaples (Badius, 1514) and the Basle edition of 1565.

The frontispiece is a photograph of the statue of Cusa in his titular church, San Pietro in Vincoli, and was executed by Andrea Bregno.

CONTENTS

Unity and Reform

INTRODUCTION

THE REVIVAL OF an interest in Nicholas of Cusa, a man who
perhaps more than any other in his century perceived the
changing relationship between the individual and the community, between medieval man and the expanding universe of the
Renaissance, has marked the beginning of one of the most
startling studies in the history of ideas. Even the vast periphery
of his scientific and philosophical achievements astounds the
modern reader. As a philosopher, astronomer, physicist, and
humanist he represents medieval man already plunged into the
social, economic, and religious flux that was the fifteenth century. As metaphysician he perfected an intellectual system
whose profundity and subtlety provides a unique relationship
to both the philosophy of the Middle Ages and that of modern
times. His emphasis on the quantitative rather than the qualitative, on the transrational rather than the rational, marks him
as a pioneer in the break-through that was to produce the pre-
vailing ideologies of man in the Western world. As an astronomer he anticipated to a certain extent the discoveries of
Copernicus and set the stage for the tremendous reappraisal
of the universe that was to culminate in the discoveries of Kep-
ler and Newton. Koyre has recently dampened some of the

3

enthusiasm felt for Cusa's astronomical doctrines, but he does praise him for his modernity. "We cannot but admire the boldness and the depth of Cusa's cosmological conceptions which culminate in the astonishing transference of the universe to the pseudo-Hermetic characterizations of God."[1]

The impetus theory as well as the entire field of dynamics were explored by him. Von Humboldt, like Regiomontanus and Campanella, found him a precursor in exposing the new cosmology. Few of the advocates of religious tolerance in the sixteenth century escaped his influence. Bodin, Postel, Castellio and d'Etaples all indicate a dependence upon him for their theories on religious pluralism. The latter speaks of his as the "summa et intellectualis theologia quae in pace veritatem indagat, et in silento docet" in contrast to the "imaginaria, quae in multiloquio perstrepit."[2] Descartes was to remark of him: "En premier lieu, je me souviens que le cardinal de Cusa et plusieurs autres docteurs ont supposé le monde infini, sans qu'ils aient jamais été repris de l'Eglise pour ce sujet."[3]

Modern philosophers have acclaimed him as the precursor of Kant as his *Learned Ignorance* parallels in purpose and scope the *Critique of Pure Reason*.[4] If some find him to be a mystic Kant, his discussions on ultimate reality and his denial of the principle of contradiction warrant the belief that he anticipated the philosophy of Hegel. Certainly Leibnitz demonstrates an affinity to his basic ideas,[5] and the French trans-

1. A. Koyre, *From the Closed World to the Infinite Universe* (Baltimore: The Johns Hopkins Press, 1957), p. 18.
2. Quoted in P. Rotta, *De Docta Ignorantia* (Bari, Italy: Laterza, 1913), p. xxx.
3. Cousin (ed.), *Lettres à Chanut*, Ep. I, 32, XX, p. 46.
4. E. Gilson, *History of Christian Philosophy in the Middle Ages* (New York: Random House, 1955), p. 536.
5. E. Vansteenberghe, *Le Cardinal Nicholas de Cues* (Paris: Librairie H. Champion, 1920), pp. 450–451.

lator of his works, Moulinier, describes him as "l'Annoncia-
teur de la Pensée moderne."[6] Martin Buber feels that Cusa
brought about a new anthropological trend in understanding
man's relationship to the universe. He writes:

> For Cusa there is not a thing which would not prefer its own being
> to all being and its own way of being to all other ways of being; all
> that it wishes in eternity is to be nothing but itself, but to be this
> one thing always more perfectly in the way proper to its nature; it is
> precisely from this that the harmony of the universe grows, for
> every being contains everything in a special 'contradiction' . . . Man
> has in himself all created things like God; but God has them in
> himself as archetypes, man has them in himself as relations and values.[7]

Karl Jaspers remarks of him: "Nicholas of Cusa is the first
philosopher of the Middle Ages whom we encounter in an
atmosphere which seems to us our own . . . His is an all-embracing thought, lovingly close to reality, yet transcending
it. The world is not circumvented but itself shines in the light
of transcendence."[8] Yet certain neo-Thomists associate him
with the dangerous nihilistic tendencies attributed to Bardaev
and his neo-Platonic symbolism.[9] Others would seem to as-
cribe to him a neo-gnostic approach to Christianity.[10]

The French historian Duhem has traced his influence upon
Leonardo da Vinci.[11] His knowledge of medicine and blood
circulation are reflected in the later discoveries of Harvey and

6. L. Moulinier, *De la docta Ignorantia* (Paris: Librairie Filex Alcan, 1930),
p. 32.
7. M. Buber, *Between Man and Man* (Boston: Beacon Press, 1955), p. 130.
8. K. Jaspers, *Way to Wisdom* (New Haven: Yale University Press, 1960),
p. 182.
9. J. Anderson, *The Bond of Being* (St. Louis: Herder, 1949), pp. 198–200.
10. A. Lidell, "The Significance of the Doctrine of the Incarnation in the
Philosophy of Nicholas of Cusa," *Actes du XIème Congrès international de
Philosophie* (Amsterdam, 1953), vol. XI, pp. 126–131.
11. P. Duhem, "Nicolas de Cues et Leonard de Vinci" in *Etudes sur Leonard
de Vinci* (Paris: Librairie Scientifique, 1909), v. 2.

Linacre in England.[12] It is interesting to note that the calendar reforms that he presented to the Council of Basle were later incorporated into the Gregorian reform of 1582 and form the basis of present-day time determination.[13] His contacts with religious recusants of the day, especially with the Muslim world, mark him as centuries ahead of his time as an authority on religious pluralism.

Thus Nicholas of Cusa occupies a unique position in the intellectual history of late medieval society. Not only his social and political works, but his philosophical writings give evidence of trends that on the one hand demonstrate his scholastic background and on the other indicate his emancipation from the metaphysical necessitarianism that was so much a part of the latter. The diversity of his thought does not, however, result in mere ambiguity or contrast, rather it gives rise to a system that while retaining the inner consistence and rigor of the schoolmen, far surpasses them in cosmological and anthropological perspective. He was perhaps more than any other in his age the symbol of that grand endeavor that sought a conception of the universe "apte à permettre la réharmonisation des facultés humaines désorbitées, la synthèse des acquisitions sociales, et le plan pour une reconstruction du monde."[14]

Yet to understand Cusa it is necessary to appraise him in terms of his times and the problems that confronted him in a world that like our own was in a period of transition.

12. R. Creutz, "Medizinisch-physicalisches Denken bei Nicolaus von Cues," *Sitzungsberichte der Heidelberger Akademie der Wissenschaften* (Heidelberg, 1939), pp. 14–31.

13. L. Pastor, *Geschichte der Päpste* (Freiburg: Herder, 1923), IX, 205.

14. F. Hermens, *Histoire Doctrinale de L'Humanisme Chrétien* (Paris: Casterman, 1948), I, 10.

It was an age in which the earlier dream of temporal unity, the theocratic vision of a unified Europe fostered by the papacy, seemed to many to be out of touch with reality. Feudalism and vassalage, once the instruments of papal direction, had become no more than worn-out symbols. The rediscovery of the ancient world had brought with it a growing suspicion that the Church, which by definition was universal, had in the historic process been confused with a small number of peoples and a limited extent of territory. "The Church, charged with leading men of every race and every background to divine salvation, had, through historical necessity, shouldered the risk of being linked to a particular civilization, and of being known only through a temporary expression of its earthly destiny, that of Western Christendom." [15] The clerical monopoly in education had been weakened and the universities themselves had been captured to a great extent by the particularism of nascent nationalism.

Yet there were also grounds for optimism. Religion was to remain the most cogent factor in the life of individuals as well as nations. The healing of the Great Schism and the spirit of the early Renaissance both heralded the hope that society and institutions, not merely individuals, could be changed for the better. There was a feeling that a free unfolding of the human spirit was ushering in a new age.

Thus to reduce Cusa to the instigator of a novel pantheism, or the prophet of a gloomy skepticism [16] is to overlook the perplexities of the century in which he lived and to fail to see

15. B. Guillemain, *The Later Middle Ages* (London: Burns & Oates, 1960), p. 117.
16. R. Stadelmann, *Vom Geist des Ausgehenden Mittelalters* (Halle: Niemyer, 1929), pp. 39–65.

him against the background of change and contrast in religion and social structure of his day. He must be measured in terms of those peculiar forces that dominated the late Middle Ages, Nominalism in theology, conciliarism in Church polity, and above all in terms of the new spirit of human progress of which he was so much a part.

Nicholas Cryfts (Krebs) was born in the village of Cusa on the Mosel in 1401, the son of an enterprising barge operator. The Rhineland was not only the commercial artery of northern Europe; it had been for centuries the melting pot into which the various elements that shaped the destiny of western Europe for a thousand years were poured and amalgamated. Here Roman, Celtic and Germanic cultural elements fused to form the prototype of the *Respublica Christiana*. It was in this region that Latin Christianity had first encountered the Nordic impulse that was to inform and strengthen it for a millennium. The Porta Nigra of Trier had echoed to the shouts of the legionnaires proclaiming Constantine emperor, and Saint Helena had enriched the city with churches and Christian shrines. Cologna Agrippinensis (Cologne) became the Rome of the north, the great metropolis of northern Europe straddling the trade routes from east to west, from north to south. Its magnificent cathedral stands today on the ruins of temples dedicated to pagan Mithras and the Matrona. The rich vineyards along the Mosel were producing their famous vintages when Coblenz (Confluentia) was yet a bastion of Roman military defenses. Charlemagne had envisioned Aix-la-Chapelle as the center of his Christian empire, the Roma Nova of the West. It was the valley of the Rhine also that was to nurture the great intellectual movements that were so formative in Western religious thought. Aquinas had sat at the feet of Albertus Magnus in the lecture halls of the University of Cologne. The Rhenish mystics Suso, Tauler, Ruysbroeck radiated a new vitality for the contemplative life and the Archpoet of Cologne gave a new direction to medieval poetry.

The lively commercial spirit of the petite bourgeoisie in nearby Coblenz, with its concomitant cultural stimulus, was not lost on the prosperous citizenry of Cusa. Like many others of the rising commercial class, Nicholas was sent to the Brothers of the Common Life at Deventer on the Lower Rhine for his early education. Pioneering in a new pedagogical experiment, the Fratres came to exert a profound influence on the educational methods of northern Europe during the succeeding century. They were to list among their later prodigies Erasmus, Pope Adrian VI, Calvin, and Luther. There is perhaps undue emphasis on the influence of the Brothers of the Common Life upon the youthful Cusa. In the years that he attended the cathedral school at Deventer it had not achieved the reputation that it enjoyed a half-century later under Alexander Heigus and Cusa's devotee, Rudolph Agricola. It is, in fact, not proper to speak of the schools of the Brothers at this early period. In 1398 the Brothers had established at Deventer a *Domus Pauperum* or hostel in connection with the cathedral school which aimed at providing young students with food and lodging in a religious atmosphere rather than with academic classes. As Paulsen remarks: "The Brothers were not a body of teachers in the sense that the Jesuits afterwards were. Certainly they were not humanist teachers."[17] Yet they inculcated a spirit of inquiry and piety that was no small factor

17. W. H. Woodward, *Studies in Education, 1400–1600* (Cambridge: Cambridge University Press, 1924), p. 83.

in the spread of learning during the period of the Renaissance
and Reformation. In the realm of education the initial impetus
of the Brethren was one of reaction and reform. Following the
ideals of their founder, Gerard Groot, they continued his attempt to strive for Christian perfection without the help of
vows, opposing the recognized principle that the monastic life
was not only superior to any other, but the only acknowl-
edged way of even aiming at holiness. The Brethren became
living contradictions of this principle. Their saintly lives, without vows, cut deeply into the façade of pseudo-piety exercised
by so many of the hypocritical religious of their day. Monas-
ticism, with its ideal of withdrawal from the world and its
rejection of so-called temporal goods, was ill adapted to the
urban mentality so active in the Rhineland. As Hyma remarks:

> The whole institution of the Brethren was a living protest against
> the decadent monasticism of the fifteenth century. Groot's brother-
> hood was one of the chief causes of that phase of the Reformation
> which in certain regions involved the disappearance of monasticism,
> and everywhere in the West produced a growing desire for more
> personal faith, more religion in the schools, more knowledge of the
> Bible, a saner method of discipline, and a reaction against all manner
> of empty formalism including a return to the use of the people's
> language.[18]

In addition to inculcating a new spirit of personal piety and
reform—a living faith as opposed to useless formalism—the
Brethren also influenced Cusa by awakening in him a desire
for the new learning that was sweeping Europe. As copyists
the Brethren did not stress the copying itself so much as the
books they copied and why. They not only copied the books
but they translated them into the vernacular. They repro-

18. Hyma, *The Christian Renaissance* (Grand Rapids: Zondervan, 1924), pp.
114–115.

duced the Bible, corrected and translated it; they copied the writings of Groot and Radewijns, the Fathers of the Church, and some of the saints. They developed the idea of collecting excerpts, *rapiaria* as they called them, or little snatches from noted authors which drove home a moral point. The outstanding example of this is, of course, the *Imitation of Christ* by Thomas à Kempis, who was with the Brethren during the same time as Cusa. The protest in the *Imitation* against formalism and "useless learning" of the early fifteenth century finds its echo in Cusa's own writings. Later in his career Cusa was to defend the Brethren and their system against the Carthusian Vincent of Aggsbach.[19]

As Jedin points out:

> The 'devotio moderna' meant personal reform through a return to Christian inwardness. As a free movement it was not limited, as were the monastic reforms, to a corporation already in existence and regulated by law, nor was it burdened by any traditions; hence it was able to develop in every direction; but it cannot be said that it exhibited any novel features: the only new thing about it was the earnestness with which it strove for the unchanging goal—the following of Christ. . . . Like all genuine religious movements it issued in active work.[20]

He adds significantly that there was a definite "lay" element in the movement,[21] a characteristic that was not without its influence on Cusa.

At least there can be no doubt that Cusa left the school at Deventer well equipped with a knowledge of the classics and the spirit of the "devotio moderna" with its emphasis on the

---

19. E. Vansteenberghe, "Autour de la docte ignorance," *Beiträge zur Geschichte der Philosophie des Mittelalters*, XIV, 2–4.
20. H. Jedin, *Geschichte des Konzils von Trient* (Freiburg: Herder, 1951), p. 116.
21. "Die devote Bewegung hatte einen stark laikalen Einschlag," *ibid.*

more personal approach to Christ. An interest in manuscripts was to engender in Cusa a thirst for research in the classics that was to rank him among the pioneers in the study of paleography and one of the outstanding bibliophiles of his time.

Cusa's matriculation at the University of Heidelberg in 1416, registering as a cleric from the diocese of Trier, marked the beginning of a university career that was to bring him in contact with some of the outstanding minds and intellectual currents of the early fifteenth century. Although his stay at Heidelberg was of such short duration that it would be presumptuous to assert that the Nominalism represented there, particularly in the tradition of Marsilius of Inghen, influenced him as deeply as his biographers contend, nonetheless, a strong element of nominalistic philosophy was encountered here, and it gradually formed part of the background over against which Cusa's theological thought was to take shape. It is evident that at least his initial contact with the "via moderna" occurred at the famous school on the Neckar. It can be assumed that the intellectual independence that was so much an ingredient of Nominalism and its disagreement with the conviction that metaphysics demand the same rigor of proof as mathematics came to Cusa's attention here. The doctrines of Inghen and Buridan, that rational or discursive proof is an approximate rather than an absolute approach to truth, left its stamp on the inquiring mind of Cusa as a result of his studies at Heidelberg.

A growing interest in the study of Nominalism during recent years has done much to dispel the disrepute in which the so-called "via moderna" is generally held. No longer tenable are the theories of such Catholic critics as Grisar, Denifle and Weis who see in Nominalism the chief factor in the break-up

of Christendom. Karl Meissinger finds that there has been a
Thomistic prejudice against Ockamism which in the light of
more searching studies is gradually giving way to the realization that late-medieval Nominalism or the "via moderna" possessed a richness and cohesion whose study may introduce a
new epoch in the history of theology.[22] Previously Gerhard
Ritter's study of Marsilius of Inghen had brought to light the
diversity of theological thought on what is termed Nominalism.[23]

Although the history of late-medieval scholasticism is an
area in which a great deal of research has been done, it remains,
like the entire fifteenth century, an unchartered field. The belief that there was one dominant thought-pattern which was
nominalist and decadent does not correspond to historical reality. Nominalism is found to be but one of several schools of
thought of this period and it means overworking the term to
apply it to a variety of movements often differing among
themselves. In spite of the late Cardinal Ehrle's warning against
the misleading vagueness of the term,[24] many continue to misuse it in sweeping generalizations. One might question the
assertion of E. L. Mascall on Bouyer's indictment of Nominalism,

. . . Bouyer is fundamentally correct in his assertion that the dead-
lock between Catholics and Protestants on the theological level has
been mainly due to their common inheritance of uncriticised, but
highly criticisable, assumptions and thought-forms from the theologically decadent late Middle Ages, and that of these by far the most

22. K. Meissinger, *Der Katholische Luther* (Berne: Francke, 1952), pp. 104–
105.
23. G. Ritter, *Studien zur Spätscholastik* (1); *Marsilius von Inghen und die
okkamistische Schule in Deutschland* (Heidelberg, 1921), pp. 165–179.
24. F. Ehrle, *Der Sentenzenkommentar Peters von Candia* (Münster: Aschendorf, 1925), pp. 108–205.

insidious and vicious, with its barren and spectral extrinsicism, was the nominalist outlook which had come to dominate philosophy and theology alike.[25]

Using the term merely to circumscribe a philosophical movement seems to place an unwarranted limit on the deep impact that Nominalism exerted in the realm of religion in the late medieval period. Nor was it a baleful influence. It was, in many respects, an evangelical reaction against the influence on Christian thought of the necessitarian doctrine of Aristotelian philosophy. As a movement it led the way to a reform of theology conceived more as a discipline of faith based on tradition and more closely aligned to the tradition of the early Fathers. It followed an eclecticism based on tradition. The basic tenet of the nominalist theologian, that the omnipotence of God, properly understood, renders deductive theology impossible, and that the absolute power of God transcends any route that theologians may devise, based only on God's few revealed acts, finds a certain echo in Cusa's later writings. It went hand in hand with his deep-felt reaction against the attempt on the part of some theologians to reduce the God of Revelation to a sterile and isolated metaphysical principle.

Oberman,[26] in a penetrating analysis of Nominalism as a theology, has indicated the pervading characteristics of this system in the realm of late-medieval religious thought, its craving for divine immediacy, divine sovereignty and human autonomy—themes that were to run through the writings of Cusa. It is particularly under the aspect of its deep sense of divine immediacy and divine sovereignty versus human autonomy

25. E. Mascall, *The Recovery of Unity* (London: Longmans, Green, 1958), p. 91.
26. H. Oberman, "The Theology of Nominalism," *Harvard Theological Review*, LIII, 47–79.

that nominalistic theology formed the background of much of his speculation. The axiom "finiti et infiniti nulla proportio" (that there is no proportion between the finite and the infinite) was to recur time and time again in his writings. His familiarity with the works of Ockham, d'Auriol and Bardwardine can leave little doubt that the notion of God's sovereignty and the autonomy of man were areas of unsolved contradiction that helped mold his presentation of theology of learned ignorance. This he attempts in terms of a better balance between reason and intellect and between contemplation and action. The need for immediacy reflected in late medieval spirituality with its activism, its concern for the tangible, gradually moved Cusa to channel this craving for closer divine contact into a system of rationalized mysticism as opposed to a mysticized rationalism. The "credo in Deum omnipotentem" of the nominalists gave way to an omnipotent Christ.

The point is not whether Cusa was a nominalist. To place him in any particular school, even such a latitudinous school as the Augustinian Platonists would be to fail to perceive his originality. There is a certain dependence on the writings of the Victorine school. Hugh of St. Victor had taught that God's omnipotence is limited only by the rule that He cannot injure Himself. Cusa, in his search for certainty, makes a clear distinction between the revelation of God Himself and the results of discursive philosophy. If his search seems to give rise to a skepticism, it is a skepticism that has the positive effect of stimulating a search for a better expression of the divine. He does not attack revelation but rather puts it into a new setting. Following the methods of the Pseudo-Dionysius and Proclus, he proposes a negative theology that is not in the least nihilistic, but rather, since it frees the positive reality of the Godhead from the conceptual limitations philosophers have placed upon it, is positivistic in the highest sense of the term. E. F. Jacob has recently pointed out:

> Our view of later medieval scholasticism has been revolutionized by appreciation of the struggle that was in progress from the middle of the fourteenth century onwards between the Ockhamist skepticism and the Platonic Augustinian tradition which, stemming from the Victorines, finds its highest expression in the intuitionist theories of Cusanus and the German school. That *docta ignorantia* should have attempted to unite the new logic and the old mysticism in a synthesis based upon mathematical principles was a notable advance in the history of thought.[27]

If philosophical pluralism was a characteristic of the fifteenth century, eclecticism was its handmaid, and here again we see Cusa as a product of his own times. His works demonstrate a blending of many influences, Meister Eckhart, Raymundus Lull, Bonaventure, and Aquinas. Both Haubst[28] and Zellinger[29] have indicated a need for better understanding the all important element of continuity in Cusa's thought. The latter writes of him: "The philosophy of the Cardinal is entirely orthodox and its integrity cannot be attacked. It is our conviction that as with Meister Eckhart a comparison with Thomistic and other approved authorities would surprisingly demonstrate his unimpeachability."[30] The revisionism in Cusa

27. E. F. Jacob (ed.), *Italian Renaissance Studies* (New York: Barnes and Noble, 1960), pp. 21–22.

28. R. Haubst, *Das Bild des Einen und Dreieinen Gott in der Welt nach Nikolas von Kues* (Trier: Paulinus, 1952).

29. E. Zellinger, *Cusanus-Konkordanz* (Munich; Heuber, 1960).

30. "Die Philosophie des Kardinals ist durch und durch orthodox, an ihrer Integrität kann nicht gerüttelt werden. Unserer Überzeugung nach ist es sicher, dass—ebenso wie bei Meister Eckhart wo ein Vergleich mit den thomistischen und anderen als autoritativ sanktionierten Lehren seine Unanfechtbarkeit in übera-schender Weise zum Vorschein brachte—dasselbe bei Cusanus der Fall sein würde." *Ibid.*, xv.

is in no way revolutionary nor a deviation from orthodoxy but rather a studied development.

Cusa expresses this need for development of what has gone before in the limited context of the *Docta Ingorantia* but it applies to his entire philosophical effort. "The immense intellectual satisfaction given by the previous consideration serves merely as an incentive to our ever-inquisitive mind to go on and discover the way to a still clearer conception of the Maximum." [31] What, perhaps, gives his writings a certain novelty is his departure from the traditional medieval summary (*summae*) presentation to a more essayist or dialogue style. To this he adds a cosmological tone that considers man as himself, "homo non vult nisi homo."

Like Gerson, whose writings he was later to defend,[32] Cusa came to see the frightful effects of "vain curiosity in matters of faith." The lack of piety and unity in theological education brought him to the conviction that the search for the divine both in practice and in theory should begin with a humble admittance of the inscrutability of the divine. A reaction against essentialistic theology engendered a belief that the grasp of human reason is limited. Unlike Gerson, who aimed at restoring unity within the realm of theology by limiting it to a humble concentration on the data of faith alone, Cusa, with his scientific mind, seeks this restoration in an effort that would transcend the partisan "school squabbles" of the time and find its basis in the more immutable and indefinite realm of mathematics. His application of geometry to the world of reality was

---

31. "Amplius, non satiabilis noster intellectus cum suavitate vigilanter per praemissa incitatus inquirit, quomodo hanc participationem unius maximi possit clarius intueri." *Docta Ignorantia*, I, 18.

32. Vansteenberghe, *op. cit.*, p. 120.

aimed at reducing the complexities of the world to distinct ideas. If the various shades of nominalistic thought that Cusa encountered at Heidelberg and later at Cologne held that metaphysical truth arrived at through deduction is, at most, tentative, his analytical mind was to find the more rigid studies in science and law at the University of Padua a fruitful field for the development of his theology.

The University of Padua was after Bologna the most celebrated school of canon law in all Europe yet there is little reason to doubt that Cusa's decision to enroll there was also motivated by its reputation as a center of scientific learning. Padua lay in the midst of those movements that were reshaping the Europe of the fifteenth century.[33] Not only was it a font of Latin Averroism and Conciliarism but it was and remained until the days of Galileo the leading scientific school of Europe. Perhaps nowhere else in Europe had a more talented and varied group of virtuosos come together than at the University of Padua during the early fifteenth century. Cesarini, the eminent canon lawyer, tempered his lectures on the Decretals with the classical ideals of Cicero. Prosdocino of Beldomandi, already renowned for his works on mathematics and astronomy, inspired a new interest in cosmology. Ugo Benzi and Jacopo of Forli, experts in medicine and Greek studies, represented Renaissance man, combining Hellenic theories with Western practices. The university's peculiar situation on the flank of the Visconti empire and within the shadow of the Republic of San Marco had exposed it to the Byzantine influ-

33. "Padua remained to the days of Galileo the leading scientific school of Europe, the stronghold of the Aristotelian qualitative physics, and the trainer of those who were to break with it. Cusanus, Purbach, Regiomontanus as well as the Italians, all studied at Padua." John H. Randall, "Scientific Method and the School of Padua," *Journal of the History of Ideas*, I, 184.

ences of the latter and the civic humanitarianism of Tuscany. Humanism had first encountered the civic world here in the previous century. It was the political and cultural center of northeast Italy and although it lost much of its power in the struggles between Milan and Venice it continued to attract the outstanding humanists of the age. Its impact on political thought and historical outlook through the writings of Vergario and Conversino continued throughout the early decades of the fifteenth century.[34]

Freed from the fetters of feudalism and devoted to sea travel and commerce, the north-Italian city-states had combined trade and civics with an interest in science and technology. Here for the first time in history an urbanized society united business acuteness with mathematical science. Here as nowhere in the West civil spirit had stuck its roots. Here medieval man in a quest for knowledge had stepped out of the narrow bounds of agrarian existence and occupied himself with the higher culture of business, art, commerce, and science. It was a civic spirit that fostered an awareness of the worth and dignity of the individual personality. Humanism was counterbalanced by the civic spirit of free institutions. There was a growing sense for the world of external experience. Platonic idealism was combined with technology to be adapted to the practical needs of urban life. As Franz Schnabel remarks: "Modern technique based on science and civic status belong together, and the craftsmen of the fifteenth century had developed understanding, exactness, and perseverance to a point where the intellectual triumphs over the emotional." [35]

34. H. Baron, *The Crisis of the Early Italian Renaissance* (Princeton: Princeton University Press, 1955), pp. 102 ff.

35. Franz Schnabel, *Unser Geschichtsbild*, "Wege zu einer universalen Geschichtbetrachtung" (Munich: Bayerischer Schulbuchverlag, 1954), pp. 145 ff.

He points out further that the conditions necessary for the development of modern technique arose in the maturation of the world of the Middle Ages in a soil formed by the talents and strengths of the Roman Germanic peoples. Copernicus and Galileo could only exist because they began as humanists and learned from the Greeks how to question nature before they moved on to their research and discovery. By the fifteenth century Western man was far beyond the knowledge of the Greeks and the Romans and yet there was not a corresponding development in their emancipation from Greek and Roman ideas of the divine. Cusa, like Copernicus and Galileo after him, saw with astonishment that the Greeks had already progressed to a causal science and had formulated natural laws. He perceived that Greek science, however, had stopped at the theory of statics formulated by Archimedes. The long process of medieval growth had brought the West Europeans to a point where the knowledge of the Greeks and Romans was emerging upon a world destined to combine causal deductions with a world of freedom. Exact science and technique were bringing the heritage of antiquity into that mold of strict thought and community of ideas that was later to enable European man to conquer the universe. It was a conquest that Cusa could envision only in terms of its creator, in terms of the Logos. As M. Foster remarks:

Modern natural science could begin only when the modern presupposition about nature displaced the Greek . . .; but this modern displacement itself was possible only when the Christian concept of God had replaced the pagan, as the object of systematic understanding. To achieve this primary displacement was the work of medieval theology, which thus layed the foundations both of much else in the modern world which is specifically modern and of modern natural science.[36]

Cusa represents, in a way, a turning point in the confluence of Hellenic and modern scientific thinking.

For six years Cusa studied in this stimulating milieu witnessing at first hand the new forces that began shifting the balance that had formed the medieval equilibrium between Church and State, and science and religion. At the age of twenty-three he received the coveted doctorate of canon law. The following year he visited the city of Rome, then being restored to the grandeur that was to make it the center of the revival of letters for the next century.

In 1425 Cusa returned to the Rhineland and was given a prebend in the city of Trier, the first of a series of benifices that were to afford him the financial independence required to continue his research. Enrolling at the University of Cologne, Cusa was deeply influenced by the Thomistic doctrines of Hymeric Van den Velde. His debt to Thomas has only recently been appreciated.[37] As a result of a legal document he prepared for the chapter at Saint Andrew's in Cologne, he attracted the attention of Cardinal Giordano Orsini, and entered the service of this humanistic prelate. From that moment on his career as an ecclesiastical diplomat was assured. In the entourage of the great humanist Cardinal, Cusa came into personal contact with the most prominent figures in the "renascentia litterarum," Poggio Brascilioni and Antonio Loschi; men convinced that with the great schism ended a

36. M. Foster, "The Christian Doctrine of Creation and the Rise of Modern Natural Sciences," *Mind* (1934), XLII, 464.
37. R. Haubst, "Zum Fortleben Alberts des Grossen bei Heymerich von Kamp and Nikolaus von Kues," *Beiträge, Studia Albertina, Festschrift für B. Geyer* (1952), pp. 420–447.

new and glorious chapter in the history of Christianity would be ushered in. The rediscovery of the ancient world gave birth to the idea of reconciling religion with the entire world. The rapid development of economic life was making social position more important than juridical status. The old order was breaking down and new groups were forming, based more on a notion of humanity than of class. There was a growing conviction that not only individuals, but society itself could be changed to make a better world.

The Council of Constance had brought churchmen into contact with this new movement for the first time. Poggio, for example, had found a copy of Plautus in a convent in the small city, just as Cusa was to make a similar discovery in Cologne, and for over a century thereafter it was largely men of this stamp who were to steer the humanistic movement into Christian channels. It was the great contribution of the oft-maligned churchmen of this period that they led what could have been a movement detrimental to organized Christianity into the very heart and center of the Christian commonwealth and impregnated it with a deep sense of religion. Cusa, le Treviran, as he was called, was well known and admired by the group of humanists that now gathered in the Curia. As Cassirer remarks: "Any study which is directed towards a study of the philosophy of the Renaissance must take its point of departure from the doctrine of Nicholas of Cusa." [38] There was a growing conviction among this group that the nature of true learning was unlimited progress of the mind. This boundless thirst for knowledge was to be combined in Cusa with a desire

38. E. Cassirer, *Individuum und Kosmos in der Philosophie der Renaissance* (Leipzig: Studien der Bibliothek Warburg, Heft X, 1927), p. 7.

for union and reform that would set him apart from most of his contemporaries as he surpassed them in depth and sincerity. Although Constance had ended the Western schism and the Pope had returned to Rome, it was indeed an uneasy peace that had followed.

The conciliar theory, which was basically an attempt to federalize and democratize the Church, with its emphasis on representation, was still very much alive. It held above all else that the Church was a corporation and that the Pope was not the sole depository of all power in the Church, but rather that authority rests with its members. The Pope and the hierarchy were not founded by Christ but were rather the result of an historical process. Authority was vested in the body of the faithful. The theory continued to operate and had now the majority backing of those who were seriously interested in a reform of the Church, a reform that Constance had not achieved. Although Cusa had come in contact with the advocates of this theory at Heidelberg and Padua, his first association with ecclesiastical politicians representing these views was at the Council of Basle.

It was here that Cusa was to make his mark both as churchman and humanist. Although originally sent to the Council as an advocate of his early patron Elric von Mandersheid in a litigation involving rival claimants to the see of Trier, his recent discovery of an important manuscript of Plautus had aroused the admiration of the humanists and his legal ability attracted the attention of Cesarini, papal legate at the Council. It was at Basle that the decisive battle between the papacy and the conciliar theory was waged, and strangely enough it was Cusa who was to draw the attention of all Europe by his famous *De*

Concordantia Catholica—probably the most original product of the conciliar epoch.[39]

Although the roots of the movement lie much deeper in the past than has usually been assumed, being traceable to the twelfth-century canonist Huguccio,[40] there is no doubt that Cusa's presentation of the theory was the most mature and harmonious of the many theories relating to papal supremacy. Cusa completed his work in 1433 and it may be summarized as a tract relating to the government of the Church and the Empire that revolves about the hierarchical doctrine of the pseudo-Dionysius. For Nicholas, the Church is a divine cosmos from the head of which, Christ, grace flows into humanity. The hierarchy itself is the depository of the priesthood in which the Pope, the bishops, and even simple priests participate. At the same time, since men are by nature free agents, obedience to ecclesiastical laws must depend upon their consent. We see here again the sense of immediacy of representation that colors all of Cusa's thought. The consent of the people, of the subordinates, is the basis upon which bishops represent their diocese and the Council represents the entire Church. For Cusa, the Pope and the bishops are equally the successors of Peter and are therefore vested with the same authority by divine right. Whatever of gradation there is in the Church refers to the use or execution of these powers. The primacy of the Bishop of Rome is in no sense a primacy of jurisdiction. His precedence, like that of Peter's, is that of an administrator. The doctrine of the Pope's plenitude of power over the Church is no more than the work of forgers. Cusa

39. H. Jedin, *op. cit.*, p. 16.
40. See Brian Tierney, *Foundations of the Conciliar Theory* (Cambridge: The Cambridge University Press, 1955).

refers to the famous Donation of Constantine, the alleged transfer of the empire to the Pope.

Long before Lorenzo Valla had exposed what has been termed "the most famous forgery in European history," Cusa had been aware of its apocryphal nature. Although its authenticity had been attacked by anti-papal writers like Wezel in the twelfth century and its legality denied in the thirteenth century by Dubois and Quidort, the support given it by the canonists was an important element in the gigantic struggle between juridical and humanistic elements in the fifteenth century. As Döllinger points out, it was

that large and inexhaustible treasury from which privileges of all sorts could be drawn whenever and however they were needed, and though a forgery, it continued to influence canon and civil law as well as theology for centuries to come—the ceremonial practices it introduced into the Roman Curia are alive today.[41]

Well aware of the historical falsity of the transfer of the empire to the papacy, Cusa continues his treatise by pointing out that supreme power, as well as infallibility, belong to the General Council, which in turn derives its authority directly from Christ as it represents the unanimous agreement of all Christians. For Cusa the difference between the papal decrees —so many of which he knew, like the Donation, to be forgeries—and the decrees of a Council, consists in the fact that the former have already secured the approval of the Church, whereas the latter still demand this approval.

In order to render this misuse of papal power and authority impossible in the future, he proposes the creation of constitutional securities based on a wider concession of powers to

41. Johann von Döllinger, *Fables respecting the Popes of the Middle Ages,* tr. Alfred Plummer (London: Rivingston, 1871), pp. 151–152.

bishops and cardinals. The cardinals should be chosen with the consent of the bishops from the various nations that are included in the Church. The ancient rights of metropolitans and the patriarchical councils should be restored.

The *Concordantia* includes all of the basic ideas of the conciliar theory—the superiority of a council over the Pope, the subjection of papal legislation and administration to the canons, the need of guarantees against misuses of the primacy and a return to "ancient laws." These ideas are cast in a speculative mold from which there issues a conception of the Church as a divine cosmos in which God's will and man's freedom are interlocked. Freedom and order that are aimed at unity are the themes of all Cusa's later writings.

Although he abandoned the anti-papal party of Basle, Cusa never quite relinquished his conciliar theories. Along with Cesarini he joined the papal group of Eugene at Florence, but he continued to maintain that the Pope exists for the "aedificatio ecclesiae," for building up the Church, and that proper measures be established for the containment of papal encroachments.

The triumph of the conciliar party at Basle was short-lived. Yet its success in reconciling certain of the Hussites, reflected in the *Compactata* of Prague, and its practical reform measures aimed particularly at the abuse of curial taxes demonstrated the sincerity of its members. In both of these areas the recommendations of Cusa were valuable. His *Epistolae ad Bohemos*, resulting from an examination of the claims of the Calixtists, brought Cusa for the first time into the arena of religious tolerance and irenicism.

The final breach between the Pope and the conciliarists

occurred during the summer of 1437 and it grew out of a problem ever dear to the heart of Cusa, church reunion. The Eastern Emperor, Palaeologus John VIII, pressed from both the East and the West by the Turkish menace, sought an alliance with the West and expressed a willingness to bring about ecclesiastical communion with Rome. Cusa, along with the archbishop of Tarentaise, was selected to journey to Greece and negotiate the preliminaries for the council. There is no doubt that it was Cusa's influence that overcame the last-minute hesitancy of the Greeks. The Council of Union with the Greeks was inaugurated in April 1438 in the Cathedral of Ferrara in the presence of the Pope and of more than seventy bishops of the West, the Byzantine Emperor, Patriarch Joseph of Constantinople, the archbishops of Ephesus, Nicaea, and Kiev, as well as representatives of the Patriarchs of Alexandria, Antioch, and Jerusalem. Financial difficulties obliged Eugene to move the Council to Florence in January 1439, and in July of that year the bull of union, "Laetentur Caeli," was read by Cardinal Cesarini in Latin and by Bessarion, the Greek humanist of Nicaea, in Greek. The union was in no small way due to the efforts of Cusa and it was therefore not without reason that a grateful Pope should entrust him with an even more important mission of Church unity, the termination of the last schism to affect the Church.

Although the remnants of the rump Council of Basle under the anti-Pope Felix V were small in number, consisting mainly of partisans in Austria, Switzerland, and sections of Bavaria, they nevertheless were represented in many of the universities, including the center of theological learning, the University of Paris. Furthermore, France and Germany, because of their

neutrality, posed an even greater obstacle to Church unification. In May 1438 a national assembly at Bourges had decided
to remain neutral in the dispute between the Council and the
Pope. The German electors had proclaimed their neutrality
at Frankfurt. A policy of neutrality based upon conciliarism
was a danger that had to be eliminated. In October 1438 Cusa
joined with Cardinal Albergati and the archbishop of Tarentaise in a commission aimed at restoring the German estates to
the papacy. Cusa himself pleaded the papal cause at the Diet of
Mainz in 1441, and finally in September of that year the Emperor Ferdinand III and the majority of the electors submitted
it to Pope Eugene. Not without reason was Cusa called the
"Hercules of Eugene" throughout the Empire. France abandoned her neutral position in 1449 and the anti-Pope Felix re-
signed, thus ending the schism. This was a victory for the
papacy in which Cusa could claim a considerable share. As a
reward for his efforts he was named Cardinal *in petto* and actually promoted to the office by Nicholas V in December
1448, with the titular Church San Pietro in Vincoli.

If unity within the Church had been achieved through the
triumph of the papal party, it had been won with a heavy burden. The reforms that had been advocated at the Councils of
Constance and Basle by the northern nations were for the
most part ignored. The conciliar group remained identified
with the party of reform and the task of channeling their influence to closer cooperation with the Holy See was now entrusted to Cusa. Few men in Western Europe were better
qualified to combine unification with reformation than the
recently-appointed German Cardinal of St. Peter in Chains.
In 1450 he was commissioned by the Pope with the title,

legatus a latere, to introduce his reform measures into the Holy Roman Empire. They were reforms that were to affect the *imperium* as well as the Church. Nowhere else in Europe were the tensions that were soon to break asunder the universalism and cultural unity of a thousand years more apparent than in Germany.

If the Christian commonwealth of the Middle Ages had been the result of an amalgamation of Latin and Germanic elements, there was growing evidence that the northern European demanded more than evasive curial promises if he was to remain in the union. The Holy Roman Empire itself was characterized by violence and civil war. The new line of Hapsburg emperors was more concerned with eastern lands in Hungary and Bohemia than it was with the modernization of the imperial administration. Feuds between cities, the emperor, and the princes blocked any real attempts to reform the government. The Turkish menace in the East and the House of Burgundy in the West, with its drive to create a new Middle Kingdom, encroaching on the territories of the Empire from the North Sea to the Jura, had all but paralyzed the central government. Plagues and business depressions had created hostility between a disgruntled proletariat and the powerful conservative forces of the old nobility, tenaciously clinging to their medieval rights and privileges. The recent introduction of Roman law with its principle that the legislator is above the law, was certainly at variance with Cusa's political axiom: "For if by nature men are equally strong and equally free, the true and settled power of one over the others, the ruler having equal natural power, could be set up only by the choice and consent of the others, just as a law also is set up by consent."

His plan for a council of regencies formed by the estates had little chance of acceptance in this centrifugal environment.

Yet the anarchy in government was almost eclipsed by the complete chaos threatening the realm of religion. Tensions between the lower clergy and the aristocratic episcopacy, between the mendicants and the corps of uneducated secular clergy, were intensified by a growing animosity between lay and cleric. An educated laity was losing patience with the rabble-rousing horde of itinerant preachers, who were only too prone to capitalize on the turbulence of the times to peddle salvation. The scholastic sermon, overloaded with theological subtleties, and more often a stereotyped version of a sermon written centuries before, had grown distasteful to the enlightened burgher. Filled with sophisms, it failed completely to touch the problems of the day, nor did sellers of indulgences and relics escape the critical eye of the city-dweller with his sober sense of marketplace value.

Cusa's works of reform are perhaps best epitomized in his *Concordantia* and his *Reformatio Generalis*.[42] In reading Cusa's *De Concordantia Catholica* or his *Reformatio Generalis* one is forcibly reminded of the text of Plato in the *Republic*, where Socrates, having delineated the features of the ideal state, somewhat nostalgically remarks: "Well, perhaps there is a pattern of it laid up in heaven for him who wishes to contemplate it and so beholding to constitute himself its citizen." [43] As Plato had wanted to reform the actual Athenian city-state according to a pattern laid up in heaven, so Nicholas of Cusa

42. This interesting document was edited in the *Historisches Jahrbuch*, by St. Ehses (1911), XXXII, 281–297.

43. Plato, *The Republic*, book IX, 592B, translated by Paul Shorey, Loeb Classical Library (Cambridge: Harvard University Press, 1935).

seeks to reform the Church in the light of the celestial model. The earthly Church, the *Ecclesia peregrina*, must incarnate the heavenly pattern if she is to be a worthy bride, "without spot or wrinkle," for the heavenly bridegroom. The pattern laid up in heaven is the very nature of the Godhead itself: diversity in unity or triune unity.[44] In the created order, but still in the realm of spirit, the angelic hierarchy is modeled on this pattern: three orders, each consisting in turn of three choirs. The angelic pattern is itself the norm for the hierarchically-structured Church on earth.

The Church is, as it were, the epiphany of the invisible divine order, or, at any rate, it should be and must strive to be so.[45] The number three recurs as a *leitmotif* in Cusa's thought: the *Ecclesia* is itself a triune unity, *triumphans, dormiens, militans;*[46] she consists of *sacramenta, sacerdotium, fideles.*[47] Even man reflects this theme of triangular diversity within unity, for he is a composite of *spiritus, anima, corpus.*[48]

The sacerdotal hierarchy which reflects the nine choirs of angels,[49] finds a correspondence in the imperial order which

44. Which Cusa speaks of as *unitas* (*Pater, aequalitas* [*Filius*], *connexio* [*Spiritus*]). Cf. *De Docta Ignorantia*, book I, ch. 9, *Omnia Opera*, ed. Hoffmann, Klibansky (Leipzig, 1932), v. 1–2.

45. Cf. book I of Cusa's *De Concordantia Catholica*, hereafter *CC*, ch. 1–10 in *Omnia Opera*, v. 14, ed. G. Kallen (Hamburg, 1939). The influence of the Pseudo-Dionysius *De caelesti hierarchia et De ecclesiastica hierarchia* at this point is plain. Cf. R. C. Petry, *Christian Eschatology and Social Thought* (to A.D. 1500) (New York: Abingdon Press, 1956), pp. 188–191, for a short discussion of pattern-thinking in Cusa. (The second and third books of the *De Concordantia* were published in 1941 and 1959.) A recent study on Marsilius of Padua points to a dependence upon this famed author for his Aristotelian quotes; see: P. E. Sigmund "Marsilius and 15th-Century Conciliarism," *Journal of the History of Ideas* (1962), XXIII, no. 3, 396–397.

46. *CC*, bk. I, ch. 4, p. 43.

47. *CC*, bk. I, ch. 6, p. 54. These correspond to the heavenly trinity of God, angels, and blessed spirits.

48. *CC*, bk. I, ch. 4, p. 46; this anthropology is borrowed from Augustine as Cusa notes. Cf. Bett, *Nicholas of Cusa* (London: Methuen, 1932), p. 144.

49. *CC*, bk. I, ch. 7, p. 62.

is itself a hierarchical ordering in which the emperor is equivalent to the Pope.[50] The *sacerdotium* and the *imperium* are related to one another as soul to body and just as the soul serves as mediational principle between the spirit and the body, so too does the priesthood serve as mediational[51] principle between the sacramental and the lay (which coincides with the imperial) orders.[52]

We begin to see how intimately, or better, organically related is the whole of reality, for through the principle of mediation Cusa is able to bind the whole of reality together.[53] Evidently, harmony in such an organic structure can not be achieved unless each element or organ fulfills its own particular function with respect to the whole.

According to Cusa's reform theology, harmony will only result when each part of the whole is functioning in the light of its particular pattern, i.e. when each member of the Church is fulfilling the obligations of his vocation within the total complex of the Church's vast life. We are here at the heart of Cusa's reform thought: the restoration of all things to conformity with their archetypes.[54] The very etymology of the word "reformare" indicates return to the purity of a pattern or model.

It is this vision which animates Cusa's reform activity as *legatus a latere* of Nicholas V in 1450–1451[55] and as Bishop of

---

50. *CC*, bk. III, ch. 1, p. 327.
51. Regarding mediation and neoplatonism, cf. Bett, *op. cit.*, pp. 102–103.
52. *CC*, bk. I, ch. 6, p. 56.
53. A treatment of Cusa's organismic philosophy may be found in J. Bohatec, *Calvins Lehre von Staat und Kirche mit besonderer Berücksichtigung des Organismusgedankens* (Breslau: G. Märtin, 1937), pp. 581 ff.
54. We might note here parenthetically the resemblance between such a conception and Plato's idea of justice in *The Republic*.
55. Cf. E. Van Steenberghe, *op. cit.*, ch. 6 and 7.

Brixen in the years following 1452.[56] His work envisions the lay, clerical, and religious elements under his jurisdiction.

Cusa's reform of the laity was aimed at calling the people back to the purity of the Gospel message and away from the corruptions of belief and superstitious practice[57] introduced to a large degree by the anxiety which gripped late medieval Christianity due to the belief that the final end was near at hand.[58] Much of the cardinal's reform work in this regard was carried on through the medium of his own personal preaching.[59]

However, the bishop's primary mode of access to his people is through his clergy and the Bishop of Brixen worked tirelessly at the reform of the diocesan clergy, though not with great success. His instrument of reform was to consist largely in the summoning of local synods, although this proved difficult due to the mountainous nature of his diocese. In spite of vigorous attempts which were quite detailed in scope, the local clergy were highly refractory in their apathy.[60]

The struggle to reform the monasteries was the most exasperating aspect of Cusa's work. Bett[61] and Vansteenberghe[62] both give fairly lengthy accounts of the most famous and difficult of these attempts: that of the monastery of Sonnenburg. A letter written in August 1452 by four mendicant orders

56. *Ibid.*, ch. 9–11.
57. One of the better-known instances of attack on superstition: cf. Bett, pp. 44–46, where the author discusses the "bloody Hosts."
58. Cf. R. C. Petry, *op. cit.*, p. 370 f., and F. M. Powicke, "The Christian Life" in *The Legacy of the Middle Ages* (Oxford: Clarendon Press, 1926), who claims that "superstition was the price paid for universality. It was due to the attempt of pagans to appropriate a mystery." P. 34.
59. Cf. R. C. Petry, "Emphasis on the Gospel and Christian Reform in Late Mediaeval Preaching," *Church History*, XVI, no. 2 (1947), 88–90.
60. Bett, *op. cit.*, pp. 50–52.
61. *Ibid.*, pp. 53 ff.
62. E. Vansteenberghe, *op. cit.*, ch. 9.

(Franciscans, Dominicans, Carmelites, Augustinians) bears witness to the discomfort which Cusa caused them in their work in his attempt to recall them to the faithful observance of their rules.[63]

We get a still clearer insight into his reform policy from his *Reformatio generalis,* which grew out of his appointment to the Papal Reform Commission, a work to which he was called by his longtime friend Aeneas Sylvius, Pius II, in 1460.[64]

To his audience of cardinals Cusa presents the figure of Christ as the ideal, the pattern of the Christian life. It is in imitating this model that the Christian becomes Christiform, i.e. re-made into the image of Christ. The cardinal stresses the need of this re-formation of those who are the eyes of the Body because evidently if they be darkness, one could hardly expect the other organs of the Body to be light.

The substratum of the fourteen rules that Cusa proposes is a principle which we have seen above: restoration of each segment of the Church's life to its *prima forma,* extending not only to clerics, monks, and laity, but to the temporal powers as well.

If one compares Cusa's reform principle to that of a nearly contemporaneous reform movement which eventually ended up outside the Church, the Hussites of Bohemia, one is confronted with a very illuminating distinction between them. The Hussite principle, as expressed by Jakoubek and Nicholas of Dresden, sought a model of purity in the Church of the Gospels and the Apostles as opposed to post-primitive Roman

63. *Cusanus-Texte IV,* "Briefwechsel des Nikolaus von Cues," J. Koch (Heidelberg, Carl Winter, 1943), pp. 111–118.
64. The date is not clear. See Pastor, *op. cit.,* II, 185.

tradition.[65] Cusa's reform movement is not essentially an historical one, i.e., a return to the primitive Church. Rather it is a return to the purity of the Church's ideals as expressed in the early canons and hence does not reject post-primitive tradition but actually affirms it.

It is also worthy of note that there is a certain spirit of nationalism behind the English reform movement of Wycliff and the Czech reform of Huss, which is absent from the reform ideas of Cusa, whose thinking always tends towards the universal and all-embracing.[66]

One of the chief obstacles to the reform envisioned by Cusa was that the Church of his day was in many respects over-institutionalized. It is not without reason that historians often overemphasize the fact that the medieval Church was in many respects a "Rechtskirche."[67] Since the middle of the twelfth century the Church in the West, particularly as a result of the investiture struggle, had gradually assumed all the elements of the Aristotelian and Ciceronian concepts of the State. The papacy itself had been dedicated to the doctrine of St. Paul in terms of government. It was an attempt to translate the "keys of the kingdom of heaven" into "the keys of the law,"

65. Cf. H. Kaminsky, "Hussite Radicalism and the Origins of Tabor (1415–1418)," *Mediaevalia et Humanistica*, X (1956), 105.

66. Cf. E. F. Jacobs, "Nicolas of Cusa," in *The Social and Political Ideas of Some Great Thinkers of the Renaissance and the Reformation*, ed. F. Hearnshaw (New York: Brentano, 1925), pp. 32–60, where a distinction is made between *Kirchentypus*, all-claiming, objective, institutional; and *Sektentypus*, restricted to groups, subjective, mystic, dependent on direct personal relations with God and between its members, p. 33. (The distinction is that of E. Tröltsch.)

67. "Das kanonische Recht und seine gelehrten Kenner erlangten im kirchlichen Leben des Spätmittelalters eine derartige Bedeutung, dass diese Kirche mit gutem Grund auch als Recktskirche bezeichenet werden darf." E. Hassinger, *Das Werden des Neuzeitlichen Europa, 1300–1600* (Brunswick: Westermann, 1952), p. 2.

to direct Europe by means of a universally binding law. Canon law after Gratian formed the "norma recte vivendi" for all members of the *Respublica Christiana*. The application of the Aristotelian categories to the "ecclesia" had given it all the appurtenances of an "ens politicum." The great popes of the period were canon lawyers. They adorned themselves with robes of purple imperial, their tiaras with a golden crown. They rode in procession preceded by imperial banners. Even the liturgy itself had taken on the over-rationalized legal terminology of law-conscious Rome. The successor of Peter was "the prince," the "true emperor." His coronation had eclipsed his consecration in importance.[68] He was not only the vicar of Peter, the vicar of Christ, he was the vicar of God.

The hierarchical apparatus of the Church had itself gradually become the prototype of the absolute and rational monarchy, and the absolutism it affected was absorbed more and more by the emerging national states so as to confront it in the sixteenth century with schism and total rejection. Theology itself became gradually saturated with juridical notions to the point that the Christ of revelation was completely submerged in an ocean of man-made rules and regulations. An angered Dante had pointed out that the chair of Peter was dominated by jurists rather than theologians. The Chancellor of the University of Paris, Jean Gerson, merely voiced the widespread conviction that the real source of the ills affecting Christendom was to be found in the misguided attempt of the papal legalists to rule the secular world in terms of decrees and papal

68. For a well-documented study of this development see E. Kantorowicz, *The King's Two Bodies* (Princeton: Princeton University Press, 1957), pp. 193–231. Also for its present-day relevancy see H. Küng, *The Council, Reform and Reunion* (New York: Sheed and Ward, 1961), pp. 134–145.

bulls.[69] The Mystical Body of Christ once symbolizing a community of believers united in a liturgical and sacramental bond was now become the expression of a juristic corporation. One of the burning questions of the day was whether the Church would be better governed by theologians or lawyers[70] and to political churchmen of the day there was no alternative to affirming the latter.

As E. Kantorowicz points out in his study of medieval political theology,

> . . . the Church which had been the mystical body of Christ, became a mystical body with its own right. That is, the Church organism became a 'mystical body' in an almost juristic sense; a mystical corporation. The change in terminology was not haphazardly introduced. It signified just another step in the direction of allowing the clerical corporational institution of the *corpus ecclesiae juridicum* to coincide with the *corpus ecclesiae mysticum* and thereby to 'secularize' the notion of the 'mystical body.'

He adds further that "in this development Aquinas himself holds a key position. For it is not devoid of some inner logic that the Doctor Angelicus on several occasions saw fit to replace straightforwardly, the liturgical idiom by a juristic term.[71]

A number of recent historians have attempted to explain the case for the canonists in the medieval period. W. Ullmann, in his penetrating analysis of juristic theology answers the criticism often voiced, that from the twelfth century onwards

---

69. "Nil magis turbat totius Christianitatis politam quam velle eadem modo gubernare hominum spiritualitatem et temporalitatem et existimare quod temporalitas proprie sit spiritualitas et jurisdictio proprie spiritualis." Jean Gerson, L. E. du Pin, *Gersonii Opera* (Antwerp, 1706), II, 149.

70. M. Grabmann, "Die Erörterung der Frage, ob die Kirche besser durch einen guten Juristen oder durch einen Theologen regiert werde," *Eichmann Festschrift* (Paderborn, 1941).

71. E. Kantorowicz, *op. cit.*, p. 201.

most of the Popes were canonists rather than theologians by stating that such criticism "is quite unjustified because it fails to take cognizance of the function of the Pope as a monarch who was primarily concerned with the translation of the *principatus* of the Roman Church into practice." He reasons that "a theologian is assuredly not qualified to govern."[72] Tierney[73] tones down Rashdall's description of canonistic science as a "marvellous jurisprudence of spiritual despotism" by pointing to the freedom of thought and expression enjoyed by the canonists themselves. Yet contemporary critics of Catholic theology still voice the conviction that the juridic element is one of the greatest obstacles to a more genuine creativity.

> Roman Catholic dogmatic uses those doctrinal traditions which have gained legal standing as the real source of systematic theology . . . This is the reason for the dogmatic sterility of Roman Catholic theology, in contrast to its liturgical and ethical creativity and the great scholarship it developed in areas of church history which are free from dogmatic prohibitions.[74]

Cusa was well aware that theology, if it were to serve its purpose, had not only to state the truths of the Christian message but also to interpret and adapt the message to each particular generation.

The late medieval Church was not only over-institutionalized and over-legalized, it was predominantly a clerical Church. The disproportionate number of clergy, constituting as they did a clerical proletariat, were not only an offense to

72. W. Ullmann, *The Growth of Papal Government in the Middle Ages* (New York: Barnes and Noble, 1953), p. 373.
73. B. Tierney, "The Canonists and the Medieval State," in *The Review of Politics*," XV, no. 3, 378 ff.
74. P. Tillich, *Systematic Theology* (Chicago: University of Chicago Press, 1951), I, 27. See also Cardinal Suhard's criticism of the juridic elements in the Church, *Growth or Decline* (Chicago: Fides, 1948), p. 28.

laymen because of their ignorance and superstition but above all because they obstructed the economic growth of the towns themselves.[75]

Perhaps an even greater source of the tensions between the Church and the secular world was the growing conviction that Catholicism was completely dominated by the Latin. The fiscal policies of the Church, perfected at Avignon, were more and more associated with the host of Italian bankers and cameral merchants, who acted as papal tax collectors and who not only drained the coffers of the municipalities at regular intervals but who were the middlemen in the profitable sale of papal compositions, absolutions, dispensations and indulgences. The Church, founded to save souls from perdition, was making salvation itself an external appliance. The remission of sins, the certainty of man's peace with God, was reduced to economic expediency. In addition it was the Latin—the French at Avignon and the Italians in Rome—who had instigated the trials and tribulations that beset Christendom from the Babylonian Captivity to the Western Schism. As Mundy remarks: "The central apparatus of the Latin Church was becoming more and more Mediterranean and more Italian."[76] Cusa was one of the last of the northern Europeans to exert an influence in the Curia and was well aware of the nationalistic trend that was weakening the universal character of the Church.

It was Cusa's aim to restore a Logos, Christ, who was neither a legalized fiction nor a fiscalized dispenser of salvation. The

75. A. Störmann, *Die städtischen Gravamina gegen den Klerus* (Münster: Aschendorf, 1916).
76. L. Loomis, ed., *The Council of Constance* (New York: Columbia University Press, 1961), p. 47 of Introduction.

Logos is organically related to the whole of reality, and harmony in such an organic structure cannot be achieved unless each element or organ fulfills its own particular function with respect to the whole. Both Empire and Church were lost in speculation on human and spiritual rights rather than concern for human and spiritual needs. The Church's great error at a time when speedily-evolving institutions were causing confusion was that it rationalized itself out of critical involvement by withdrawing into the stratified hierarchy of an earlier period. It was a withdrawal that produced a false ascetic distance, instead of an awareness of temporal needs. Based upon a limited notion of humanity, it was a failure to realize that man has a horizontal as well as a vertical dimension. The answer was not legal subordination but rather the spirit of cooperation and toleration flowing from the conviction that any organism, political or ecclesiastical, is composed of interests that must be conditioned by mutual dependence. Whereas Augustine meant to warn his readers against the earthly city, Cusa wants to save and improve it by extending the whole concept of humanity and by impregnating the concept with more vitalized notions of Christ's humanity—

> This humanity, being maximal humanity, embraces the total power of the species and is so much the source of being of each man as to stand far closer to him than ever could brother or friend. For the maximal of human nature so works that each man adheres to Him by formed faith. Christ is that man in perfect union while man's individuality remains untouched.[77]

Thus Cusa finds his fundamental conception of humanity embodied in the idea of Christ. The humanity of Christ becomes the bond of the world and the highest proof of its inner

77. See p. 75.

unity; for it is Christ's humanity which bridges the chasm between the infinite and the finite, between the creative first
principle, and the created. Cusa, following the Pauline teaching, that in Christ, "Everything which is in heaven and on
earth is united," holds that if every man is a microcosmos, then
Christ is the same in a maximal way, and therefore, the completion and the goal of the universe and of mankind. Cusa
addresses his works to the Renaissance man with his awareness
of this microcosmic condition.[78] He speaks to the urbanite
rather than to the men of the university with their "school"
partisanship. His reforms are aimed at the world of the technician, the engineer, the artist, the merchant. The "Idiota" or
the "layman" is the spokesman in his dialogue on wisdom and
on cosmology, his *De Docta Ignorantia* is a kindly bypassing
of the theology of the schoolmen and his *De Pace Fidei* is a
silent appeal for tolerance without reference to organized religion.

The religious universalism that he fosters in this new approach is remarkably lacking in the juridic and formalistic
concepts that the layman found oppressive in the over-
organized religion of his day. It is a universalism that is accessible to the world of mathematics, to natural science, to
physics. It presents a new and dynamic approach to the meaning of history in opposition to the theory of Augustine and
the Middle Ages. The Church must become the hidden dynamic of history and only a deified humanity will accomplish
this. Man is for Cusa a "Deus occasionatus" because he is a free
creature—*liber est qui sua causa est*—and is God-like in so far

78. R. Haubst, *Die Christologie des Nikolaus von Kues* (Freiburg: Herder, 1956), p. 307 f.

as he is a being creating his own entity. Humanity is, as it were, the ladder upon which the creature must climb to the divine. For Cusa, the Christian, in spite of his transcendent vocation, had to integrate himself into the transitory world of which he was so much a part. This he could accomplish only by convincing himself that Christ by His Incarnation had consecrated the entire universe through and through. Like St. Paul, he was profoundly aware that in Christ are contained in germ all the mysteries of creation, as well as the mystery of the Trinity Itself. It is in unfolding these mysteries, visible as well as invisible, that man fulfills his noblest task.

In many respects the theology of the late Middle Ages had shifted away from its original Christocentric moorings. If Aristotelian metaphysics had, in a certain sense, recognized the supernatural as an intruder and forced the separation of philosophy and theology, Augustinianism was also a failure in fitting Christ into the material universe. The "Golden Age" was always something in the past; Christ would never again take on human flesh, pursue His public ministry, or give His life for the salvation of souls. There is much to be said of Toffanin's assertion that, ". . . in the long centuries of patristic decadence, that indifference, implicit in Augustinian Platonism, toward all that which, in man, is nature, grew into a real contempt for science, into an exacerbated pessimism, a slighting of the religious value of the cosmic order. . . ." [79]

It is perhaps this conviction that prompted the great student of Cusa, Ernst Cassirer, to remark:

> Cusanus became to a certain extent the exponent of the intellectual circle, which in Italy of the fifteenth century, represented, alongside

79. G. Toffanin, *History of Humanism* (New York: Las Americas, 1954), p. 7.

the declining scholastic and the rising humanistic culture, a third specifically modern form of knowledge and direction of research. . . . Here everything was directed toward a concrete, technical, artistic purpose for which a theory was sought. In the midst of creative artistic activity, the demand arose for a deeper understanding of the nature of that activity.[80]

The key to understanding that activity and research Cusa finds in Christ, a Christ Who is the Principle of all creative activity both human and divine. It is Christ Himself Who is the great Artist, the great Technician.

In placing a new emphasis upon Christ as Creator, Cusa stimulated or at least revived a different approach to appreciating the triune nature of God. It is not without reason that Hoffman can claim it was Cusa who turned men's minds once again to this central mystery of revelation.[81] The assumption that the humanity of Christ ceased to be after His death is evident in speculation that identified the divine law with a prime mover and that envisioned God as a far-away sovereign only causally related to His creation. If Christ had been over-legalized by canon lawyers, theologians had diminished His mediating role by accommodating Him to the convenient filing system of Aristotle in a way that completely obscured His vital role in all creation as well as in all creative activity.

To reduce grace to a "habitus" or to express the revealed mysteries in hylomorphic terms ran the risk of creating a barrier between God and man. Cusa, convinced that doctrines lose their vitality unless they affect the soul as well as the mind,

80. E. Cassirer, *op. cit.*, p. 7.
81. "Cusanus war derjenige philosophische Denker des Mittelalters, dessen Lehre als Ganzes grundsätzlich im Begriff der vollen Trinität, ja vorzüglich im Begriff des heiligen Geistes gegründet war." Quoted in E. Hoffman, "Nikolas von Cues als Philosoph," in *Heidelberger Akademie der Wissenschaft* (1929), I, 8.

unless they move society as well as individuals, attempts to show the Trinity as a revelation that goes beyond a mere rational or metaphysical conceptualization. The endeavor to make divine revelation more accessible, more intelligible, is one that has always run the risk of over-emphasizing the rational. Aquinas may have changed the water of philosophy into the wine of theology but the doctrinaire intoxication that followed was leaving Christ more and more out of the total picture. Nor was Cusa the first to warn against the dangers of the Aristotelian siren. Tertullian had thundered against Valentinus in the third century: "Unhappy Aristotle! who invented for these men dialectics, the art of building up and pulling down, an art so evasive in its propositions, so far-fetched in its conjectures, so harsh in its arguments, so productive of contentions. . . ."[82] Abelard had confessed, "nolo sic esse Aristotles ut secludar a Christo." To this Cusa would add, ". . . the learning of the dialecticians is but an incentive to constant strife. It seeks for a victory of words, it puffs us up with pride and only increases the distance between ourselves and God and the peace that emanates from this union." His philosophy attempts to go beyond the limits of discursive reasoning, and to envision the Trinity with the soul as well as the mind. He feels that the dogmas of Christianity possess a supra-rational element that transcends the very principle of contradiction. As with Anselm and Eckhart before him, the question that Cusa proposes to answer is not whether God exists. In his writings he rather attempts to enrich the concept of God by placing it in a mathematical rather than an analogical setting. He

82. Tertullian, "On the Prescription of Heretics," 7, adapted from the translation of Peter Holmes, *Ante-Nicene Fathers*, Oxford Translation, ed. Cope (Buffalo: 1884–1886), III, 246.

wants to avoid the danger of circumscribing the divine with the finite. To reduce Aristotelian arguments—that are at most approximates to metaphysical proof—to absolute norms ran the risk of increasing the gap between God and the soul.

Taken as a whole Cusa in his theology continually emphasizes a vital and more immediate orientation to revelation and especially to the Christological doctrine of John and Paul. The prologue of the Johannine Gospel runs through his theology from beginning to end, combined with the Pauline insistence on the unique eminence of the humanity of the Logos in His role as Mediator. To this end he applies the acuteness and analytical ability of his mind in terms which because of their mathematical precision avoid the ambiguities of traditional discursive processes. It is not his intention to substitute speculative faith for divine revelation, but rather to bring into clearer vision what is contained in the mystery, the depth, and the width of Scripture. Because he tries, in developing this system, to avoid the fruitless strife between various schools of philosophy that had reduced the cogency of theology in his day, he skims off the cream of tradition and refreshes it with a blend of his own genius. The end result is a picture of Christ that although less logical than the traditional one is one that is both more pervading and personal. It is a view of Christ that comprehends the great wealth and beauty of the visible world here below as well as the beatitude to come. It is a view more congenial to a generation swiftly changing its attitude towards the universe from one of survival and escape to one of conquest and development—"The Universe reproduces the Absolute Maximum in the greatest possible way."[83] For both

83. See *Docta Ignorantia*, II, 4.

the Church and the Empire harmony will be achieved only as
the result of each part of the whole functioning in the light of
its particular pattern. The heart of Cusa's reform both individually and collectively is the restoration of all things to conformity with their archetypes. It is basically a restoration that
is Christiformal, that is, remade into the image of Christ. It is a
restoration of each segment of society to its *prima forma*. It is
a rededication of all creation to the figure of Christ, wherein
the disparate elements of his time achieve diversity in unity
and unity in diversity.

Probably the most solvent ingredient in the change that
transformed the world of Cusa—and certainly the most revolutionary—was the new evaluation of time and of man's relationship to the temporal. This new evaluation of time has
transformed and modified Western thought as perhaps no
other. It still remains an unchartered area in both philosophical
as well as historical studies, and yet it carried the seeds of the
idea of human progress, human advancement, to which Cusa
was to fashion his re-interpretation of the universe. It underlay his shift from the qualitative to the quantitative as the infinity of time underlay the infinity of the universe. For the
medieval world, the traditional Augustinian concept of time
as the exponent of fragility had fostered the degradation of
whatever was temporal or secular. Time in Averroistic Aristotelianism became the symbol of eternal continuity and the
proper evaluation of an infinite continuity began to revive
traditional feelings concerning the limitations of time and the
transitoriness of human institutions. It was from this milieu
that the idea of progress took its origin rather than in the atmosphere of the Enlightment as is often held. It was in this

same environment of rapid change that Cusa saw the danger of the shifting attention from the kingdom-to-come to the kingdom of this world. The fifteenth century gave strong evidence of movement from a world centered around Christ to a world centered about man.

As Baillie points out:

The modern belief in progress is essentially a product, though a late appearing product, of the movement of the Western European mind, known to us as the Renaissance. That movement was many-sided and took many forms, but its distinguishing characteristic is a certain shift in the previously existing relation between man's sacred and secular interests.[84]

The emphasis on the individual which "had appeared as a ripple in the twelfth century" became almost a tidal wave by the close of the fifteenth century. In the thirteenth century Aquinas had stressed the dignity of man's rational nature and Dante had glorified the "earthly and the temporal," yet both of them were much farther from reconciling the world of men with the world of God than they suspected. The reconciliation between Hellenism and Christianity constructed by Aquinas rested on a shaky basis. It lacked the dynamism and the energy that the emerging *Volksgeist* of Europe demanded.

Men were beginning to question the sacral institutionalism that had developed out of the medieval synthesis. The institution that had formed itself in response to the historical opportunities of the time was no longer a community which was distinguished from other communities because its members were motivated by a mutual love for one another and for all mankind. It was no longer an organic community with communal relationships. Thomas had incorporated the legacy of

84. John Baillie, *The Belief in Progress* (New York: Scribner, 1950), p. 96.

the ancient Church into the feudalistic order, and while changing the way of Christian faith and life he was persuaded that he was loyal to an unchanging divine order. That his outlook was historically conditioned and influenced by his own times was overlooked by his followers. Any system that operates outside the scope of history tends to ossify and to lose its vitality. As the sense of history and philosophy developed, the humanists began to question the medieval synthesis.

The fourteenth and fifteenth century was

> . . . a protest against the otherworldliness of the Middle Ages. In both their practice and their precepts the men of the Renaissance asserted that human life here and now has an undeniable meaning. Man's earthly existence must not be regarded as an anteroom for heaven.[85]

There was a growing conviction that history follows a continuous and orderly course and that the course of change had brought and would continue to bring improvement to the condition of mankind.

For Cusa it was even more apparent that the fifteenth-century bourgeois was unlikely to share in Augustinian pessimism. There was a joy in activity that had replaced the mystical desire to flee the world. The deep psychological effect of the movement from farm to town, already evident in the commercial revolution of the thirteenth century had gathered tremendous momentum in the succeeding centuries. As Sellery points out,

> The medieval *bourgeois* was not prone to be an Augustinian. It was not easy for him, living in a town which he and his fellows had created and adorned, to regard work as a penalty for sin or this good

---

85. J. A. Hutchison, *The Two Cities, A Study of God and Human Politics* (Garden City, N. Y.: Doubleday, 1957), p. 84.

earth as place of exile, a vale of tears, as the preachers taught. It was the bourgeois . . . who was the first medieval man to recognize this world as good. Homesickness for the other world inevitably became more rare.[86]

This bourgeoise resentment had come out in the open by the time Cusa began his reformatory efforts. The discovery of new interests and values did not eliminate a desire to deny the claims of eternal rewards, but concomitant with it was a claim also to the independent cultivation of secular interests. Knowledge was not merely to serve the clarification of theological speculations, nor was the civil order merely a temporary framework accommodated to the operations of the Church as a body politic. Wisdom for Cusa "cries out in the very streets of the city."

There was a growing interest in life *per se.*

St. Augustine had carefully defined the nature of the Christian involvement in the amenities of our earthly existence. We are not, he said, to value them for their own sake, but only to make such use of them as is inevitable, while we wait for the redemption which is to come; and on this distinction between *uti* and *frui*, between use and enjoyment, the whole of his Christian wisdom rests. In his view the succeeding ages had consistently followed him. . . . This does not mean that everybody throughout these ages lived according to this rule, but only that they knew they ought to, and were ashamed of themselves or shame-faced before others when they did not.[87]

This optimism is later reflected in the better known works of Ficino and Pico della Mirandola. The melancholy of the medieval man is replaced by a conviction that he can share here below in the joy to come hereafter. The optimism revolved around a deep belief in the solidarity of mankind. Thus Ficino

86. C. Sellery, *The Renaissance, its Nature and Origin* (Madison: University of Wisconsin Press, 1939), p. 175.
87. Baillie, *op. cit.*, p. 96.

asks: "How does it help you, O Theologian, to attribute eternity to God, if you do not attribute it to yourself in order that you may enjoy divine eternity through your own eternity?" [88] Pico, writing on the dignity of man, expresses the theme of Cusa that freedom to choose one's way of life is God's greatest gift to mankind. After God had created the universe and its creatures, He desired "someone to ponder the plan of so great a work."

At last the best of artisans ordained that that creature to whom He had been able to give nothing proper to himself should have the joint possession of whatever had been peculiar to each of the different kinds of being. He therefore took man as a creature of indeterminate nature and, assigning him a place in the middle of the world, addressed him thus: 'Neither a fixed abode nor a form that is thine alone nor any function peculiar to thyself have we given thee, Adam, to the end that according to thy longing and to thy judgment thou mayest have and possess what abode, what form, and what functions thou thyself shall desire. The nature of all other beings is limited and constrained within the bounds of laws prescribed by Us. Thou, constrained by no limits, in accordance with thine own free will, in whose hand We have placed thee, shalt ordain for thyself the limits of thy nature. We have set thee at the world's center that thou mayest from thence more easily observe whatever is in the world.' [89]

Cusa, perhaps more than the later humanists, foresaw the possible gulf between literary intellectuals and the growing technological scientists of his time. Long before Swift in the eighteenth century and Polanyi in our day, he perceived the need for a superior guide, a transcendent religious reconciliation, that would not isolate scientific knowledge but use it to achieve harmony over the whole range of knowledge. He

88. Quoted in P. Kristeller, *Studies in Renaissance Thought and Letters* (Rome: Edizioni di storia e letteratura, 1956), p. 270.
89. E. Cassirer, *et al.*, *The Renaissance Philosophy of Man* (Chicago: University of Chicago Press, 1948), pp. 219–222.

makes man a "second God" because in the midst of the chaos of changing phenomena he alone is capable of unifying all things in a vast mutually interrelating system. The explanation of the visible world is no longer a mere tieing of an event to an eternal prototype of existence, categorizing forms and essences, but rather an establishing of the laws of evolution and progress, of weighing data with an ever-tightening web of mathematical precision. The value of temporal things is thus recreated by man himself who enhances them by the utility he finds in them. Like the banker whose bills of exchange he himself endorses, man endorses the material world and its value lies not so much in possession as it does in this radical capacity to determine value. We see here the conviction that man can best know and honor all the works of creation by examining and exploring them. This is in no way a denial of the priority of eternal interests but rather a preparation for a wider and deeper appreciation of the eternal. There is a note of joy in Cusa's proclaiming man's responsibility, " . . . to know and honor all His works with his best tools and techniques, that so we may be more easily led to many things that are yet hidden from us."

A St. Francis of Assisi had sung a Canticle of the Sun in praise of Mother Earth, Brother Fire and all of nature. Dante had written the *Convivio* and the *De Monarchia*, wherein, " . . . for the first time in Christian thought we find the earthly and temporal city regarded as an autonomous order." [90] Both had spoken at the end of a long period during which human nature and the material universe had been dwarfed by the

90. C. Dawson, *The Dynamics of World History* (New York: Sheed and Ward, 1956), p. 243.

shadow of eternity. Cusa, spokesman for a new era, combined admiration for the physical world with an inquisitive search for certitude; his work provided an ideological basis for defending the autonomy of man in an expanding universe, "a universe whose center is everywhere and whose circumference is nowhere."

It was his lifelong endeavor to achieve organic unity out of multiplicity, to lessen the tensions rending the *Respublica Christiana*, by putting the Logos, the Life of the world, in a more universal framework. He would give Christ a horizontal as well as a vertical dimension.

Yet the ills that weakened the unity of the West had advanced too far and too deeply. There was little hope for religious reform from a Curia that had surrendered universalism to conformism, that had, so to speak, turned itself inward upon itself. There was even less hope for the *renovatio imperii*, where nascent nationalism had conspired with particularism to threaten Christendom from within, as the Turk was threatening it from without. The new social classes, the merchant, the artisan, the scientist, to whom Cusa had addressed his writings, were gradually absorbed into elite groups, only to perpetuate an aristocratic Europe, wedded to Absolutism, for centuries to come.

Above all, the religious forces, the spiritual dynamism, upon which he had based his metastasis, had been exhausted to a point where a more radical, a more revolutionary movement was needed to revive them. Cusa was no revolutionary, as d'Etaples eulogizes him: "Venerentur igitur omnes, et detrahatur nemo." The reconciliation which he sought between the *imperium* and the *sacerdotium*, between science and faith, through a coincidence of opposites, remained in an empty tomb. The world would continue to search for them in a seeming unending cycle of disappointments, yet like the disciples of old, it would have to hear again the angelic message that Cusa so often reiterates: "Why seek ye the living among the dead?"

Cusa died in Umbria in 1464 and was buried in his titular church in Rome. The lovely neo-classic monument in the left nave of San Pietro in Vincoli, executed by Andrea Bregno, has captured much of the poignancy of his character. The inscription below it, "Delixit Deum, timuit ac veneratus est, ac illi soli servivit, promissio retributionis non fefellit eum," epitomizes his life.

OF LEARNED IGNORANCE

CUSA composed his most famous work, *De Docta Ignorantia,* during those months of comparative peace and quiet that followed his intense activity at Basle and Florence. The work was completed in February of 1440 and dedicated to his friend and former teacher at Padua, Cardinal Cesarini. The more immediate reaction to the doctrine of learned ignorance, that it was heretical, irreligious, and would lead to the destruction of systematic theology has been modified with the passing of the centuries. Recent studies and a widening knowledge of Cusa's other writings have demonstrated that his doctrine is rooted much more deeply in biblical and patristic tradition than has generally been assumed. His system is in no way a substitute for divine revelation but is rather a sincere attempt to bring into clearer light the central and anthropomorphic position of Christ. This he accomplishes with daring excursions to the very limit of controlled thought. From the wealth of patristic and medieval thought he carefully selects whatever will correspond to a more vital image of Christ not only in the individual soul but in the universe itself.

It is Cusa's hope that the method of learned ignorance will

overcome all the inadequate "ratiocinationes" of contemporary philosophers. He is well aware of the great difficulty in weening them away from Aristotle and he feels that it would take some sort of a miracle, a religious conversion (ut sit miraculo simile, sicuti sectae mutatio) to see one of them reject Aristotle and rise up to something better. The logic of Aristotle was no fitting instrument to investigate a universe created by the infinite God of Christianity. His is a system that is spontaneously adapted to the needs of its own times. By stressing the role of Christ as Mediator, an office ever present and individual in each person as well as in the universe rather than an historical fact accomplished once and for all, Cusa impresses the personal reality of Christianity as a vital and organic force through all ages. In Christ the Maximum is most fully actualized because this actualization involves both God and nature, and because man, through Christ, attains his maximum, the ultimate antithesis between God and nature is finally transcended. Therefore not only through Christ, but in Christ does man realize the Maximum.

DE DOCTA IGNORANTIA
The Third Book

We have set down this much about the restricted nature of the universe, to the end that we may enquire in learned ignorance into the maximum at once absolute and restricted, Jesus Christ, ever blessed, to the increase of our faith and perfection. Let us further elucidate to your admirable attentiveness, as briefly as possible, the consideration of Jesus. We pray Him Who is truth to be our way to Him, that through faith to fruition we may be made to live in Him, by Him Who is Himself eternal life.

CHAPTER I. THE UNSURPASSABLE MAXIMUM, EVEN IF LIMITED
TO THIS OR THAT GENUS OR SPECIES, CAN EXIST ONLY IN
THE ABSOLUTE

In the first book it was shown that there endures eternally, equally and immovable itself, an Absolute Maximum incommunicable and never to be contracted or overwhelmed. In the second place was shown the contracted entity we call the universe, for only in limitation can things in plurality hope to exist. The unity of the maximum is absolutely in itself; the unity of the universe is in the restriction called plurality. The plurality of things in which the universe finds its actual limitation could never contain the highest equality for it would then be no longer in plurality.

57

Things must be distinguished by genus, species and number, or by species and number, or by number simply; that each may repose in its own number, weight and measure. Wherefore are all things separated into degrees, that no two may absolutely coincide.

No limited thing may share in the precise degree of limitation of another; everything necessarily exceeds or falls short of every other thing. All limited things, therefore, have their station between the maximum and the minimum in such a fashion that at any point a larger or smaller degree of limitation may be added. But this process may not be continued to infinity; an infinity of degrees is impossible, for it is no more rational to postulate an actual infinite number of degrees than to postulate no degrees at all; as was shown of numbers in our First Book. In limited things, therefore, it is impossible to rise to the absolute maximum or to sink to the absolute minimum. The divine nature, the Absolute Maximum, cannot be diminished into a finite and limited thing; nor can a limited thing be shorn of all limitation and become the Absolute Maximum.

No limited thing, therefore, since it can suffer further or lesser limitation, can ever reach the confines either of the universe or of a genus or a species. The first general limitation of the total universe is into the plurality of genera, and these branch out into further differentiations. Now genera actually exist only in their species and species only in their individuals; it is these last that alone have concrete existence. As it is admissible to seek the nature of individuals only within the confines of their species, so, conversely, no individual may hope to stretch to the full range of genus and universe; different degrees of perfection must be found among the many individuals of one species. In other words, no individual of a given species can be so completely perfect as to make any higher perfection impossible, nor so utterly imperfect as to exclude the possibility of further imperfection. Nothing stretches to the uttermost confines of its species.

There is but one limit of species and genera and of the universe, and it is the centre, circumference and bond of all things. The universe does not exhaust the infinite and absolutely maximal power of God, like some simple maximum putting a limit to God's power. Consequently the universe does not arrive at the limits of absolute greatness, no more than genera reach the limits of the universe or species the limits of genera or individuals the limits of species. The result is that, between the maximum and the minimum, all things are what they are in the best way possible, with God as the beginning, middle and end of the totality and each member of it, so that all things, whether they rise or sink or tend to the centre, may approach God. That all in their endless variety may be bound together, He makes the bond among them all. Wherefore, among the genera that limit the one universe there is this link between higher and lower that they meet in the middle, and among the different species such is the bond, that the highest species of one genus coincides with the lowest species of the genus immediately above, making one universal and perfect continuity.

The connecting link between species is a thing of degrees and the maximum is never reached, which is God. Therefore species of different genera are not linked by some indivisible third that admits of no greater and less but by a third species whose individuals shade off from one species to the other, no one individual, however, sharing equally both species as being a composite of both. The individual rather shares the nature of its own species in its own individual degree, so that, put side by side with others, it looks like a composite of the higher and the lower species—though never equally of both, for no composite can be formed of exactly equal elements. And placed as it is midway between two species, in its composition one species, the higher or the lower, necessarily prevails. Examples of this are found in the works of philosophers, on oysters, sea shells and other things.

No species then sinks so low as to become the minimum of a particular genus, for before it reaches that minimum it is changed into another; and similarly with species that rise. They, too, change into another before they become the maximal of the genus. When in the genus, animal, the human species strives to reach a high place among beings endowed with sensibility, it is caught up into the new connection of an intellectual nature; but the lower part still prevails, and for that reason it is still named animal. There may well be other spirits—I have mentioned them in *De Coniec-turis*—that are broadly classed with the animal because they possess a nature that has something of the sensible in it. But because in them the spiritual nature prevails they are named spirits rather than animals, although the Platonists regard them as intellectual animals. Species, then, must be conceived as being of the nature of an orderly progressive number, necessarily finite, that order, harmony and proportion may characterize the vast variety of creatures, as we pointed out in the First Book. And whether we count down to the lowest species of the lowest genus, than which there is actually no smaller, or to the highest species of the highest genus, than which similarly a greater or higher is not in fact to be found—although still smaller and greater are not possible without postulating a progress into infinity—we must set out from the absolute unity which is God, that our starting-point may be the principle of all things. As we move from the minimum which is the maximum, or from the maximum to which the minimum is not opposed, we shall see species as numbers that meet us on the way. In the universe there is nothing that does not enjoy a certain singularity that it shares with no other. Nothing can prevail over all that is in all things so as to turn their differences into sameness, for never can complete sameness exist in any two things. If at one time one thing is smaller and at another time larger than another throughout the change it preserves its singularity so that never does it pass through a moment of exact equality. A quadrangle inscribed in a circle may grow to one that encloses a circle, that is, from one smaller to one greater than a circle, without ever touching exactly the same dimension as a circle. An angle of incidence can change from one smaller to one greater than a right angle, without ever touching the mean of equality. More things of this kind will be set forth in the Book of Conjectures.

Individuating principles do not meet in precisely the same harmonious proportion in one thing as in another; every one is meant to be a unity and in its nature perfect. In each species, the human for example, some are counted more perfect and more excellent than others, as Solomon excelled in wisdom, Absalom in beauty, Samson in strength; and those who outclassed their fellows in mental power were deemed worthy of special honour. All this notwithstanding, differences of view following varieties of religion, sects and lands are responsible for different standards of comparison, so that what is praiseworthy here may be odious there. Whence, incapable of an exhaustive study of even one of these candidates for honour, and totally ignorant of the greater number of them throughout the world, it is quite beyond our power to pronounce anyone to be excellent above the rest of mankind.

This is a divine arrangement, in order that each, though he admire others, should be content with the manners of his own people, with his own tongue and all else of his home, and should find something peculiarly dear to him in the soil that gave him birth. In such a spiritual ground there grow unity and peace without envy, as far as may be here below. For this unity is fully present only among them that reign with Him Who is our peace surpassing all understanding.

CHAPTER II. THE MAXIMUM AS LIMITED AND ABSOLUTE TOGETHER, AT ONCE CREATOR AND CREATURE

It has been sufficiently shown that the multiplicity of the universe is its limitation and that this multiplicity so lies that none of its parts can ever attain to the simple maximum. I will add further that if it were possible for the maximum to become contracted to an actually existing species, this maximum would actually be, according to that contraction, all that it was in the power of that genus or species to become. The absolute maximum is the realization of all possible being and thus is absolutely infinite. The maximum contracted into genus and species is similarly the realization of all possible perfection of that given contraction, and, since a greater perfection of that contraction is not thinkable, it is no less than the infinite embracing every nature of that given contraction. The minimum coincides with the absolute maximum; and the minimum contracted coincides with the maximum contracted.

The clearest illustration of this is to be found in the maximum line. It has no opposite; it contains all figures and is the equal of all the figures it can contain; and, as was shown in the First Book, with it the point coincides. Wherefore, if anything could be presented as the maximum limited individual of a particular species, that thing would necessarily be the plentitude of that genus or species as way, form, reason and truth, in the fullness of perfection of all possibles of that species. Such a contracted maximum, being the final term of every nature within that limitation and including in itself every perfection of that limitation, would, beyond all proportion, hold the highest equality with any given individual, neither greater nor smaller than any, but including in its fullness the perfections of all.

From which it is clear that such a contracted maximum could not exist as a purely contracted thing, for we have already shown that no thing could touch such fullness of perfection in a state of contraction. Nor could such a contraction be God, Who is absolutely illimitable. It would have to be the maximum in a state of limitation, that is, God and creature, the absolute and the limited, and this by a limitation which could only subsist by the subsistence of the absolute maximum. For, as we showed in the First Book, there is only one maximal in which a limited thing could be called the maximum. If maximal power were to unite limitation with itself with the closest union compatible with the preservation of both natures—the limitation being safeguarded which was the fullness of the contracted created species—so that in virtue of the hypostatic union it would be God and all things, such an admirable union would surpass all our understanding. To conceive it as a union of diverse things would be to misunderstand it. The absolute maximum cannot be thought of as other and diverse; for it is all things. To think of it as two things once apart and now united would also be a misconception. For the divine being has no relation to past and future, nor is it rather this thing than that; nor could the limited thing have been describable before the union as this or that, like an individual person subsisting in himself. Neither can the union be described as of parts united to make a whole, for God could never be part of anything. Nor again may anyone conceive this most admirable union as one of form and matter, for the absolute Deity is incapable of being mingled with matter or of informing it.

This union would be higher than all intelligible unions, for here the limited thing—since it is also a maximum—can subsist only in the absolute maximum itself, while it adds nothing to that in which it is, for that is itself the absolute maximum; nor can it pass into the nature of that maximum, for it itself is limited. The limited must here so subsist in the maximum that, if we conceive it as God we deceive ourselves, for the limited cannot change its nature; if we imagine it as creature, we are again mistaken, for the absolute maximum, which is God, does not abandon His nature. If, lastly, we present it to ourselves as a composite of both we are again in error, for between God and creature, between the limited and the absolute maximum, a composition is impossible. We should have to conceive such a being as being at once God and creature, creature and creator—creator and creature both, without composition and with confusion. Who shall be raised so high as to conceive diversity in unity and unity in diversity? Such a union, therefore, would surpass all understanding.

CHAPTER III. HUMAN NATURE AND ONLY HUMAN NATURE
PECULIARLY ADAPTED TO BE THIS MAXIMUM

What the nature of the contracted maximum itself ought to be is a question that can be easily solved in the light of our previous remarks. Such a maximum is necessarily one, as the Absolute Maximum is absolute unity; at the same time it is limited to this or that. Now the order of things clearly presents some things as inferior by nature, as lacking life and intelligence, some superior by nature because intelligent, and some between these two. If, therefore, the Absolute Maximum is the most universal being of all things, and not more of one than of another, it is clear that that being is more capable of union with the maximum which shares the nature of the largest number of things.

Consider what would happen if a thing of inferior nature were elevated to the maximum. It would be both God and itself. Let us take the example of a maximal line. That line is infinite in absolute infinity and maximal by the maximum to which it is necessarily united; it is God by its maximality and a line by limitation. It would thus be all that a line could become. But a line does not involve either life or intelligence: which means that a line would have reached the maximum itself, while it lacked the natures above it! It would be the maximum while lacking certain perfections; it could become greater!

A similar pronouncement must be made about the highest nature that comprises no inferior; for the union of inferior with superior is greater than is either separately. Now it befits the maximum—with which the minimum coincides—so to unite with one thing that it does not exclude another but rather embraces all. Therefore, a nature in the middle which is the link between inferior and superior is alone most suitable for elevation by the power of the maximal and infinite God. It comprises in itself all natures, the highest of the inferior and the lowest of the superior;

so that if it rise together with all that is in it to union with the maximum, it is plain that in it all natures and the whole universe have touched, in every way possible to them, the highest itself.

Now, human nature it is that is raised above all the works of God and made a little lower than the angels. It contains in itself the intellectual and the sensible natures, and therefore, embracing within itself all things, has very reasonably been dubbed by the ancients the microcosm or world in miniature. Hence is it a nature that, raised to union with the maximum, would exhibit itself as the fullest perfection of the universe and of every individual in it, so that in this humanity itself all things would achieve their highest grade. But humanity has no real existence except in the limited existence of the individual. Wherefore it would not be possible for more than one real man to rise to union with the maximum; and this man assuredly would so be man as to be God, would so be God as to be man, the perfection of all things and in all things holding the primacy. In him the smallest things of nature, the greatest and all between, would so coincide in a nature united with the absolute maximum, as to form in him the perfection of all things; and all things, in their limitation, would repose in him as in their perfection. This man's measure would also be that of the angel and of every one of the angels, as St. John says in the Apocalypse (XXI, 17), for he would be the universal contracted entity of each creature through his union with the absolute, which is the absolute entity of all things. From him all things would receive the beginning and end of their limitation. By him who is the maximum in limitation, all things are to come forth into their limited being from the Absolute Maximum, and by means of him revert to the maximum. For he is the first beginning of their setting forth and the last end of their return.

Source or cause of the being of all things, God is the creator of all, and all are made for him. To this highest, maximal and absolute power of creating all things, the nature of humanity would be united. In consequence, God Himself would by this assumed humanity become all things in their limitation in that humanity, as He is the absolute power behind the beings of all things. This man, therefore, since He would subsist by union in the highest equality itself of all being would be the son of God and would be the Word in which all things were made, i.e. the equality itself of all being; and, as was shown earlier, this is what the son of God is called. But He would not cease to be the son of man nor cease to be man, as shall be shown below.

It is in no way incompatible with God, Most excellent and most perfect, that these things can be done by Him without any variation, diminution, or any lessening of His nature. It rather fits in with his immense goodness that all things should be created by Him and for Him in the most excellent and most absolutely perfect fashion and in an order suited to its unimprovable perfection. Now this is not so, and no one can reasonably deny, unless he deny God Himself or perfection itself, that all things could be more perfect. From Him who is the highest good and whose work can contain no defect we must put far away every invidious criticism. As He is the maximum, His work, as far as this is inherently possible in creatures, approaches the maximum. But the power of the maximum is exhausted only by and in itself, there is nothing outside it and it is infinite. In no creature therefore could it be so exhausted that this infinite power could not, given any creature whatsoever, create a better and more perfect. But if a man be elevated to unity with this power in such fashion as to be a creature subsisting not in himself but in union with this infinite power, this power terminates not in the creature but in itself. Herein lies the most perfect activity of the maximal power of God, infinite and inexhaustible, and which can never fail; for if it could, there would be neither creator nor creature. For how could the creature exist, as something limited from the divine being, if that very limitation was incapable of union with him? By this creature all things, coming from him who is absolute, are to exist. They in their limitation are from him to whom their limitation is united in the closest union. First, then, stands God the creator. Next is God and man, whose created humanity has been assumed into the most intimate possible union with God, and, as being the universal limitation of all things, is hypostatically and personally united with the absolute power behind the being of all things; that he may exist by the most absolute God through the universal limitation, which is humanity. In the third place all things are in their limited being, so that what they are that they might be in still better order and manner.

Now this order must not be regarded as a temporal one, as though God had preceded in time the first-born of creation, or as though that first- born, God and man, had preceded the world in time. It is rather an order that by nature and perfection transcends time, so that he who exists with God above time and before all things, in the fullness of time and after many cycles of ages, appeared in the world.

CHAPTER IV. THIS BEING IS JESUS, EVER BLESSED, GOD AND MAN

We have reached the point where, with full trust in the deductions we have made, we may hold without hesitation that the conclusions we have set forth are strictly true. We shall now add that Jesus, ever blessed, with the coming of the fullness of time, is the first-born of all creation.

In His earthly life He worked wonders above earthly powers and, found always true in all He said, He affirmed certain things concerning Himself; moreover those who consorted with Him bore like witness and sealed it with their blood. We are, therefore, justified in affirming with unshakable constancy, what indeed has long been proved by irrefutable arguments, that He it is whose coming all creation awaited from the beginning, and who had Himself by his prophets predicted His appearance in the world. He came to fulfil all things. He restored all to health by His will as one having power over all things, He unfolded the hidden and secret things of wisdom, He took away sin like a God, raised the dead to life, transformed nature, commanded spirits, the sea and the winds, walked upon the water and gave to men a law that was the complete fulfilment of all laws. In Him—as witnessed that most distinguished preacher of truth Paul, enlightened from above in an ecstasy—we possess every perfection, 'redemption and remission of sins; who is the image of the invisible God, the first-born of every creature, for in Him were all things made in heaven and on earth, visible and invisible, whether thrones or dominations or principalities or powers, all things were created by Him and in Him. And He is before all and by Him all things consist. And He is the head of the body, the Church, He is the beginning, the first-born from the dead, that in all things he may hold the primacy; it hath pleased Him that all fullness should dwell in Him and by Him to reconcile all things to Himself.'

Such indeed and many other testimonies of the saints are offered us to the effect that He is God and man. In Him the humanity itself is united to the Word in the divinity itself, so that the humanity does not subsist in itself but in the divinity. Henceforth humanity cannot dwell in perfect fullness except in the divine person of the Son.

In order that we may, above all our intellectual comprehension and as it were in learned ignorance, come to know this person who has united man with himself, let us raise our mind higher and consider the following:

God is in and through all things and all things are wholly in God, as we have already shown. Now these two aspects, both that God is in all and that all are in God, must be taken together and coupled with the fact that the divine nature is of the highest equality and simplicity. Whence, while He is in all things, God is not there by degrees or by a particular measure of communication; and at the same time, because these things cannot be except in diversity of degrees, they are with their natural diversity of degrees in God. In all things and all in Him, God is there, without any variation of His absolute power to create, in unity with the maximal humanity of Jesus; in Him the maximal man cannot exist except in the maximal fashion. Jesus is thus the absolute creative power of God and in Him as in the Son, the middle person, the eternal Father and the Holy Spirit dwell. All things are in the Word; in that most high and most perfect human nature which mightily embraces all creatable beings, all things exist, that all fullness may dwell in Him.

The mind can be gently conducted to the understanding of these things by the following illustration:

Sense knowledge is a limited kind of knowledge; the senses know only the individual. By comparison with sense-knowledge intellectual knowledge, which is of the universal, is absolute and abstracted from the limitations of the particular. Now, sensation is found in various degrees of keenness in different animals and by this they are classed in different grades of nobility and perfection. We have shown that the human, the highest species of the genus animal, cannot rise to the degree which is simply the highest; nevertheless, here the senses behave in such fashion that this animal is also a being of intellect. For man is his intelligence. In him the sense limitation is in some sense supposited in the intellectual nature. While the latter is a kind of abstracted and separate divine thing, the senses remain temporal and corruptible according to their nature.

This bears a certain (though not very close) analogy with what we are now considering in Jesus. In Him the human nature is supposited in the divine, for not otherwise could it exist in its maximal fullness. The intelligence of Jesus, altogether the most perfect in existence, can be personally supposited only in the divine intellect which alone is actually all things. Intellect in man is potentially all things and grows by steps from potency to act, so that the further it grows the less is it in potency. But the maximal intellect, the actually full term of the potency of every intellectual nature, could not exist unless it were also God, who is all in all things. It is as though a polygon inscribed in a circle were human nature and the circle were the divine nature. If the polygon were to become the maximum, than which no greater could exist, it could never exist by itself in finite angles, but only as a circular figure. In consequence it would not have a figure of its own proper being separable even intellectually from the external circular figure itself.

The maximal perfection of human nature must be sought in substantial and essential things, in intellect, which the bodily functions serve. Hence the maximally perfect man need not be found eminent in accidentals, but only in intellect. It is not required that he should be a giant or a dwarf or a man of this or that stature, complexion, figure or other accidental. This only is necessary, that his body so avoid extremes as to be a most apt instrument of his intellectual nature, and that it obey without resistance, murmur or fatigue. Our Jesus, in whom even in His earthly life all the treasures of wisdom and of knowledge were hidden as a light in darkness, is credited with having, for the purposes of that most eminent intellectual nature, a body most apt and most perfect, and to this the holy companions of His earthly life bear witness.

CHAPTER V. THAT CHRIST WAS CONCEIVED OF THE HOLY GHOST
AND WAS BORN OF THE VIRGIN MARY

It must further be considered how this most perfect human nature, which now subsists by the subsistence of the Word, does not in any way exceed the bounds of its species, since it is a finite nature at the peak point of perfection. Like begets like, and so the begotten proceeds from its begetter in a similarity of nature. But to a term that is termless there can be neither limit nor comparison. For that reason the maximal man cannot be born in the natural way, and yet the species, of which he is the end and perfection, must have some beginning. His generation, therefore, partly followed human nature, since he is a man. Since, however, he has no causal relation but only a relation of the highest origin to a principle to which he is immediately united, that principle, creating or generating, is his Father, the immediate source of his origin; and the human principle is there as the passive one providing the receptive matter. Hence is he from a mother without male seed.

Every operation proceeds from some kind of spirit and love, uniting the active with the passive, as we have shown somewhere above. Hence the maximal operation, outstripping all proportion of nature, by which the creator is united with the creature must necessarily arise from the highest uniting love, that is, from the Holy Spirit, who is love itself. By him alone, with no help from a limited agent, could the mother conceive, within the latitude of the species, the Son of God. Thus the Father, who fashioned all things out of nothing by the Holy Spirit, so that they proceeded into being from non-existence through Him, now through the same most Holy Spirit achieves this purpose, working a most perfect work.

An illustration may help our ignorance. When some most excellent teacher wishes to reveal his thought in order to feed his pupils with the truth of his mind, he takes care to clothe that thought in sound; thought is not communicable except in a sense-garb. The natural spirit of the teacher fashions the air into an audible shape suited to the thought; the spoken word lives in the thought, so that when it falls upon the ears it reproduces the thought.

The analogy is a slight one, but it does help to raise us in meditation above our natural understanding. The eternal Father, wishing to reveal to us His Son, the Eternal Word, the riches of His glory and immense goodness and the fullness of knowledge and of wisdom, took pity on our weakness. He perceived that only in a sense-form and in one like to ourselves could we grasp the truth, and to make a revelation adapted to our capacity, He clothed His Son in human nature by means of the Holy Spirit, who is consubstantial with himself. And this Holy Spirit, as a

word is formed from the air by the breath of man, fashioned the
animal body from the pure and fruitful virginal blood, adding reason, that he might be a man, and united the Word of God the
Father with this man interiorly, so that the Word became the
very centre of subsistence of that human nature. And this was
done not in stages, as happens in our human conceptions in time,
but instantaneously and timelessly and in accordance with a will
at one with infinite power.

No one can doubt that this mother, filled with such virtue and
privileged to supply such material, surpassed all other virgins in
every spiritual perfection and was endowed with an ampler blessing than all other fruitful mothers. In every way prepared for this
single and most excellent virginal childbirth, she was necessarily
free from everything that might stand in the way of the purity,
the vigour and the unity of so excellent a bringing-forth. For, unless of the most choice and elect virginity, she could not have been
capable of virginal conception without the seed of man. If not
herself most holy and most highly blessed by God, she could never
have provided the workroom of the Holy Spirit in which he
fashioned a body for the Son of God. Had she not remained a virgin after this birth, she could not have furnished to this birth a
centre of maternal fecundity in its full perfection, but only one
shared and diminished and unworthy of the supreme uniqueness
of such a Son. Since, then, this most holy Virgin surrendered herself wholly to God and brought to the action of the Holy Spirit
the complete concurrence of her most bountiful fruitfulness,
there remained with her her virginity, immaculate before birth,
during birth and after birth and unsullied above all common natural begetting.

From a Father eternal, therefore, and a mother temporal, the
most glorious Virgin Mary, was born Jesus Christ, God and man;
from a Father who is the maximum and absolute fullness of being
and from a mother of the fullest virginal fecundity and filled in
the fullness of time with the highest blessing. He could not be a

man, born of a mother, a virgin, except in time; nor could he be begotten of the Father except eternally. But his temporal birth demanded within time the fullest perfection, as it demanded in his mother the fullest fruitfulness.

When, therefore, the fullness of time was come, since a man could be born only in time, he was born in time and in a place admirably suitable, but completely hidden from all creatures. For the divine decrees stand outside all proportion to normal human experiences. Hence was there no indication by which any reason could apprehend these decrees, although in a certain most secret prophetical inspiration divers dark intimations wrapped up in human analogies had been given out, by which wise men might forecast by a process of deduction the incarnation of the Word in the fullness of time. But only the eternal Father foresaw the exact time, place and manner; and he brought it about that, in the depth of the night, when the profoundest silence held all things, the Son should come down from the high citadel into the womb of the virgin and at the most fitting appointed time should manifest Himself to the world in the form of a servant.

CHAPTER VI. THE MYSTERY OF JESUS' DEATH

It will not be out of place to interpose here a short digression to clarify what has gone before and to enable us the more aptly to set forth the mystery of the Cross. It is beyond question that man is made up of sense and intellect, with a reasoning power between that joins these two together. Order subjects sense to reason and reason to intellect. Intellect is itself not of time and space, but entirely free from them, while sense is completely dependent upon time and space informations. The reason lies as though horizontal to the intellect but at an angle to the senses, that those things that are within and those that are outside time may here coincide.

The senses being animal are quite incapable of understanding things spiritual and outside time. The animal understands not the things of God, for God is a spirit and more than a spirit. Where-fore sense-knowledge is in the darkness of ignorance of eternal things and occupies itself with the flesh and with the desires of the flesh in the concupiscible powers, and with repelling obstacles in the irascible powers. The reason, more noble in its nature because it shares the intellectual nature, is endowed with certain rules wherewith it restrains the passions and desires and reduces them to comparative quietude, lest, placing his whole desire in sense things, a man should be bereft of the spiritual aspirations of the intelligence. It is the first of all laws that a man should never do to others what he would not wish to be done to himself; that eternal things should have precedence over temporal things, and pure and holy things over impure and fleeting things: and the laws framed by most holy legislators from reason itself and promul-gated according to divers times and places as counterweights to those who sin against reason, all co-operate to this end.

At a higher level the intelligence recognizes that, even when the senses are subjected to reason by the denial of the passions which are so natural to it, man would still be incapable of attaining by himself the end of his intellectual and eternal aspirations. For man is begotten of the seed of Adam by carnal pleasure which in the act of propagation triumphs over the spirit. And therefore, his nature, originally rooted in carnal delights—for through these did man take origin from his parents—remains quite impotent to tran-scend temporal things in order to embrace spiritual. Wherefore if the weight of carnal delights drags down reason and intelligence to consent by non-resistance to these movements, it is clear that a man is thereby turned away from God and robbed of the enjoy-ment of the highest good, which is upward, eternal and of the spirit. If, then, reason controls the senses, it is still more imperative that intellect should control reason, and that in faith fashioned above reason a man should adhere to the Mediator and be drawn by God the Father to glory. No man was ever yet able of himself to rise above himself and above his own nature, so subject from its origin to carnal desire, and, thus freed, ascend to eternal and heavenly things, save He who came down from heaven, Jesus Christ. He it was who also ascended by His own power, for in Him human nature, born not of the will of the flesh but of God, presented no obstacle to His most powerful flight to God His Father.

In Christ then, human nature itself by its union with God is raised to the highest power and escapes the weight of temporal and downward-dragging desires. Christ Our Lord willed to mortify and, in mortifying, to purge out in His own body all those crimes that drag us down to earth, not for His own sake, for He did no sin, but for us; that all men, of the same human nature with Himself, might find in Him complete purification from their sins. That willing and most innocent, that most shameful and most cruel death of the man Christ on the cross was the extinction, satisfaction and purgation of all the carnal desires of human nature. All that is possible to human nature in the way of love of one's neighbor stands out as most generously achieved in the perfect charity of Christ, who gave himself to death even for His enemies.

The humanity of Christ Jesus then atoned for the deficiencies of all men. This humanity, being maximal humanity, embraces the total power of the species and is so much the source of being of each man as to stand far closer to him than ever could brother or most intimate friend. For the maximal of human nature so works that in each man that adheres to Him by formed faith Christ is that man in perfect union, while the man's individuality remains untouched. Whence the truth of His own words: 'Whatsoever you did to the least of my brethren, you did to me.' And conversely, whatever Christ merited in His Passion they also merited who are one with Him—this in the degree of merit that attaches to diverse degrees of union with Him by faith formed in charity. Hence in Him are the faithful circumcised, in Him baptized, in Him do they die, in Him are they quickened to life again by resurrection, in Him at last are they united to God in glory. Our justification then is not from ourselves but from Christ. He is all

fullness and therefore if we possess Him we possess all things. It is
by formed faith that we belong to Him in this life; and it is by faith
that we can be justified, as shall be said at greater length later. This
is the ineffable mystery of the Cross and of our redemption, in
which, beyond what has already been touched upon, Christ shows
us that truth and justice and the divine virtues must be preferred
to temporal life, as the eternal before the passing and perishing. In
the most perfect man the highest constancy, courage, charity and
humility should dwell, since the death of Christ reveals the presence of all these virtues in the maximal degree in the maximal
Jesus. The higher, then, a man rises in these immortal virtues, the
closer a resemblance bears he to Christ. Here the maximal and
minimal coincide: maximal humiliation with exaltation, the most
shameful death of the virtuous man with the most glorious life;
and so with the rest, all of which are laid bare to us in the life,
passion and crucifixion of Christ.

CHAPTER VII. THE MYSTERY OF THE RESURRECTION

Mortal and capable of suffering, Christ could reach the glory
of the Father, who, being absolute life, is immortality itself, only if
His mortal part put on immortality. And this could be done only
by death. How else could mortal put on immortality except by
being shorn of his mortality? and how could that be cancelled
except by the payment of the debt of death? Truth itself pro-
nounced those dull and slow of heart who did not understand that
Christ must die and so enter into His glory.

We have shown earlier that Christ died a most cruel death for
us. It now remains to say that, since it was fitting that human nature should be led to the triumph of immortality by no way but
by a victory over death, He underwent this death in order that
with Him human nature might rise to eternal life and that animal
and body might be rendered spiritual and incorruptible. As
true man He must needs be mortal, nor could He convey mor-

tal nature into immortality but in crushing mortality by death.

How neatly Truth itself inculcates this necessity when He says: 'Unless the grain of wheat falling upon the earth die, it remains itself alone; but if it die, it beareth much fruit.' If Christ had remained always mortal, even if He had never died, how could He have bestowed immortality upon the human race? Dying not, He would have continued mortal without death. It was needed, therefore, that he should be liberated from the possibility of death by dying, if He were to bear abundant fruit, so that lifted up He might draw all things to Himself; for His power was not only over a world and earth corruptible but also a heaven incorruptible.

Our ignorance may achieve some understanding of this if we keep in mind what was said above. For we showed there that the maximal man Jesus could not have a personal subsistence in Himself separately from the divinity because He is maximal. For this reason an interchange of attributes is allowed in (our speech about) Christ and the human things in Him coincide with the divine. For his humanity is inseparable from his divinity, being indeed in the most intimate union with it; it is, so to speak, clothed in, and caught up into, the divinity and is incapable of separate personal existence. A man consists of body and soul in closest union and the destruction of this union is death. Wherefore the maximal of humanity, whose existence is a divine person's, could not be separated, either body or soul, from that divine person, during the divorce of body and soul called death, for without the divine person the man Christ had no existence.

Christ therefore did not die in such fashion that His person was dissolved. In death there was no local separation from the centre in which His humanity was rooted, and He remained hypostatically united to the divinity. The lower nature, which could suffer the division of soul and body, in the temporal and local sense suffered that division, so that at the hour of death, body and soul were in time and place apart. But corruption was impossible either to body or to soul, for both were united to the eternal. That which was born in time was subject to temporal death and separation, but when the temporal composite had completed the circle of its return to dissolution and the body was now freed from time modifications, His true humanity, which is timeless, remained united incorruptible with the divinity and reunited as essential His true body and soul. The shadowy image of the true man, which had appeared in time, departed that the true man freed from all capacity to suffer might rise. The same Jesus, now exempt from temporal change and destined to die no more, now most truly rose by the reunion of soul with body, and now lives out of reach of temporal change. True incorruptible humanity could not have been hypostatically united to the divine person without confusion of natures, except by this union of body and soul.

Let Christ's illustration of the grain of wheat come to the rescue of our ignorance and small wit. The grain corrupts numerically while the specific essence remains whole for it is by means of this latter that nature will raise up many grains. If the grain were the maximal and most perfect possible, dying in a most excellent and fruitful soil, it would bring forth not a hundredfold nor a thousandfold but the total possibility comprised in the whole nature of that species. This is what Truth says when He says that it would bring forth much fruit; muchness or multitude is finite, but without number. Consider it more narrowly still. The humanity of Jesus must, in the very thought that it is contracted in the man Christ, be thought of at the same moment as united to the divinity. As united to the divinity it is absolute; as being that concrete man, Christ, it is limited, that through His humanity He may be a man. And thus the humanity of Jesus is as though midway between the purely absolute and the purely limited. Consequently it is only under certain aspects that we can call it corruptible; in itself and apart from particular circumstances it was incorruptible. It was corruptible in the time medium to which it had been contracted; but free from time and above time and united with the divinity, it was incorruptible.

Truth contracted to time is as a sign and image of supra-temporal truth. The truth of the body contracted to time is as the shadow of the truth of the supra-temporal body; and the truth of the contracted soul is as the shadow of the soul freed from time. While it is in time, the soul appears more like sense and reason than intellect; here below it cannot apprehend without pictures. But when it is freed from time the intellect is relieved of the need of pictures. Since Jesus' humanity was supernal, rooted indivisibly in the divine incorruption, at the end of corruptible time the resolution of soul and body could be made only in the direction of that root of incorruptibility. Wherefore at the end of the time-movement—which end is death—when all those things were removed which appertain to the truth of human nature only in its temporal aspect, the same Jesus rose, not with a body of weight and corruption and of the shadowy, passible qualities that belong to composition in time, but with a true, glorious, impassible, agile and immortal body, as was demanded by truth shorn of time-conditions. The truth of the hypostatic union of the human nature with the divine imperiously required this union. Whence Jesus, ever blessed, must rise from the dead as He Himself said: 'It behoveth Christ so to suffer and the third day rise from the dead.'

CHAPTER VIII. CHRIST THE FIRST-FRUITS FROM THE DEAD
ASCENDED INTO HEAVEN

From the above it will readily be seen that Christ is the first-born from the dead. None might rise from the dead before him, since human nature in time never yet attained the maximal or never united as in Christ with incorruptibility and immortality. All men were powerless until he should come who would say: 'I have power to lay down my life and to take it up again.' In Christ therefore, human nature put on immortality; and he is the first-born of them that sleep.

There is but one indivisible humanity and specific essence of all men by which all individual men are men numerically distinct each one from each. The same humanity is that of Christ and of all men, the numerical distinction of individuals remaining unblurred. Hence it is clear that the humanity of all men, who in the temporal order came before or after Christ, has in Christ put on immortality. We may, therefore, patently conclude:—Christ has risen: therefore all men shall rise, when all flow of corruptible time shall cease, and shall be for ever incorruptible. But while there is but one humanity of all men, there are various and divers individuating principles which contract that humanity to this or that subject; and in Jesus Christ alone these were most perfect and most powerful and closest to that essential humanity which was united to the divinity. In virtue of His humanity Christ was able of His own power to rise from the dead; and this power came to His humanity from the divinity, which is why God is said to have raised Him from the dead. Being God and man he rose by His own power, and save Him, no man may rise like Christ, except in the power of Christ, who is also God.

Christ it is, then, by whose human nature our human nature has put on immortality and by whom above time we shall rise in His likeness. . . . This shall be at the end of the world, when motion, in which we are born and immersed, shall have ceased. Christ whose birth from His mother only was temporal, did not await the complete flowing away of time before he rose; for time had no comprehension of his nativity. Observe that nature has put on immortality in Christ; wherefore we shall all rise by Christ but not all like Him, and in Him by union; these last shall be only those who are Christ's by faith, hope and charity.

If I mistake not, you now perceive that there is no perfect religion leading men to the last and most desirable end of peace, which does not embrace Christ as the mediator and saviour, God and man, the way, the life and the truth. See what senseless credulity the Saracens are guilty of, who confess Christ to be the greatest and most perfect of men, born of a virgin and caught up into heaven, but deny Him to be God. Blind indeed are they, for they assert the impossible. From what has gone above it must be clearer than light to every intelligent man, that no man could be in all things most perfect and the maximal of man born above nature of a virgin, unless he were also God. But these are senseless persecutors of the Cross of Christ and ignorant of his mysteries. They shall not taste the divine fruit of the redemption, indeed by their law they look not for it; for their law promises nothing but the indulgence of sensual desire. We hope for the crushing out of such desire in the death of Christ; we sigh for the possession of incorruptible glory.

The Jews also like these confess the Messias to be the maximal and most perfect and immortal man but, fixed in the same diabolical blindness, they deny him to be God. They also hope not for the supreme beatitude of the enjoyment of God, as do the servants of Christ; nor shall they achieve it. But, what to me is still more strange, both Jews and Saracens believe that there will be a general resurrection, but do not preceive that it is made possible only by a man who is also God. It might, indeed, be urged that when the movement of generation and corruption ended there could be no perfection of the universe without a resurrection. Human nature is the one essential element in the universe, without which it would be neither perfect nor even a universe, and hence, if time stopped, it would be necessary for men to rise to incorruption, if the whole universe is not to perish. In men, it might be urged, the nature of all mediants is completed, and it would not be necessary that other animals should rise, since man is their perfection. And it might further be submitted that resurrection is necessary that the whole man may receive from a just God the due reward of his deeds. But in addition to all this it is above all necessary to believe in Christ, God and man, by whom alone human nature can attain to incorruptibility.

Blind then are all who believe in a resurrection, and believe not in Christ who alone can make it possible. Faith in the resurrection is in fact the affirmation of the divinity and humanity of Christ and of the death and resurrection of Him who is the first-born from the dead, as was said above. He rose that by an ascension into heaven He might enter into glory. I am forced to conclude that this ascension must be one over all movement of corruption and all influence of the heavens. As God He is everywhere but He is more closely to be associated with that place where never is any change, suffering, sadness etc., such as are found among the things of time. And this place of eternal joy and peace we must assert to be above the heavens, although it is neither conceivable nor describable nor even definable as a place.

He is the centre and circumference of intellectual nature, and since the intellect embraces all, he is above all. But in holy rational souls and in intelligent spirits, who are the heavens that declare His glory, He reposes as in His temple. Thus we conceive Christ to have gone up above all place and all time to His incorruptible mansion, above all that can ever be said, inasmuch as He ascended above all the heavens that He might fulfil all things. As God, He is all in all things; and He reigns in the heavens of those intelligences, for He is truth itself; but not as located, that is, as in the circumference, but as in the centre he sits, for He, as being their life, is the centre of all rational spirits. Wherefore He himself affirms this kingdom of heaven to be also in men, for He is to souls the fountain of life and their last end.

CHAPTER IX. CHRIST, THE JUDGE OF THE LIVING AND THE DEAD

Who more just a judge than He who is justice itself? Christ, the fountain-head of every rational creature is Himself the maximal reason, from which flows all reason. Now it is reason's role to exercise discriminating judgment. Hence rightly is he the judge of the living and the dead who with all rational creatures assumed reasoning human nature, and all the while remained God, who is the rewarder of all. Above all time He judges all things by Himself and in Himself, for He embraces all things, being the maximal man, and in Him are all things since He is God. As God He is infinite light in which there is no darkness, and this light illumines all things so that in the light all things are most manifest to the light. And this infinite intellectual light embraces in its timelessness the present like the past and the living as the dead—as bodily light is the hypostasis of all colours. Christ is as the most pure fire which is inseparable from the light, subsisting not in itself but in the light. He is that spiritual fire of life and understanding which consumes all things and involves all in Himself and so, proves, tries and judges all things, like the judgment of the material fire which probes all things through and through. In Him are judged all rational spirits, like all material that is capable of burning. Some such is transformed totally into the very image of fire; like the best and most perfect gold which, remaining gold, is so intensely fired that it seems no longer gold but fire. Other kinds of material like alloyed silver or brass or iron share not such intensity of heat, though all seem transformed into fire, each in its own degree. Now this discrimination is made by the fire only and not by the different materials. For everything soaked in flame apprehends only that most intense heat and not the particular degree of heat it can stand. When we inspect molten gold or silver or copper in very intense fire, their transformation into the form of white heat makes it impossible for us to distinguish these metals. But if the fire itself had a mind, it would understand the degree of perfection of each metal and would adjust its intensity to the nature of each.

Certain ignitable materials can remain indestructible in fire and so, in various degrees of intensity can become capable of shedding light and heat in consequence of their transformation into the very likeness of fire. Others by reason of their alloys can be heated but not to the white heat of light. Christ our Judge, in one most simple and undivided judgment, in one moment most justly and without invidious distinction, communicates to each one, as in the order of nature, not in the order of time, the heat of created reason, that he may pour in upon that reason the light of God's intelligence, so that God be all in all things, and all things in God through this mediator himself, and all grow as much to his stature as their capacities allow. But some, because they are simpler and more unified, can receive both heat and light, others heat in some degree but no light; and all this is dependent upon the capacity of the recipient.

Since that infinite light is eternity and truth itself, it is imperative that the rational creature who desires to be enlightened by Him should rise above earthly and corruptible things and turn to things true and eternal. Corporal things and spiritual things work differently. The vegetative power of a body transmutes the nourishment it receives from outside into the nature of the creature nourished; the animal is not turned into bread, but bread into the animal. But the intelligent spirit, whose action is supra-temporal and, so to speak, upon an eternal level, when he turns to eternal things, cannot change them into himself. Nor can he, as being himself incorruptible, change into them and cease to be an intelligent substance. But he can be transformed into them in such fashion as to be absorbed into a likeness of eternal things; this, however, only in degrees. The greater and more fervent his preoccupation with them the more fully and deeply is he perfected by eternal things, and the more profoundly is his being hidden in the eternal being. Now Christ is more than immortal. He liveth, and He is the life and the truth. Whosoever turns to Him turns to life and to truth, and the more ardently He does this the higher is He raised above mundane and corruptible things to eternal things, until His life becomes hidden in Christ. Virtue is eternal. Justice endureth for ever and ever; and so also is it with truth. He that turneth to virtue, walketh in the ways of Christ, which are the ways of purity and immortality. Virtues are divine illuminations. He, therefore, that in this life turneth by faith to Christ who is virtue, shall be freed from this temporal life and shall be found in the purity of spirit, that he may enter into the joy of eternal possession.

CHAPTER X. THE JUDGE'S SENTENCE

It is clear that no mortal can understand that judgment and the sentence of that Judge. It is one outside all time and movement; it is not conducted by the weighing of pros and cons, by parallel cases, by discourses and deliberation that involve drawn out session and delay. In a Word were all things made—for, he spoke and they were made—in the Word, which is itself reason, are all things judged. Nor shall there be any interval between the judgment and the carrying it out. Resurrection, final decision, the glory of the accepted sons of God, the damnation and exclusion of souls averted from him, all shall be accomplished in an instant.

An intelligence is above time and unsubjected to temporal corruption, for by its nature it embraces within itself incorruptible forms. Such, for example, are the abstractions of mathematics—and even of physical things, which the mind buries in itself and readily transforms into abstractions or spiritual realities. All this is to us an indication of the mind's own incorruptibility, for the habitat and natural container of incorruptible things must itself be incorruptible. Now this intellect has a natural movement towards the most abstract truth as being the end of all its desires and its final and most delectable object. Now this ultimate object is in all things, for it is God; and the immortal and incorruptible human intelligence is insatiable till it attains him, for it is satisfied only with an eternal object.

But if, freed from the body in which it was subject to the conjectures of time, the intellect reaches not its desired end but falls into ignorance; if, made for truth and in its deepest desire seeking truth not in shadows and signs but rather with certitude and face to face, it now, turned in the hour of its dissolution from truth to the corruptible, pursues corruptible desires, it is rightly said to fall into intellectual death. For it is now occupied with uncertainty and confusion in the dark chaos of mere possibility, in which there is no firm actuality. It is the function of the intellect to know being, and this knowledge is its life. Wherefore, as to know at last the stable, eternal desired object is its life, so is it eternal death for it to be separated from that immutable desired thing and to be thrown into the very gulf itself of confusion where it will for ever, in some way possible to it, be tormented by fire. Its manner of suffering is not to us intelligible other than as the deprivation of its vital nourishment of truth and well-being, together with the loss of all hope of ever attaining to them, so that, without extinction and without end, it ever dies in agony.

This is a life bitter above all imagining, for it is death in life, it is being in nothingness, and knowledge more empty than ignorance. It was shown above that the resurrection of mankind is a rising above movement, time and quantity and all else that is subject to time. Here the corruptible becomes incorruptible, the animal is rendered spiritual, the whole man becomes his intelligence which is spirit and his body (still truly a body) is absorbed into the spirit. The body is no longer in itself as in its corporal and quantitative measurements, but buried in the spirit—a process which is the exact contrary of our state here, where no intellect is seen but only the body, wherein the intelligence seems to be imprisoned. But there the body is in the spirit as the spirit is in the body here; and as here the soul is weighed down by the body, there the body is lightened by the spirit. Hence, just as the spiritual joys of intellectual life are there keenest and in them the glorified body shares, so the sadness of that hell of spiritual death is most terrible, and in it the body in the soul has its share. Our God when apprehended is Himself eternal life and intelligible above all intellect. And therefore, those eternal joys, exceeding all understanding, are greater than words can ever convey.

Similarly, the sufferings of the damned are beyond all thinkable or describable sufferings. All those suggestions of joy, happiness and glory that the Fathers offer us from the analogy of earthly melody and harmony as pointers from things we know to the unknown joys of eternal life, are but pale sense-suggestions, infinitely distant from the truth, of that spiritual good that no imagination can picture. And similarly, the sufferings of hell which they liken to sulphurous fire and pitch and other sense-pains are very faintly described by these analogies, for these sufferings are fiery spiritual agonies; from all which may Our Lord Jesus Christ, our life and salvation, Who is for ever blessed, deign to preserve us. Amen.

CHAPTER XI. THE MYSTERIES OF FAITH

Our ancient writers are at one in asserting that faith lies at the root of all understanding. In every science certain things must be accepted as first principles if the subject matter is to be understood; and these first postulates rest only upon faith. He who wishes to rise to knowledge must first believe those things without which knowledge is impossible. Says Isaias: 'Unless you believe you shall not understand.' Faith, therefore, embraces every intelligible thing. Understanding is the unfolding of what was wrapped up in faith. The intelligence is therefore directed by faith; and faith is extended by understanding. Without sound faith then there is no true understanding. There is no mistaking the kinds of conclusions that are reached from faulty principles and from a weak foundation: and on the other hand, there is no faith more perfect than that which is founded upon the truth itself, which is Jesus.

Everyone knows that a right faith is the most excellent gift of God. The Apostle John tells us that faith in the Incarnation of the Word of God leads us into truth, that we may become the sons of God. He first sets forth this faith simply and only then narrates many works of Christ in accordance with this faith, that the intelligence may be enlightened in faith. And at the end he suggests the conclusion: 'These things are written that you may believe that Jesus is the Son of God.'

Now this most wholesome faith in Christ, constantly strength-
ened in simplicity, can, in our accepted doctrine of ignorance, be
extended and unfolded. The greatest and profoundest mysteries
of God, though hidden from the wise, may be revealed to little
ones and humble folk living in the world by their faith in Jesus:
for in Jesus are hidden all the treasures of wisdom and of knowledge, so that without Him no man can do anything. For He is
the Word, and the power by whom God made the world, He
the most high having alone power over everything in heaven and
on earth. He cannot be apprehended within the context of this
world. Here we are led by reason, opinion, or doctrine from the
better known to the less known by symbols; whereas he is grasped
only when movement ceases and faith takes its place. By this faith
we are caught up into simplicity above all reason and intelligence
to the third heaven of most pure simple intellectuality; that in the
body we may contemplate him incorporeally, because in spirit,
and on the earth in an entirely unearthly fashion and rather in a
heavenly and incomprehensible manner, whereby we perceive
that He cannot be comprehended because of the immensity of His
excellence. And this is none other than that very learned ignorance—by which the blessed Paul himself, raised higher and into a
closer knowledge, perceived that the Christ with whom he was
at one time acquainted, he never really knew.

We, then, believers in Christ, are led in learned ignorance to
the mountain that is Christ, which our animal nature is forbidden
to touch; and when we endeavour to gaze upon Him with the eye
of the mind we fall into darkness, knowing that in that very darkness is the mount in which He is pleased to dwell for the sake of all
those who live a life of the spirit. But if, in the constancy of a
firmer faith we approach Him, we are snatched away from the
eyes of them that live by sensuality, to perceive with interior hearing the voices and the thunder and the dread signs of His majesty.
We are given to realize that he alone is the Lord whom all things
obey. And step by step we come close even to certain incorrupti-

ble footprints of Him (as to most divine characters) in which, hearing the voice not of mortal creatures but of God Himself in His holy organs and in the words of His prophets and saints, we come, as in a cloud of more transparent quality, to perceive Him more clearly.

At this point the believer, moving ever upwards in more ardent desire, is caught up into intellectual simplicity and leaps above all sensible things, as though passing from sleep to watchfulness and from hearing to sight; there are things seen which cannot be revealed, because they are above all that mortal ever heard and above all the speech of man. For if these revelations came to be told, unutterable things would be framed in human speech, things beyond all hearing would fall upon human ears; for what is there seen is beyond mortal sight. For there is heard incomprehensibly and as surpassing all speech, Jesus for ever blessed, the term of all understanding because He is the Truth, of all sense for He is Life, the finality of all being as He is Being itself, and the perfection of creation for He is God and man. From Him all speech came and to Him it all must return, for all that is true in speech is from Him. For all speech if for instruction, and therefore to Him it must belong Who is wisdom itself. 'Whatever is written is written for our instruction.' Writing is but speech that has been given permanent shape. 'By the word of the Lord the heavens were firmly set up.' All created characters therefore are representative of the Word of God. Spoken word stands for the word of the mind; and this incorruptible word is reason; which is Christ himself, the incarnate Reason of all reasoning; for the Word was made flesh. Jesus therefore is the end of all things.

To the man who rises to Christ by faith such things become clear by degrees. Now the divine efficacy of this faith cannot be explained; for if it be strong, it unites the believer with Jesus so that he ascends above all that is not in union with Jesus. For such a man, if he have full faith in the power of Jesus to whom he is united, exerts a power over movement and nature and commands even the evil spirits; and, as the acts of the saints often witness, marvellous things are wrought, not by him himself but by Jesus in him and through him.

This perfect faith of Christ should be most pure, most intense and, as completely as possible, formed in charity. It does not admit of any admixture or alloy, for it is a faith in the most pure truth that can do all things. Very often in the course of this work we have found the minimum to coincide with the maximum. It is thus with a faith which is simply and purely maximal in act and possibility; it cannot be found in an earthly being unless he be also a heavenly one, as Jesus was. If an earthly soul wished to possess the maximal faith of Christ in pure actuality, such faith would have to be of such indubitable certitude that it were no longer faith but the highest unhesitating certitude in every point.

Here is the all-powerful faith which is the maximum and the minimum and embraces all that is to be believed in him who is the Truth itself. And if the faith of one man does not attain the degree of another's because equality is impossible—just as a thing seen is not seen as exactly the same by several different people—this nevertheless is essential, that each one believe to the full power of belief that is in him. Then, even if he exhibit by comparison with others the faith only of a grain of mustard seed, so great is the power of that faith that it exacts obedience from the mountains themselves; for it commands by the power of the Word of God, to whom he is, in his measure, strongly united by faith: and none can resist that power.

Such by the power of Christ will become the force of your intellectual spirit, if it adhere to Him above all things and be so nourished by Him and be so one with Him by union as to become—its individuality always reserved—as it were, supposited in His life. But if this is brought about only by the complete turning of the spirit—which draws the sense with it—to Him in strongest faith, that faith itself must be formed in unitive Charity. Complete faith is not possible without charity. Every living thing loves life and every intellect loves to know. How then could Jesus, immortal life itself and infinite truth, be believed in and not loved with the most ardent love. Life of itself is lovable; if Jesus therefore is believed to be eternal life, it must be impossible not to love Him. For faith without charity is not living faith but dead, and ultimately, not faith at all. But charity is the form of faith and that which gives it true being; indeed it is the sign of the most unshakeable faith. When all things are abandoned for His sake, when body and soul themselves are reckoned as nothing by comparison with Him, then have you certificate of a most powerful faith.

Nor can faith be strong without the holy hope of enjoying Jesus. There would be little surety in a faith that did not hope for the promises of Christ. If a man does not hope to possess the eternal life which Christ has promised to believers, can he be said to believe in Christ? Can he be said to hold Christ to be the truth? If he has not an unshakeable hope in the promises, how could he choose death for Christ, having no hope of immortality? It is because he holds that Christ abandons none that hope in Him, but bestows upon them eternal beatitude, that the believer judges it well to suffer all things for Christ and to await so great a reward for so little.

Great indeed is the power of faith which fashions a man in Christ's mould so that he forsakes sensible things, denudes himself of the contagions of the flesh, walks in fear in the way of the Lord, follows in the footsteps of Christ with joy, and willingly and even exultantly takes up the cross. Such a one is as a spirit in the flesh; to him for Christ's sake this world is death, and life lies in its removal that he may be with Christ. Of what spirit is he in whom Christ dwells by faith? What is that amazing gift of God which by faith raises us, poor pilgrims in frail flesh though we be, to such power above all that is not Christ by union. Let us brace ourselves that each one aspire by daily mortification to rise by steps to union with Christ, even, as far as may be, to the deep union of absorption in him. Such a one, leaping above all visible and mundane things, reaches the complete perfection of his nature.

Here is the perfected nature which, the flesh and sin being destroyed, we may attain in a transformation into the image of Christ. This is far removed from those occult practices of certain necromancers who claim that a man may be raised by faith to a close union with a spirit who is his familiar, and by the spirit's power be able to work wonders in fire or in water, to effect strange transformations with the help of magical musical incantations, or to reveal the closest secrets of nature. It is quickly recognized that in all these things the soul is seduced and turned aside from life and truth. Such souls become completely fettered to these dark spirits and their faith issuing in deeds they offer them, with incense, the worship that belongs only to God. This worship they discharge with abject reverence and much incantation, as to one capable of granting their requests. And their trust does sometimes bring them their earthly desires; but they are held close to a spirit to whom, divided eternally from Christ, they will for ever adhere in torments.

God be praised that he has by his Son redeemed us from the darkness of such ignorance and has taught us that all is false and a lie, howsoever produced, that comes to us from any other mediator than Christ who is the truth, and from any other faith but that of Jesus. There is but one Lord Jesus, the master of all things, who fills us with every blessing and who alone makes ample satisfaction for all our deficiencies.

CHAPTER XII. THE CHURCH

The nature of the church may be gathered from what has gone before but I shall add a brief word upon it to complete this work.

Faith of necessity enters into and dwells in different souls in different degrees; and no man may hope to attain the maximal faith, than which no greater could exist, as similarly none can reach the maximal charity. Maximal faith, than which none could be greater, if it dwelt in a soul here below, would at once render him a sharer of the beatific vision; for the maximal in any genus, as it is the ultimate terminal of that genus, is thereby the initial point of the genus next above. Whence maximal faith can simply not be in any man who is not also in the state of comprehensor. Similarly maximal charity cannot be in a lover who is not at the same time the Beloved Himself. Whence neither faith nor charity in the maximal degree are predicable of any man but of Jesus Christ, Who is both viator and comprehensor, at once the man who loves and the God who is beloved. Within the maximal are all things included for it embraces all. In the faith of Jesus Christ, all true faith and in His charity all true charity are comprehended, each in its distinct degree. These distinct degrees lying below the maximum and above the minimum, no man, even if he possess, as far as could be, the maximal faith of Christ, could reach that maximal faith by which he might comprehend Christ, God and man. Nor could any man so love Christ that He could not possibly be loved more; for Christ is love and charity itself and consequently infinitely loveable. No one, that is, could either here or hereafter love Christ so much as to become Christ and man. All then who are united to Christ either by faith and love here below or by taste and embrace hereafter, are united to Him in a particular degree, and this degree determines the intimacy of the union; and none subsists in himself apart from this union, nor does the union destroy the individual's degree.

Now this union is the church, the gathering together of many into one, as the many members are gathered into one body, each in his own degree. One member is not another, but each with the others is one body which unifies them all. None can enjoy life and existence apart from the body, while none can claim to be the body except as dwelling in the body. While we journey here below the truth of our faith can subsist or continue to be only in the spirit of Christ, while the order of believers remains a high diversity in agreement, in one and the same Christ. And when we sink out of the church militant at death, we shall afterwards rise only by the power of Christ, so that the church triumphant shall also be one, with each in his own hierarchical niche. Then shall the truth of our flesh be not in itself but in the truth of the flesh of Christ, the truth of our body shall be in the truth of Christ's body, and the truth of our spirit in the truth of the spirit of Christ Jesus, like the branches of the vine; so that there shall be but one humanity in all, the humanity of Christ, and one spirit, that of Christ, in all spirits, and that each may dwell in Him in such fashion that there is but one Christ in all. Hence, in this life to receive one of all that are Christ's is to receive Christ, and to do unto the least of His is to do unto Him. To wound Plato's hand is to wound Plato; if a foot is caught in the smallest snare, the whole man is thereby caught. In the heavenly country to rejoice in anything however small is to rejoice in Jesus and to see Jesus in everything: for by him is God ever blessed. Thus by His Son shall our God be all in all things, and each member in His Son and through him united with God, and with all things, that joy may be full without envy or any defect.

While we sojourn here our faith can continually increase as can also charity. Each it is true is in such a degree that at a given moment and given his nature he may not be in another; but while he is in one degree he is in potency to another, though never in potency to the infinite charity of Christ. But we must, by the grace of our Lord Jesus Christ work to actualize our total possibility, and to move from virtue to virtue and from degree to degree, by him who is faith and charity. Of ourselves, as ourselves, we can without him do nothing. But all that we can do, we can do in him who alone can make up for our deficiencies, that in the day of resurrection we may be found to be integral and noble members of him. Believing and loving with all our power, we can confidently beg of Him this grace of increased faith and charity, in tireless prayer approaching His throne with great trust. For He is infinitely merciful and loving and permits none to be defrauded of His holy desire.

Dwell upon these things as they are, and you shall be flooded to the depths of your soul with a gracious sweetness of spirit and shall scent the inexpressible goodness of God in an interior taste and most aromatic incense, which, passing, He will minister to you; and with which you shall be satisfied when His glory shall appear. You shall be satisfied, I repeat, and with no disgust of satiety, for this immortal food is life itself. And as the desire to live increases ever, so the food of life is eaten ever, but never to become the nature of the partaker. That food sets up disgust which oppresses the stomach but does not bestow immortal life, for it fails of its nature and becomes the nature of the feeder. But the desire of our mind is to live by mind, which is continually to enter more and more into life and joy. But life and joy are infinite; and the blessed are borne into life and joy by ardent desire. They who drink of the fountain of life are satisfied in such fashion as still to thirst; and as this drink never becomes a past thing, for it is eternal, ever are they blessed both drinking and in thirst, and never shall that thirst and its satisfaction pass.

Praised be God who has given us a mind that cannot be satisfied with the temporal. Its desire having no limits, it recognizes itself as above all time immortal, from its insatiable desire within time. It perceives that it cannot be satiated with the desired intellectual life except in the fruition of the most excellent and highest good that can never fail. The enjoyment of that good can never become a thing of the past, for appetite can never grow less. To offer an illustration from the body, it is as if a starving man sat at a great king's table, to be plied with the one food that he longed for, the nature of which food was to sharpen the appetite the more it filled. If such food never gave out, it is clear that in being filled, the feeder would continue to long for the same food and be ardently moved to continue to seek it. A man would always

long for a food whose power was to stimulate the feeder to seek
it with greater and greater desire. Such is the power of an intellectual nature, that receiving life into itself, it is transformed
into that life, to the degree of its power of transformation. The
air which receives into itself the ray of the sun becomes itself
light. The intellect becomes the thing it understands; but it understands only the universal and incorruptible and enduring
things, for incorruptible truth is its object; and to this is it by
its nature moved. And this truth it apprehends in the still peace
of eternity in Christ Jesus.

Such is the Church Victorious in which is our God for ever
blessed. There is Christ Jesus, true man, united with the Son of
God in such supreme union that the humanity has no foothold
in existence except in the divinity: and in such ineffable hypostatic union that the truth of his humanity could not bear a deeper
or more simple union and continue to be. Furthermore, if every
rational nature were in this life turned to Christ in deepest faith
and hope and charity, while the personal reality of each remained
intact, all would be so united to Christ that all, angels and men,
would have no existence apart from Him. By Him the reality of
the body of each one is to be drawn in and absorbed in God
through its own proper spirit, so that each one of the blessed,
the reality of his own being untouched, should be in Christ,
Jesus Christ Himself, and through Him God in God, and that
God Himself, remaining the absolute maximum, should be in
Christ Jesus, Jesus Himself, and the all in all things through Him.

In no other way can the Church be completely one. For the
church means the unity of the many, with the preservation of the
personal reality of each, without confusion of natures or degrees.
Now the more the church is one, the greater she is. But this
Church is the Church at its greatest possible point. This Church
then, the Church of the eternally triumphant, is the most vast because a greater union in her is not conceivable. Gaze deep into
this union where the union is absolutely maximal and divine, and

where is found the unity of Godhead and humanity in Jesus and the unity of the Church of the victorious blessed with the Godhead of Jesus. Nor is absolute unity itself greater than the unity of the natures in Jesus or of the blessed in heaven. For it is the maximal unity, which is the union of all unions and that which is all unions, receiving neither less nor more, and proceeding, as was shown in the First Book, from unity and equality. Nor is the union of the natures in Christ greater or less than the unity of the church triumphant, since, being the maximal union of natures, it suffers in this neither greater nor less.

Whence all diversities that become united take their unity from that very maximal union of the natures in Christ. By this, the unity of the Church is what it is. But the unity of the Church is the maximal ecclesiastical unity. And being maximal, it coincides with the hypostatic union of the natures of Christ above it. And the union of the natures in Jesus coincides with the absolute unity which is God. Thus the unity of the Church, which is the union of subjects with her, although it does not seem as perfect as the hypostatic union, which is one of natures only, or as the first divine simplicity, in which no otherness or diversity could exist, is nevertheless resolved by Jesus into the divine unity from which it first took its rise. This shall be better seen if we recall what has often been insisted upon earlier. The absolute unity is the Holy Spirit. The maximal hypostatic union coincides with the absolute unity. From this it follows that the union of natures in Christ is by the absolute, which is the Holy Spirit, and exists only in it. Now, as we have shown, the unity of the Church coincides with the hypostatic union; whence, in the spirit of Jesus, who is in the Holy Spirit, lies the union of the triumphant souls in heaven. So says Truth itself in St. John: 'The glory which thou gavest me I have given to them; that they may be one as we are one, I in them and thou in me, that they may be made perfect in one.' In consequence the church in eternal peace will be so perfect that it could not be more so, and so transformed in the light of glory that in all things only God shall appear. To this church of so great love and triumph do we aspire, imploring God the Father Himself with suppliant hearts that by His Son, Our Lord Jesus Christ, and in Him by the Holy Spirit, that He would grant us of His immense love this union, that we may eternally enjoy Him Who is for ever blessed.—Amen.

CONCERNING WISDOM

THE TWO BOOKS, *De Sapientia*, have been acclaimed by critics as the "most important discussion of wisdom in the late Middle Ages." [1] They form as it were, a bridge between the *Learned Ignorance* and the *Vision of God* in Cusa's endeavor to bring the entire Trinity into his philosophical system and to give the Logos a more dynamic setting in the speculative pursuit of Wisdom. Written during the summer of 1450, the two treatises reflect the somber joy of the year of Jubilee in Rome of the restored Papacy. We find here the recurring theme of all his writings, the Pauline insistence that the knowledge of this world which seems to surpass all others is in fact a stumbling block as it puffs man up rather than humbles him. Wisdom is not to be found in books, she cries out in the streets proclaiming to all that she dwells in the very highest places. The object of our knowledge is the recognition of our ignorance. It is to perceive that Wisdom Itself is higher than all knowledge and utterly unknowable. To recognize this condition is the greatest wisdom and in itself absolute precision. For Cusa the Logos is an infinite intellectual form and the actuality of all formable

1. E. Rice, *The Renaissance Idea of Wisdom* (Harvard, 1958) p. 19.

forms, the formal principle of all creation from which and back to which all existing things flow. God created all things by His Word, Who is God and Who is Wisdom. For to assert that God made all things in Wisdom is no more than to say that God created all things in His Word. Thus for Cusa, as for Aquinas divine Wisdom is identical with the Word of God with Whom we can communicate by participation but who remains in Himself transcendent and unattainable as He is in Himself.

DE SAPIENTIA

BOOK ONE

Author: A certain citizen or private individual met in the Roman Forum a very wealthy Orator whom he smilingly though courteously addressed in the following manner.

Citizen: I am quite amazed at your pride, for even though you have worn yourself out with the continual reading of innumerable books, you are none the less not moved to humility. This can be for no other reason than that the knowledge of this world wherein you believe you have surpassed all others, is actually foolishness in the sight of God, and has the effect of puffing men up, whereas true knowledge humbles them. I wish that you would advert to this fact because it is the treasure of all happiness.

Orator: This is certainly a great presumption on your part that being a poor citizen and completely unlearned you should underestimate the pursuit of learning without which no one progresses or improves himself.

Citizen: It is not so much presumption, O great Orator, but rather charity that keeps me from remaining silent; for I perceive that you are entirely given over to the pursuit of wisdom and with much wasted effort and it is from this that I would, if I am able, like to rescue you, so that you might see your error. I am convinced that once you have escaped from this trap you would truly rejoice. The opinion of authority has led you astray and you are like a horse who, though being by nature free, is tied with a halter to a stall and is fed only what is given to him. Your mind, bound as it is by the authority of writers, is nurtured on strange and oftimes unnatural food.

Orator: If the food of wisdom is not to be found in the books of wise men, then where is it to be found?

Citizen: I do not say that it is not found there but rather that one does not find in books the natural food of wisdom. Those who first endeavoured to write of wisdom did not apply themselves to nonexisting books but rather by natural nourishment were brought to a state of perfection, and it is quite evident that they have surpassed all those who believe they have profited from books.

Orator: Although it is perhaps possible that some things may be known without the study of letters, nevertheless, difficult and important matters cannot possibly be known since learning is increased by additions.

Citizen: I have already pointed out that you are led by authority and in this way you are deceived. Someone writes something and you believe him. I wish to say that wisdom cries out in the very streets and her cry is how she dwells in the highest.

Orator: From what you have said so far, you seem to think that you are yourself wise and yet you are nothing more than a simple citizen.

Citizen: This is perhaps the real difference between you and me. You consider yourself wise when actually you are not, and are proud of the fact. I, however, realize that I am a simple citizen and am consequently more humble and as a result more learned.

Orator: How can you as a simple citizen be brought to a knowledge of your own ignorance?

Citizen: Not by your books but by the books of God.

Orator: What are they?

Citizen: They are those which He has written with His own finger.

Orator: Where can they be found?

Citizen: Everywhere.

Orator: Do you mean in this very marketplace?

Citizen: Certainly, for I have already said that wisdom cries out in the very streets.

Orator: I would certainly like to know how.

Citizen: If I could perceive that you are really desirous to learn and not motivated by mere curiosity, then I would gladly make these great matters known to you.

Orator: Can you do this in a cursory manner so that I might get a taste of your meaning?

Citizen: Certainly I can.

Orator: Might I suggest that we withdraw from the street here and go over to this little barbershop so that we discuss this in more quiet surroundings.

Author: This was agreeable to the citizen and so they withdrew, and seating themselves in this secluded place the citizen, facing the marketplace, began his discussion.

Citizen: Since I have already pointed out that wisdom cries out in the very streets and her message is that she dwells in the very highest places, I will try to prove this. First of all tell me what you see here in the marketplace.

Orator: Over in one place I see money tellers, in another produce being weighed, and right opposite us I see oil being measured as well as other things.

Citizen: There are actually operations of reason whereby man surpasses the beast. For the beast can neither enumerate, nor weigh, nor measure. Now consider for a moment by what and in what these things are accomplished.

Orator: By making distinctions.

Citizen: You are quite right. But by what means is distinction achieved? Is it not by one?

Orator: What do you mean by that?

Citizen: Is not one times one one, two times one two, and three times one three, and so on?

Orator: I'll have to admit that.

Citizen: Therefore all enumeration is based on one.

Orator: It seems that way.

Citizen: Since then one is the beginning of enumeration, then the least weight is the beginning of weighing, and the least measure the beginning of measuring. Let us call therefore the least weight an ounce, and the least measure an inch; then as we number by one, so we weigh by the ounce, and measure by the inch. In the same manner enumeration proceeds from one, weighing from the ounce, and measuring from the inch. Likewise in one is enumeration, in an ounce is weighing, and in an inch measuring. Isn't this so?

Orator: Certainly.

Citizen: But how then do we attain unity? By what inch or by what ounce?

Orator: That I am not able to say. Yet I am sure that unity is not attained by number since number comes after one. In the same manner neither is the ounce arrived at by the weight nor the inch by measure.

Citizen: What you say is quite correct; for just as that which is simple is in nature before what is a composite, so the composite is in nature after the simple. And hence it is that the composite cannot measure the simple, but rather the contrary is true, and we may conclude from this how that by which, of which, and in which everything enumerable is numbered, is not attainable by enumeration. It is also evident that that by which, of which, and in which everything weighable is weighed is not attainable by weight and likewise that by which, of which, and in which every measurable thing is measured is not to be attained by measure.

Orator: I can see this quite clearly.

Citizen: Transfer then this cry of wisdom in the streets into the highest place where wisdom dwells and you will find things more delectable than even the most ornate books contain.

Orator: Unless you explain what you mean by this I'm afraid I can't follow you.

Citizen: And unless your request comes from affection I cannot make them known since the secrets of wisdom are not to be opened to everyone indiscriminately.

Orator: I am certainly anxious to hear more from you; for the few things you have already related have enkindled my interest. And from what you have already mentioned there is evidence of even greater to follow. Therefore I earnestly entreat you to continue with what you already have begun.

Citizen: I am not sure that I can easily reveal these great secrets and demonstrate their deep profundity. Yet I will go along with your request. The highest wisdom consists in this, to know, using the above mentioned simile, how that which is unattainable may be reached or attained unattainably.

Orator: What you say is quite amazing but not quite consonant.

Citizen: This is the very reason why these secret things ought not to be revealed to everyone, because when they are made known they appear to many as absurdities. You wonder why it is I speak things that seem to contradict one another; yet you will hear and taste the truth. That which I have already said relating to unity, the ounce, and the inch must likewise be predicated of all things as they relate to the beginning of all things. For the beginning of all things is that by which, in which, and of which everything that can have a beginning has a beginning, and is yet attainable by what has a beginning. This it is by which, in which, and of which every intelligible thing is understood and yet remains itself unattainable by any understanding; that it is by which, in which, and of which everything spoken is spoken and yet which of itself is ineffable in any language. It is that by which, in which, and of which every terminable thing is determined and every limitable thing limited and yet itself remains interminable by any terms, unlimited by any limit. You can make almost an unlimited number of such true propositions and fill all the oratorical volumes even to the point of adding to them indefinitely to show how wisdom dwells in the highest. For that is the highest which cannot be higher; and only infinity reaches that altitude. Hence it is that wisdom (which all men by their very nature desire to know and consequently seek after with such great affection of mind) is known in no other way than that it is higher than all knowledge and utterly unknowable and unspeakable in all language. It is unintelligible to all understanding, immeasurable by all measure, improportionable by every proportion, incomparable by all comparison, infigurable by all figuration, unformable by all formation, immovable by all motion, unimaginable by all imagination, insensible to all sensation, intractable to all attraction; untastable in all taste, inaudible in all hearing, invisible in all sight, inapprehensible in all apprehension and unaffirmable in all affirmation, undeniable in all negation, indoubtable in all doubt, inopinionable in all opinion; and because in all speech it is unexpressable there can be no limit to the means of expressing it, being incognitable in all cognition by which, in which, and of which are all things.

Orator: There can be no doubt that these things are far beyond what I had expected to hear from you. Please continue and proceed to where we may be able to test some of these high and sublime theories. It is quite evident that you will never be quite satisfied in speaking of this wisdom, and I am convinced that the great sweetness contained therein is to be tasted only with an inner taste. Otherwise the attraction would not be so great.

Citizen: It is then wisdom which tastes and there is nothing sweeter to the understanding. Nor are they to be considered in any way wise who speak the word only and not by the taste. And they speak with gusto of wisdom who through it know all things in such wise that they know nothing at all; for by wisdom and in it and of it is all the internal relish and taste. Yet because it dwells in the highest it is not tastable by any relish or taste. Therefore, it is tasted untastably in so far as it is higher than all that is tastable, sensible, rational, or intellectual. To taste in an untastable manner is as it were to savor something from afar as, for example, if we could say by the aroma of something we get a foretaste of it. For just as the aroma of something odoriferous is multiplied and picked up or acquired by another and thus attracts us to the race to run to the anointed in the odor of the ointments, so the eternal and infinite Wisdom shining in all things invites us, with a certain foretaste of its effects, to be borne to it with a wonderful desire. For in a similar way life itself is an intellectual spirit having in itself a certain innate foretaste through which it searches with great desire the very font of its own life. Without that foretaste it could neither seek after it nor know when it had acquired it. It is due to this that it is moved toward it as its proper life. Every spirit finds it sweet to ascend continually to the very principle of life even though this be inaccessible. For a persistent and continued ascent to life is the constituent element of increased happiness.

In this search for life when it finally sees that it is something infinite, there occurs a corresponding increase of joy proportionated to its vision of immortality. In this way it comes to pass that the very inaccessibility or incomprehensibility of its infinite life becomes that which is most desired and longed for. It is as if a man discovers that the treasure of his life is innumerable, unweighable, and immeasurable. And this very awareness of the incomprehensibility is most desirable not because it refers to the one comprehending but to the most lovable treasure of his life. In loving something lovable he finds that in it there is to be found the infinite and inexpressable causes of love. This is the lover's most joyful comprehension, when he comprehends the incomprehensible loveliness of the thing loved. For he would never choose as an object of his love something comprehensible if he compared it with what is utterly immeasurable, indeterminable, and completely incomprehensible. This is how I express the most joyful comprehensibility of the incomprehensible.

Orator: Let me see whether or not I have correctly understood you. It seems to be your intention to point out that our beginning by which, in which, and of which we are and are moved is then tasted by us as the beginning, middle, and end. When its vital sweetness is intastably tasted by the affection and incomprehensibly comprehended by the understanding, then he who makes an effort by way of taste to taste it and by comprehension to comprehend becomes utterly without taste as well as understanding.

Citizen: You have understood me quite correctly. For they who think that wisdom is nothing other than that which is comprehensible by the understanding, and happiness nothing else than what they can attain are quite far from true eternal and infinite wisdom. They are turned to that which is finite and finding there a certain determinable rest they think this to be the happiness of life. But it is not. Once they discover their deception they are greatly disturbed for where they thought to find happiness and towards which they have directed all their efforts they find only sorrow and death.

Wisdom is the infinite and never failing food of life upon which our spirit lives eternally since it is not able to love anything other than wisdom and truth. Every intellect seeks after being and its being is living; its living is to understand; its understanding is nurtured on wisdom and truth. Thus it is that the understanding that does not taste clear wisdom is like an eye in the darkness. It is an eye but it does not see because it is not in light. And because it lacks a delectable life which for it consists in seeing, it is in pain and torment and this is death rather than life. So too, the intellect that turns to anything other than the food of eternal wisdom will find itself outside of life, bound up in the darkness of ignorance, rather dead than alive. This is the interminable torment, to have an intellect and never to understand. For it is only the eternal wisdom in which every intellect can understand.

Orator: What you say is both beautiful and seldom said. Now pray tell me how I can be lifted up to some taste of the eternal wisdom.

Citizen: The eternal wisdom is tasted in every tastable thing; it is delight in everything delightful. It is beauty in all that is beautiful. It is the appetite in every appetible thing and is so with regard to all desirable things. How can it possibly not be tasted? Is not your life pleasant to you when it corresponds to your desire?

Orator: Yes, but is that all?

Citizen: Since, therefore, this desire of yours does not exist except through eternal wisdom from which and in which it is and in the same way this happy life itself is naught else but from the eternal wisdom in which it resides and without which it cannot be, it follows that in whatever you desire of the intellectual life you desire nothing other than the eternal wisdom which is the fulfillment of your desire, the beginning as well as the middle and end of it. If, therefore, this desire for immortal life, this desire to live eternally happy is sweet to you, you have already found within yourself a certain foretaste of the eternal wisdom. For there is really nothing that is desired that is not already known. Among the Indians there are certain types of apples but since we have no foretaste of them we have no desire for them. Since we cannot live without nourishment we have a certain innate desire for it. In fact we have a certain foretaste for nourishment so that our physical life can continue. A child has a certain foretaste for milk in his natural makeup and when he is moved by hunger naturally seeks milk. For we are nourished by those very elements by which we are made. In like manner the understanding has its life from the eternal wisdom and it has accordingly a certain foretaste of what must nourish it. Hence in all nourishment which it needs for life it is not moved to feed upon anything other than that from which it receives its intellectual being.

If, therefore, in every desire of the intellectual life you would consider the source of the intellect, through what it is moved and towards what it moves, you would discover in yourself that the sweetness of eternal life is that which renders this desire of yours so sweet and delectable.

If you take the example of the iron and the magnet you will find that iron has in the magnet a certain beginning of its own effluence. While the magnet by its presence attracts the heavy and ponderous iron, the iron, with a marvelous desire, is drawn contrary to the motion of nature whereby it should press earthward, and is moved upwards by uniting itself to its beginning. Except for the fact that there is in iron a certain natural foretaste of the magnet, it would no more be attracted to the magnet than to any ordinary stone, and except for the fact that there is in the magnet a greater inclination towards iron than to copper there would be no attraction and drawing.

Accordingly our intellectual spirit has from the eternal wisdom a principle of being thus intellectually and this makes it more in conformity with wisdom than any non-intellectual being. That is why the irradiation or immission into a holy soul is a most desirable movement towards and awakening of the soul. For he who seeks after wisdom with intellectual motion is already inwardly touched by the foretaste of the sweetness and its reception into the body renders the body almost incorporeal. The weight of no sensible thing can hold him down until he unites himself to the attracting wisdom, and this causes the soul to forsake the senses and to appear mad in that it no longer concerns itself with anything other than this wisdom. For such a person it is sweetness to leave this world and this life in order the more readily to be carried into the wisdom of immortality.

It is this foretaste that makes what is ordinarily delightful to appear abominable to holy men who bear patiently all kinds of bodily torments to obtain it sooner. This teaches us that once our spirit turns to it, it can never fail. For since our very body is unable by any corporeal tie to contain the spirit, but freeing itself from all the duties of the body it urgently seeks the eternal wisdom, then certainly, though the body fail, it will never fail. For this assimilation, which abides naturally in our soul, and which without this wisdom is a source of disquietude, is as it were a certain living image of the same. For the image is not at rest unless it be in the presence of that which it reflects and from which it has its beginning, middle, and end. This living image by its very life stirs up a motion toward the Exemplar in which it alone can rest. The life of the image is unable to find rest in itself since it is the life of the life of truth and not its own. Thus it is moved toward the Exemplar as toward the truth of its being. If, therefore, the Exemplar be eternal, and the image have life, in which it has a foretaste of the Exemplar, it will be moved towards it with great desire. Since this vital motion cannot find rest except in that infinite life which is the eternal wisdom, the motion will not cease in the attainment of the finite which never touches the infinite. It is moved with a continual desire to reach it and the delightfulness of the attraction is never lessened. For wisdom is such a pleasant food that it satisfies without diminishing the appetite and thus provides a delight that never ceases.

Orator: I certainly understand what you have presented in such a masterly fashion. However, I find a great discrepancy between the taste of wisdom and what we generally predicate of our sense of taste.

Citizen: I think that you are right in that respect and your words certainly please me. Just as any knowledge of the taste of something we have never actually tasted is quite empty until we do taste it, so the taste of this wisdom cannot be acquired by hearsay but by one's actually touching it with his internal sense, and then he will bear witness not of what he has heard but what he has experimentally tasted in himself. To know of the many descriptions of love which the saints have left us without knowing the taste of love is nothing other than a certain emptiness. Thus it is that it is not enough for him who seeks after eternal wisdom to merely read about these things, but it is absolutely necessary that once he discovers where it is by his understanding he make it his very own. He who finds a treasure hidden in a field cannot rejoice or enjoy that treasure if it is in another man's field. For that reason he sells all he has and purchases the field, that he may have the treasure in his own field. The eternal wisdom will not be obtained unless the possessor keeps nothing of his own. That which we have of our own are our vices and that which we have of the eternal wisdom are nothing but good things. The spirit of wisdom does not dwell in a body that is a slave of sin or in a soul inclined towards evil. The spirit of wisdom dwells in his own pure field and in his sapiential pure image. Where the eternal wisdom dwells, there is the Lord's field which bears immortal fruit. It is the field of the virtues which wisdom tills and from it are produced the fruits of the Spirit, Righteousness, Peace, Fortitude, Temperance, Charity, Patience and the like.

Orator: You have sufficiently explained these matters. Yet I have another question to pose. Is it not God who is the beginning of all things?

Citizens: Who doubts this?

Orator: Is the eternal wisdom anything else but God?

Citizen: Far be it from us to say that it is anything else.

Orator: But did not God form or create all things by His Word?

Citizen: He did.

Orator: Is the Word God?

Citizen: It is.

Orator: Is wisdom so?

Citizen: To assert that God made all things in wisdom, is no more than to say that God created all things by His Word. Consider how all that is might be able to be, and might be so and actually is. God who gives it the actuality of being is, and in Him is that potency wherewith a thing may be produced from non-being to being. He is God the Father whom we might also call Entity or Unity, because He necessitates being out of what did not exist (through His omnipotence). God gives it a determined form of being so that it is this or that, as, for example, heaven, and nothing else. This is the Word, the wisdom, the Son of the Father, and we might call Him the equality of Unity or Entity. Then there is being and being so united that it exists and this proceeds from God Who is the nexus that unites all things together. This is the Holy Spirit, for it is the Spirit that unites and binds together all things in the Universe, as well as in ourselves. And thus it is that nothing begets unity but it is the first beginning never begun. So nothing begets the Father who is eternal. Equality proceeds from unity as the Son from the Father and the bond proceeds from both unity and its equality. Thus the Holy Spirit proceeds from the Father and the Son. Hence everything, in order to have being and to have such and such a being, has need of a unitrine principle, namely God of three and one. Of this we could add further discussion if time permitted.

Wisdom which is itself the equality of being is the word or reason of things. It is, as it were, an infinite intellectual form and the form that gives the formed existence to a thing. Therefore, an infinite form is the actuality of all formable forms and the most precise equality of them all. It is just as if there were an infinite circle; it would be the true type of all figurable figures and the equality of the being of every figure. For it would be a triangle, a hexagon, a decagon, and so on. It is the most adequate measure of all of these, even though it is itself a most simple figure. Infinite wisdom is simplicity, embracing all forms and being at the same time the most adequate measure of them all. The perfect idea of the omnipotent art should be the art itself and the basic form of everything formable by art. If you look upon the form of man you will discover the form of the divine art. It is so precise an example thereof that it appears that no other form approaches it more closely. If you turn your attention to the form of heaven and convert yourself to the form of the divine art you will be able to discover no other than the exemplar of this form of heaven. It is the same with all forms either formed or formable. The art or wisdom of God the Father is the most simple form and yet it is the only and most equal example of infinite formable forms, regardless of how variable they may be.

O, how admirable is then, that form whose infinity is so simple that all formable forms cannot exhaust its implications. It is only he who elevates himself with sublime understanding above all opposition who sees its utter truthfulness. If one observed the natural power that it has in unity, he would see it, in so far as it is in act, as a certain form perceptible to the understanding alone and then only as at a distance. Since the power of unity must be most simple, it must be simple infinity. Furthermore, if one were to turn to the form of numbers, whether considering dualities or decimals, and would then return to the actual power of unity, he would see that form which is held to be the actual power of unity as the most precise example of duality, tennality, or any other numerable number. The infinity of that form which is called the power of its unity produces this effect, that while you consider the duality, the form itself can be neither greater nor smaller than the form of the duality of which it is the most precise example.

In this way you can see that the one and same simple wisdom of God, since it is infinite, is the truest example of all formable forms and this is its attainment by which He reaches all things limited or unlimited and disposes them.

It is in all forms as the truth in the image, the example in the thing exemplified, the form in the figure, the precision in the assimilation. And even though it literally communicates itself to all things as something infinitely good, yet it cannot be received by any as it is because in other things it is not identically received. Yet even though it is received in other things in a different manner this reception is still the best possible one. Non-multiplicable infinity is better explicated in a variety of recipients. A great diversity is the best expression of non-multiplicivity. Wisdom being in diverse forms is diversely received. Thus it is that every form called to Identity is a partaker of wisdom in so far as it can. Some of the participants, since they receive it in a spirit quite distant from the first form, hardly receive more than an elementary being. Where the spirit is more formed we find mineral being, others more nobly fashioned are vegetable life, still higher sensible life, the scale then leads to imaginative power, then a rational, and finally an intellectual life. This latter is the highest level and is nearest the image of wisdom. This alone is that level or degree that has an aptitude or ability to lift itself up to the taste of wisdom. Because in those intellectual natures the image of wisdom is the living intellectual life whose power consists in being able by itself to exercise a motion whereby it advances by understanding to its proper object, absolute truth or eternal wisdom. This advance, since it consists in understanding, is to taste intellectually. Apprehension with the understanding is actually to attain quiddities as well as possible with a certain agreeable taste. For just as in the sense of taste which does not reach the quiddity of a thing there is nevertheless a certain sweetness which comes from the quiddity, so by the understanding there is tasted in the quiddity an intellectual sweetness. This is the image of the sweetness of eternal wisdom which is the quiddity of quiddities and an improportionable comparison of one sweetness to another.

Because of the brevity of the time what has been discussed should be sufficient to point out that wisdom is not to be found in the art of oratory, or in great books, but in a withdrawal from these sensible things and in a turning to the most simple and infinite forms. You will learn how to receive it into a temple purged from all vice and by fervent love to cling to it until you may taste it and see how sweet that is which is all sweetness. Once this has been tasted, all things which you now consider as important will appear as vile and you will be so humbled that no arrogance or other vice will remain in you. Once having tasted this wisdom, you will inseparably adhere to it with a chaste and pure heart. You will choose rather to forsake this world and all else that is not of this wisdom, and living with unspeakable happiness you will die. After death you will rest eternally in that fond embrace which the eternally blessed wisdom of God Himself vouchsafed to grant both to you and to me.

BOOK TWO

Author: It happened that the Roman orator, after hearing these words from the citizen concerning wisdom, was filled with great admiration and after finding him in the area of the Temple of Eternity he spoke to him in this fashion.

Orator: O, sir, most sought after, please help my weakness that I may with greater ease feed upon those difficulties that transcend my mind. Otherwise, it will avail me little to have heard so many profound ideas from you.

Citizen: There is no difficulty easier than to speculate upon divine things where the difficulty coincides with the delight. But tell me, what do you want?

Orator: I want you to tell me, since God is greater than can be conceived of, how I ought to conceive of Him.

Citizen: It is just as you would do in conceiving.

Orator: What do you mean by that?

Citizen: You have heard that in every art of conceiving he who is unconceivable is conceived; therefore a concept comes from a conception to him who is unconceivable.

Orator: How then can I make a more precise concept?

Citizen: Conceive precision itself, for God is absolute precision.

Orator: What must I do once I decide to form a right concept of God?

Citizen: You must turn your mind to rectitude itself.

Orator: And if I decide to seek after a true concept of God, what must I do?

Citizen: You must consider truth itself.

Orator: To arrive at a just concept, what must I do?

Citizen: You must turn yourself to justice.

Orator: And when I endeavor to obtain a good concept, what must I do?

Citizen: You must lift up the eyes of your mind to goodness.

Orator: The direction you give me in each case is a source of wonderment to me.

Citizen: You see how easy the difficulty in divine things is, in that it always offers itself to the inquirer in the same way that it is sought.

Orator: Certainly there is nothing more wonderful.

Citizen: Every question concerning God presupposes the thing questioned, and what the question presupposes must be answered in every question concerning God. For God, although He cannot be signified, is signified in each signification of terms.

Orator: Could you kindly expatiate on this a little for I am so carried away that I can hardly hear what you are saying.

Citizen: Does not the question whether or not a thing is presuppose entity?

Orator: It certainly does.

Citizen: Therefore, whenever you are asked whether or not God exists you should answer that which is presupposed, namely that He is, for this is the very entity presupposed in the question. Thus if anyone asks you, what is God, you will answer, realizing that our question presupposes a quiddity that God is absolute quiddity itself. This applies to everything else also. Nor should there be any hesitation or doubt in this matter, for God is the absolute presupposition itself which presupposes all else, just as in every effect the cause is presupposed. See therefore, O Orator, how really easy theological difficulty is.

Orator: Certainly this is a great and marvelous facility.

Citizen: God, I tell you, is the infinite facility itself and it is not at all agreeable to Him that He should be an infinite difficulty. For it is necessary, as you will shortly hear, concerning curved and straight lines, that difficulty passes into facility if it is to agree with the infinite God.

Orator: If that which is presupposed in every question is in matters divine the answer to the question, then there cannot be, properly speaking, any question concerning God, since the answer coincides with the question.

Citizen: You have made a good inference. And you might add to this that since God is an infinite straightness and an absolute necessity, a doubtful question cannot reach Him, but in Him all doubt is certainty. Whence we must also infer that any answer to a question concerning God cannot be, properly speaking, a precise answer. For precision is nothing other than what is one and infinite and this applies to God alone. Every answer participates in the absolute answer which is infinitely precise, but what I have mentioned as to how, in theological questions, the answer is presupposed, must be understood in this same manner that the question is posed, and taken in this sense it will be sufficient. As with God neither the question nor the answer is able to attain precision, so in the same manner wherein the question approaches precision, in just that way the answer presupposes. And this is our sufficiency which we have from God: knowing unattainable precision cannot be reached except in a limited fashion that partakes the manner of absolute precision. And among the various and manifold ways of participating in the one mode of precision, the one we have just mentioned approaches the closest to the absolute facility. This is our sufficiency because we cannot attain any other that is easier and more true.

Orator: Who would not be amazed at hearing these wonderful things? For whereas God is absolute incomprehensibility you say that our comprehension approaches Him in the same proportion and manner as it increases in its participation in the facility.

Citizen: Anyone who considers, as I do, that the absolute facility coincides with the absolute incomprehensibility cannot but conclude as I do. This is why I certainly affirm that a universal approach to all questions relating to the formability of God is easier and in proportion is truer and more convenient in so far as it considers God in this affirmation.

Orator: Please explain this.

Citizen: Even though we admit that some things may be spoken affirmatively of God, yet in that theology which denies all concerning God we must speak otherwise. For there the more truthful answer is always a negation. But in that way we are not led to a knowledge of what God is, but what He is not.

There is, furthermore, a consideration of God that is neither affirmation nor negation (nec positio nec ablatio) which is agreeable to Him since He is above affirmation and negation. This then is an answer that denies both the affirmation and the negation as well as the combination of the two. In answer then to the question whether God is, the affirmative would flow from the presupposition that He is and that in so being He is also the presupposed Entity. But according to the way of negation it would be answered that He is not, since by this way not one of all the things which can be spoken would lie in accordance with the unspeakable. Hence, following the way that is above both the affirmative and the negative, it must be answered that He is neither, namely absolute Entity; neither that He is not, nor simultaneously is and is not, but rather that He is above both of these. Now I think you can understand what I mean.

Orator: I now perceive that what you wish to say is that in speaking theologically, where we admit that God speaks, the power of language is not entirely excluded. Thus you have brought the sufficiency of difficulties into the facility of the manner of forming truer propositions concerning God.

Citizen: You have understood this well. For if I would make known to you the concepts I have of God, then my speech, if it is to be of any use to you, must be made up of significant words, so that by virtue of the words of which we have a common understanding, I may lead you to what is sought after. The thing that we now seek is God. This is, therefore, an instructive or discursive theology whereby I will endeavor, by the power of language, to lead you to God in the simplest and truest way I know.

Orator: Let us return now to those things that you promised earlier, and explain them in an orderly fashion. In the first place you remarked that the conception of conception, since God is the conception of conception, is the conception of God. Isn't it rather true that it is the mind that conceives?

Citizen: Without the mind there is no concept.

Orator: Since to conceive is proper to the mind then certainly to conceive an absolute concept is nothing other than to conceive the art of the absolute mind.

Citizen: Go ahead, you are on the right path.

Orator: But the art of the absolute mind is nothing other than the form of all formable things. Thus I see how the concept of a concept is naught else but the concept of the idea of divine arts. If I am right tell me.

Citizen: You speak exceedingly well; for an absolute concept can be nothing other than the ideal form of all things which can be conceived, which is the equality of all things formable.

Orator: This concept, as I understand it, is termed the word (logos) of God or reason.

Citizen: Regardless of what learned men may call it, in that concept are contained all things. Just as those things which, without previous reason, do not come into existence, we say none the less that they exist beforehand in the reason. And everything that we can possibly conceive has its own reason, so that is what it is and not something else. Therefore, whoever looks with a deep mind into the simplicity of absolute reason, which by way of priority embraces all things in itself, arrives at a concept of conception itself or an absolute concept—and this is exactly what I promised.

Orator: Enough of this. Now proceed to demonstrate how the concept of absolute precision is a more precise concept of God.

Citizen: Time does not permit me to go over the same thing in detail, nor do I consider it appropriate since by opening the door to one consideration I have already opened them all. But, nevertheless, listen to what I have to say briefly. Precision, straightness, truth, justice and goodness, of which you have heard, are the same thing. Certainly you do not believe that I want to say that all theological speculation is a sort of circular course wherein one of God's attributes may be verified of the other, as for example when we say that the greatness of God comes from the necessity of His infinite simplicity, or that the greatness of God is His power or vice versa, and so of all the things that we attribute to the essence of God. But these things of which I presently speak we find by experience to coincide with our ordinary verbal expressions. For whenever we hear someone express something, we say that he expresses it precisely or rightly, or truly or justly, or well, and thus you see how our daily speech conveys this idea. He who admits that a person does something precisely or rightly means nothing other than that he expressed something truly, justly, and well. You will have to admit that what you consider to be true consists in his having said neither more nor less than he ought to have said and this can be predicated of all else. For precision is nothing else than to say what is neither more nor less. In the same way what is right or true or just or good is limited by the less or the more. For how can that be precise, right, true, or good that is less than precise, right, true, or good? And just as that which is less than precise is not precise and what is less than right is not right, and less than true not true, less than just not just, and less than good not good, so it is quite evident that where more is predicated of what is precise, or right, or true, just or good, this is not predicated in an absolute manner.

Orator: In those things then that admit of more or less a concept of God cannot be properly formed.

Citizen: Your inference is quite correct. For since God is infinite, any description that admits of a more or less cannot be predicated of Him. Hence, in this area we cannot ascend or descend 'ad infinitum' as in the case with numbers or the division of an extended quantum.

Orator: We have to assume then that in this world there is really no precision or rightness, or truth or justice, or goodness, since we see by experience that one thing is more precise than another, as for example one picture is more precise than another. In the matter of rightness, one thing is more right than another, one thing is more true than another, one is more just, another better.

Citizen: You have understood me quite well for those things, since they are absolute and not limited by the 'more' and the 'less' are not of this world. For it is impossible to find anything so precise that it cannot be more precise, or so straight that it cannot be more straight, or so true that it cannot be truer, or so just that it cannot be more just, or so good that it cannot be better. Whatever of precision, rightness, truth, justice, or goodness that is found in this world is but participation of those absolutes and images of which these are examples. I use the plural since we refer to them, the various reasons, and norms of different things, yet they are actually from one Exemplar, since they coincide to that which is absolute.

Orator: I would certainly like to hear more on this particular point—how it is possible to have one absolute Exemplar of so many varieties of things.

Citizen: Whoever is but little versed in these theological problems would find this extremely difficult, but to me there is nothing easier and more delightful. For the absolute Exemplar is in nothing other than absolute precision, rightness, truth, justice, and goodness. It embraces or contains all examplificable things of which there can be precision, rightness, truth, justice, or goodness, in a manner much more perfect than your own face contains the formable elements of its own image. For all images of your face that are painted are precise, right, and true only in so far as they partake of and imitate the living image of your face. And although it is impossible that any one of these should be identical or lacking in difference, as precision is not of this world, and whatever is distinct exists differentially, yet all of these truths need only one Exemplar.

Orator: You speak quite well in explaining the unity of the Exemplar, but not sufficiently in explaining equality. For although my face is the measure of the truth of the picture, since it is judged by comparing it to my actual face, yet how can it be an adequate criterion of the size, more or less, of the face? It is not true that my face is the most adequate measure of all its representations in every manner since it is always either greater or lesser.

Citizen: What you say of the face is quite correct, for since it has quantity and thus a capacity for more or less, it is not precision and an adequate measure of another thing. In this world, lacking in adequate precision, it is impossible to have measure and likeness. But if you will conceive of an absolute Exemplar it is otherwise. For that is neither great nor small for these things cannot be of the ratio of the Exemplar. An ant for example when it is painted is no less an exemplar than a mountain that has to be painted and vice versa. Wherefore, an absolute exemplar that is not capable of, more or less as it is, precision and truth cannot be either greater or less than the thing exemplified. That, therefore, which cannot be the less, we call the minimum, and this is the greatest degree of smallness; and that which cannot be greater we call the maximum. Free the maximity from the greatest degree of the minimum and the greatest degree of the maximum and you will see the maximity itself uncontracted in a lesser or smaller degree. You will see that maximity precedes greatness and smallness so that it can be neither the greater or the lesser but is rather the maximum in which the minimum coincides. Therefore, such a maximum, since it is the absolute exemplar, cannot be either greater or lesser than any possible exemplification, and that which is neither greater nor less we call equal. Therefore, the absolute exemplar is equality, precision, measure, or justice—which is the same as truth and goodness and which is the perfection of all things that can be exemplified.

Orator: Could you please explain to me how infinity can agree with absolute rectitude or rightness?

Citizen: I'll do that willingly. You are aware that the greater a circle is, the greater is its diameter.

Orator: I am aware of this.

Citizen: Although a circle, since it has a capacity for being greater or smaller, cannot be the maximum or infinite, yet let us suppose that such a circle were infinite. Would not then the diameter be an infinite line?

Orator: This would necessarily follow.

Citizen: And the circumference, since it is infinite, would be the diameter. But we cannot have two infinites, for the addition of one to the other makes this the greater. And the circumference cannot be a curved line for this would present the impossibility of its being lesser or greater than the diameter. Since the proportion of all curved circumferences is one and the same in relation of all circles to the diameter, it is a proposition that is more than threefold. If, therefore, the circumference is equal to the diameter, it will also be the diameter itself and a straight line. For this same reason you can see that the arc of a greater circle is more like a straight line than the arc of a smaller circle, and because of this the circumference of an infinite circle must be straight. Thus it is evident that whatever is curved, since it is capable of more or less, is not found in the infinite but only straightness or rightness.

Orator: What you have said certainly pleases me because your words lift me up to what I seek. Would you kindly show me how infinite straightness or rightness is the exemplar?

Citizen: You are quite capable of perceiving this yourself. Infinite rightness has the same relation to all things as an infinite line, if it existed, would have to all figures. For if infinite rightness, which is of necessity absolute, were contracted to a line, it would in this contracted state include precision, rightness, truth, measure and the perfection of all measurable figures. Therefore, absolute rightness, considered absolutely and uncontracted to any line, or any other thing whatever, is likewise in an absolute sense the exemplar, precision, truth and perfection of all things.

Orator: What you have just said leaves no doubt in my mind. However, could you show how an infinite line is the precision of all figures? Yesterday you told me how an infinite circle is the exemplar of all figures. This I failed to understand and I came here desiring to be better informed. Yet now you say that an infinite line is precision and this I understood even less.

Citizen: You have already heard how an infinite line is a circle and in the same manner so is a triangle, a quadrangle, a pentagon. In fact, all figures coincide with an infinite line. For an infinite line is the exemplar of all figures that can be made out of lines because an infinite line is an infinite act or form of all formable figures. If you would look at a triangle and then elevate yourself to an infinite line you will find that it is actually the finest exemplar of a triangle. Consider, for example, an infinite triangle. This triangle is neither greater nor lesser than the aforesaid triangle. For the sides of an infinite triangle are infinite and an infinite side being the maximum in which the less coincides is neither greater nor less than the given side. So the sides of an infinite triangle are neither greater nor less than the sides of the given triangle. So neither the whole triangle is greater or less than the given triangle. Hence it is that an infinite triangle is the precision and absolute form of a finite triangle. But the three sides of an infinite triangle must of necessity be one infinite line because there cannot be a plurality of infinite lines. Therefore, we have it that an infinite line is the most precise exemplar of the given triangle. And what I have said of the triangle applies to all other figures.

Orator: What an amazing facility for solving difficulties. I can now see that all these things follow immediately, once the notion of an infinite line is accepted. From this follows the fact that it is the exemplar, precision, rectitude, truth, measure or justice, goodness or perfection of all figures that are figurable by a line. I also see that in the simplicity of its straightness all things figurable are contained most truly, formally and precisely, lacking all confusion and defect, and that they are in the infinite more perfect than can possibly be configured.

Citizen: Blessed be God, who has used me, a most ignorant man, as an instrument, such as it is, to open the eyes of your mind to see Him with such amazing facility in the way He has made Himself visible. For when you transfer your consideration from straightness contracted to a straight line to absolute infinite straightness, you will perceive that it includes all that is formable, and the species of all things, as we have explained in the case of figures, and in the same way that straightness is itself the exemplar, or justice or goodness or perfection of all things that are or can be, so also with the precise and unconfused actuality of all things that either are or have potential existence. Regardless of what you perceive, so long as you elevate your mind to the infinite straightness, you will find it to be the most precise and indefectible exemplar of truth itself. If you consider an individual person who is both right and true, you will see that he is nothing other than straightness, truth, measure and perfection, contracted and terminated in himself. And if you consider his straightness which is finite and then focus your consideration on the infinite straightness, you will immediately perceive how infinite and absolute straightness can be neither greater nor less than that straightness contracted in this man, whereby this man is straight and true and is the truest, most just, and precise, of that absolute straightness.

Thus infinite truth is the precision of finite truth, and, being absolutely infinite, is also the precision, measure, truth and perfection of everything that is finite. What we have said of the individual person may be predicated of all other things.

You now have what is granted to contemplate eternal wisdom, that you may behold all things in a most simple rectitude, most truly, precisely, unconfused and perfectly, even though enigmatically. For the vision of God is not seen in this world without mystery until He will make Himself visible without darkness. And this is the facility of the difficulties of wisdom which in proportion to your fervor and devotion may God grant each day an increased clarity both to you and to me until He lifts us up into the glorious fruition of the truth, where we shall remain eternally.

Amen

THE VISION OF GOD OR THE ICON

AT THE REQUEST of the Benedictine monks of his diocese at Tegernsee, Cusa composed this little work on mysticism in October of 1453, in which he suggests an "Easy path to mystical theology." As in all his works, Nicholas leads his reader experimentally from concrete experience to sacred obscurity where he will feel the presence of an invisible light and whence he will try to emerge with intensive effort so as to acquire a foretaste of the ultimate happiness to which we are all called. The entire series of spiritual exercises, despite occasional variations, are grounded in the same fundamental doctrine he so often expounds, namely, an intellectual ascension from the obscurity of Learned Ignorance by admitting the blending of contraries beyond which lies the Infinite. God's indisputable help, which gives us knowledge prior to the desire of finding Him, pursues us through revelation. Here for the first time in his writings he brings into strong relief his location of God, not in the region where contraries blend, but away beyond it. It is a step forward from the earlier introduction to his basic work on Learned Ignorance. Socrates' psychological axiom "Know Thyself" gives way to that of

129

the Stoic moralist, "Be thine own master." Like the latter he advocates the conquest of liberty to assure the sovereignty of reason. This is not, however, the halting point. Reason's criterion for the Christian is not nature in the rigidity of its laws and the universality of its application, it is a Personal God whose will is manifested in natural laws intimately present in each of us. Here we see his constant aim at illucidating the 'Instant,' the punctual participation of the concrete duration of the Eternal Itself. His expressions reverberate with Pauline echoes. There is a categorical rejection of all concepts of God as a far off Sovereign whose creatures enjoy nothing more than an accidental dependence. In the inner recess of each conscience God is present as the active foundation of all mental operations.

We perceive in Cusa a new blending of the Hellenic and Semitic tradition. For the Semitic mind, "to know" was primarily an active experience of an object. It is a concrete and intimate personal relationship rather than an abstraction. For the Hebrew, the knowledge of God is the experience of God in history and human life. There is no recognition of any human process, for God is not only the object, He is the means of this knowledge. For the Greek, "to know" an object meant to know it as it is in itself, involving a process of abstraction, of purification that approximates impersonal contemplation. The fact that Aristotelianism had little appeal for Nicholas is inherent in the system itself. The mystic needs a human construct that allows him to conceive and express his experience of contact with God. Platonism, with its identification of real existence with intelligible being conceived by thought, is well suited to this. Aristotelianism, on the other hand, refuses to consider any problem of existence aside from an empirically given existent. Platonism provides the mystic with the immediacy he is looking for. There is real contact between the knower and the known, the mind "goes out" to the object known.

The confluence of these two streams, the Hebraic and the Platonic, provide Cusa with a metaphysics in terms of which he could reflect upon, express his experience of, the Christian mysteries. But Greek metaphysics came to Nicholas through the transforming hands of the Neoplatonists. Proclus was a great favorite of the cardinal, especially the *Element of Theology* and the commentary on the *Parmenides*. So the work contains the typically Neoplatonic outflow and return of things to God, the negative theology so familiar since Pseudo-Dionysius, and the dialectical tension of opposites of Plotinus, which had found more recent expression in Eckhart's reconciliation of contraries in God. This structured world with its hierarchy of beings will seem strange to the modern mind. It is necessary to keep in mind the Platonic notion of knowledge, and to realize that in the Neoplatonic metaphysics, the underlying assumption is that logical classes reproduce the structure of reality.

An awareness of this Neoplatonic influence will prove useful in understanding the cardinal's emphasis on vision. The reader who is familiar with mystical writings knows that the mystic, in an effort to express the non-rational or supra-rational character of his experience, has frequent recourse to symbolism related to the senses of touch, taste, and the like. The infrequent shift from visual imagery in this work of Cusanus probably finds its expression here. In Neoplatonism there is a fusion of the spiritual and intellectual lives. If there is a logic in the universe, if there are mathematical laws, in a word, if the universe is intelligible, then the philosopher, if he "purifies" himself, should be able to attain an ever clearer vision of the ultimate Rationality. We find, therefore, in the Platonic tradition a definite reluctance to admit that for man the supreme experience of the Divinity must always be in terms of "contact" rather than "vision." This treatise of Nicholas of Cusa is significant in the shift from what has been called the "theological and objective mysticism" of the first centuries to the "psychological and subjective mysticism" that has developed since the Middle Ages.

The present translation is an accommodation by E. Salter of the English version of Giles Randall published in London in 1646 and entitled *The Single Eye*. The beautiful English of the time seems to enrich a work wherein is unfolded the Mystery of Divine Presence.

DE VISIONE DEI

THE BOOK OF THE MOST REVEREND FATHER AND LORD IN CHRIST,
THE LORD NICHOLAS OF CUSA, CARDINAL-PRIEST OF SAINT PETER IN
CHAINS, BISHOP OF BRIXEN, TO THE ABBOT AND BRETHREN OF
TEGERNSEE, CONCERNING THE VISION OF GOD, OR THE ICON

I will now show you, dearest brethren, as I promised you, an easy path unto mystical theology. For, knowing you to be led by zeal for God, I think you worthy of the opening up of this treasure, as assuredly very precious and most fruitful. And first I pray the Almighty to give me utterance, and the heavenly Word who alone can express Himself, that I may be able, as ye can receive it, to relate the marvels of revelation, which are beyond all sight of our eyes, our reason, and our understanding. I will endeavour by a very simple and commonplace method to lead you by experience into the divine darkness; wherein while ye abide ye shall perceive present with you the light inaccessible, and shall each endeavour, in the measure that God shall grant him, to draw ever nearer thereunto, and to partake here, by a sweetest foretaste, of that feast of everlasting bliss, whereunto we are called in the word of life, through the gospel of Christ, who is blessed for ever.

PREFACE

If I strive in human fashion to transport you to things divine, I must needs use a comparison of some kind. Now among men's

133

works I have found no image better suited to our purpose than that of an image which is omnivoyant—its face, by the painter's cunning art, being made to appear as though looking on all around it. There are many excellent pictures of such faces—for example, that of the archeress in the market-place of Nuremberg; that by the eminent painter, Roger, in his priceless picture in the governor's house at Brussels; the Veronica in my chapel at Coblenz, and, in the castle of Brixen, the angel holding the arms of the Church, and many others elsewhere. Yet, lest ye should fail in the exercise, which requireth a figure of this description to be looked upon, I send for your indulgence such a picture as I have been able to procure, setting forth the figure of an omnivoyant, and this I call the icon of God.

This picture, brethren, ye shall set up in some place, let us say, on a north wall, and shall stand round it, a little way off and look upon it. And each of you shall find that from whatsoever quarter he regardeth it, it looketh upon him as if it looked on none other. And it shall seem to a brother standing to eastward as if that face looketh toward the east, while one to southward shall think it looketh toward the south, and one to westward, toward the west. First, then, ye will marvel how it can be that the face should look on all and each at the same time. For the imagination of him standing to eastward cannot conceive the gaze of the icon to be turned unto any other quarter, such as west or south. Then let the brother who stood to eastward place himself to westward and he will find its gaze fastened on him in the west just as it was afore in the east. And, as he knoweth the icon to be fixed and unmoved, he will marvel at the motion of its immoveable gaze.

If now, while fixing his eye on the icon, he walk from west to east, he will find that its gaze continuously goeth along with him, and if he return from east to west, in like manner it will not leave him. Then will he marvel how, being motionless, it moveth, nor will his imagination be able to conceive that it should also move in like manner with one going in a contrary direction to himself. If he wish to experiment on this, he will cause one of his brethren to cross over from east to west, still looking on the icon, while he himself moveth from west to east; and he will ask the other as they meet if the gaze of the icon turn continuously with him; he will hear that it doth move in a contrary direction, even as with himself, and he will believe him. But, had he not believed him, he could not have conceived this to be possible. So by his brother's showing he will come to know that the picture's face keepeth in sight all as they go on their way, though it be in contrary directions; and thus he will prove that that countenance, though motionless, is turned to east in the same way that it is simultaneously to west, and in the same way to north and to south, and alike to one particular place and to all objects at once, whereby it regardeth a single movement even as it regardeth all together. And while he observeth how that gaze never quitteth any, he seeth that it taketh such diligent care of each one who findeth himself observed as though it cared only for him, and for no other, and this to such a degree that one on whom it resteth cannot even conceive that it should take care of any other. He will also see that it taketh the same most diligent care of the least of creatures as of the greatest, and of the whole universe.

'Tis by means of this perceptible image that I purpose to uplift you, my most loving brethren, by a certain devotional exercise, unto mystical Theology, premising three things that be serviceable thereunto.

CHAPTER I. THAT THE PERFECTION OF THE IMAGE IS VERIFIED
OF GOD THE SUPREMELY PERFECT

In the first place, I think, it should be presupposed that there is nothing which seemeth proper to the gaze of the icon of God which doth not more really exist in the veritable gaze of God Himself. For God, who is the very summit of all perfection, and greater than can be conceived, is called Θεός from this very fact that He beholdeth all things. Wherefore, if the countenance portrayed in a picture can seem to look upon each and all at one and the same time, this faculty (since it is the perfection of seeing) must no less really pertain unto the reality than it doth apparently unto the icon or appearance. For if the sight of one man is keener than that of another among us, if one will with difficulty distinguish objects near him, while another can make out those at a distance, if one perceive an object slowly, the other more quickly —there is no doubt but that Absolute Sight, whence all sight springeth, surpasseth in keenness, in speed, and in strength the sight of all who actually see and who can become capable of sight.

For, if I examine sight in the abstract, which I have dissociated in my mind from all eyes and bodily organs, and consider how abstract sight in its limited state—that is, as sight in seeing persons— is narrowed down to time and place, to particular objects, and to other like conditions, while sight in the abstract is in like manner withdrawn from these conditions, and absolute, then I well perceive 'tis not of the essence of sight to behold one object more than another, although it inhereth in sight, in its limited state, to be unable to look on more than one thing at a time, or upon all things absolutely. But God is the true Unlimited Sight, and He is not inferior to sight in the abstract as it can be conceived by the intellect, but is beyond all comparison more perfect. Wherefore the apparent vision of the icon cannot so closely approach the supreme excellence of Absolute Sight as our abstract conception. And so there can be no doubt that whatever seemeth to exist in that image the same doth really and supremely exist in Absolute Sight.

CHAPTER II. THAT ABSOLUTE SIGHT EMBRACETH ALL
MODES OF SEEING

Following on these considerations thou mayest perceive sight to differ in those who see by reason of its varied forms of limitation. For our sight followeth the affections of our eye and mind, and thus a man's looks are now loving and glad, anon sad and wrathful; first the looks of a child, later, of a man; finally, grave, and as of an aged man. But sight that is freed from all limitation embraceth at once and the same time each and every mode of seeing, as being the most adequate measure of all sights, and their truest pattern. For without Absolute Sight there can be no limited sight; it embraceth in itself all modes of seeing, all and each alike, and abideth entirely freed from all variation. All limited modes of seeing exist without limitation in Absolute Sight. For every limitation existeth in the Absolute, because Absolute Sight is the limiting of limitations, limiting not being limitable. Wherefore limiting pure and simple coincideth with the Absolute. For without limiting naught is limited, and thus Absolute Sight existeth in all sight, because through it all limited sight existeth, and without it is utterly unable to exist.

CHAPTER III. THAT THE ATTRIBUTES OF GOD ARE NOT
REALLY DIFFERENT

Thou mayest in consequence remark how all attributes assigned to God cannot differ in reality, by reason of the perfect simplicity of God, although we in divers ways use of God divers words. But God, being the Absolute Ground of all formal natures, embraceth in Himself all natures. Whence, although we attribute to God sight, hearing, taste, smell, touch, sense, reason and intellect, and so forth, according unto the divers significations of each word, yet in Him sight is not other than hearing, or tasting, or smelling, or touching, or feeling, or understanding. And so all Theology is said to be stablished in a circle, because any one of His attributes is affirmed of another, and to have is with God to be, and to move is to stand, and to run is to rest, and so with the other attributes. Thus, although in one sense we attribute unto Him movement and in another rest, yet because He is Himself the Absolute Ground, in which all otherness is unity, and all diversity is identity, that

diversity which is not identity proper, to wit, diversity as we understand it, cannot exist in God.

CHAPTER IV. THAT THE GAZE OF GOD IS CALLED PROVIDENCE, GRACE, AND LIFE ETERNAL

Approach thee now, brother contemplative, unto the icon of
God, and place thyself first to the east thereof, then to the south,
and finally to the west. Then, because its glance regardeth thee
alike in each position, and leaveth thee not whithersoever thou
goest, a questioning will arise in thee and thou wilt stir it up,
saying: Lord, in this image of Thee I now behold Thy providence
by a certain experience of sense. For if Thou leavest not me, who
am the vilest of men, never and to none wilt Thou be lacking. For
Thou art present to all and to each, even as to those same, all and
each, is present the Being without whom they cannot exist. For
Thou, the Absolute Being of all, art as entirely present to all as
though Thou hadst no care for any other. And this befalleth because there is none that doth not prefer its own being to all others,
and its own mode of being to that of all others, and so defendeth its
own being as that it would rather allow the being of all others to
go to perdition than its own. Even so, Thou, Lord, dost regard
every living thing in such wise that none of them can conceive
that Thou hast any other care but that it alone should exist, in the
best mode possible to it, and that each thinketh all other existing
things exist for the sole purpose of serving this end, namely, the
best state of him whom Thou beholdest.

Thou dost not, Lord, permit me to conceive by any imagining
whatsoever that Thou, Lord, lovest aught else more than me; since
Thy regard leaveth not me, me only. And, since where the eye is,
there is love, I prove by experience that Thou lovest me because
Thine eyes are so attentively upon me, Thy poor little servant.
Lord, Thy glance is love. And just as Thy gaze beholdeth me so
attentively that it never turneth aside from me, even so is it with

Thy love. And since 'tis deathless, it abideth ever with me, and Thy love, Lord, is naught else but Thy very Self, who lovest me. Hence Thou art ever with me, Lord; Thou desertest me not, Lord; on all sides Thou gardest me, for that Thou takest most diligent care for me. Thy Being, Lord, letteth not go of my being. I exist in that measure in which Thou art with me, and, since Thy look is Thy being, I am because Thou dost look at me, and if Thou didst turn Thy glance from me I should cease to be.

But I know that Thy glance is that supreme Goodness which cannot fail to communicate itself to all able to receive it. Thou, therefore, canst never let me go so long as I am able to receive Thee. Wherefore it behoveth me to make myself, in so far as I can, ever more able to receive Thee. But I know that the capacity which maketh union possible is naught else save likeness. And incapacity springeth from lack of likeness. If, therefore, I have rendered myself by all possible means like unto Thy goodness, then, according to the degree of that likeness, I shall be capable of the truth.

Lord, Thou hast given me my being, of such a nature that it can make itself continuously more able to receive Thy grace and goodness. And this power, which I have of Thee, wherein I possess a living image of Thine almighty power, is freewill. By this I can either enlarge or restrict my capacity for Thy grace. The enlarging is by conformity with Thee, when I strive to be good because Thou art good, to be just because Thou art just, to be merciful because Thou art merciful; when all my endeavour is turned toward Thee because all Thy endeavour is turned toward me; when I look unto Thee alone with all my attention, nor ever turn aside the eyes of my mind, because Thou dost enfold me with Thy constant regard; when I direct my love toward Thee alone because Thou, who art Love's self, hast turned Thee toward me alone. And what, Lord, is my life, save that embrace wherein Thy delightsome sweetness doth so lovingly enfold me? I love my life supremely because Thou art my life's sweetness.

Now I behold as in a mirror, in an icon, in a riddle, life eternal, for that is naught other than that blessed regard wherewith Thou never ceasest most lovingly to behold me, yea, even the secret places of my soul. With Thee, to behold is to give life; 'tis unceasingly to impart sweetest love of Thee; 'tis to inflame me to love of Thee by love's imparting, and to feed me by inflaming, and by feeding to kindle my yearnings, and by kindling to make me drink of the dew of gladness, and by drinking to infuse in me a fountain of life, and by infusing to make it increase and endure. 'Tis to cause me to share Thine immortality, to endow me with the glory imperishable of Thy heavenly and most high and most mighty kingdom, 'tis to make me partaker of that inheritance which is only of Thy Son, to stablish me in possession of eternal bliss. There is the source of all delights that can be desired; not only can naught better be thought out by men and angels, but naught better can exist in any mode of being! For it is the absolute maximum of every rational desire, than which a greater cannot be.

CHAPTER V. THAT SIGHT IS TASTING, SEEKING, PITYING, AND ACTING

O how great and manifold is Thy sweetness which Thou hast hidden up for them that fear Thee! It is a treasure that may not be unfolded, in the joy of fullest gladness. For to taste that Thy sweetness is by the touch of experience to lay hold on the sweetness of all delights at its source, 'tis in Thy wisdom to attain unto the reason of all things desirable. To behold Absolute Reason, which is the reason of all things, is naught else than in mind to taste Thee, O God, since Thou art very Sweetness, the Being of life, and intellect. What else, Lord, is Thy seeing when Thou beholdest me with pitying eye than that Thou art seen of me? In beholding me Thou givest Thyself to be seen of me, Thou who art a hidden God. None can see Thee save in so far as Thou grantest a sight of Thyself, nor is that sight aught else than Thy seeing him that seeth Thee.

I perceive, Lord, in this image of Thee how ready Thou art to show Thy face unto all that seek Thee, for never dost Thou close Thine eyes, never dost Thou turn them away. And albeit I turn me away from Thee when I turn me utterly to some other thing, yet for all this dost Thou never move Thine eyes nor Thy glance. If Thou beholdest me not with the eye of grace, the fault is mine, who have cut me off from Thee, by turning aside, and by turning round to some other thing which I prefer before Thee; yet even so dost Thou not turn Thee utterly away, but Thy mercy followeth me, that, should I at any time be fain to turn unto Thee again, I may be capable of grace. If Thou regardest me not, 'tis because I regard not Thee, but reject and despise Thee.

O infinite Pity! how unhappy is every sinner who deserteth Thee, the channel of life, and seeketh Thee, not in Thyself, but in that Which in itself is nothing, and would have remained nothing hadst Thou not called it out of nothingness! How demented is he who seeketh Thee, who art Goodness, and, while seeking Thee, withdraweth from Thee, and turneth aside his eyes! All seekers seek only the good, and every seeker after the good who withdraweth from Thee withdraweth from that he seeketh.

Every sinner, then, strayeth from Thee and departeth afar off. Yet so soon as he return unto Thee Thou dost hasten to meet him, and before he perceiveth Thee, Thou dost cast Thine eyes of mercy on him, with fatherly love. For with Thee 'tis one to behold and to pity. Accordingly, Thy mercy followeth every man so long as he liveth, whithersoever he goeth, even as Thy glance never quitteth any. So long as a man liveth, Thou ceasest not to follow him, and with sweet and inward warning to stir him up to depart from error and to turn unto Thee that he may love in bliss.

Thou, Lord, art the companion of my pilgrimage; wheresoever I go Thine eyes are always upon me. Now with Thee seeing is motion. Therefore Thou movest with me and never ceasest from motion so long as I move. If I am at rest, there Thou art with me also. If I ascend, Thou ascendest, if I descend, Thou descendest; whithersoever I turn me, there Thou art. Nor dost Thou desert me in the day of trouble; as often as I call upon Thee, Thou art near. For to call upon Thee is to turn unto Thee, and Thou canst not fail him that turneth unto Thee, nor could any turn unto Thee wert not Thou already at hand. Thou art present before I turn unto Thee. For, unless Thou wert present and didst entreat me, I should know naught at all of Thee, and how could I turn unto Thee whom I knew not at all?

Thou, then, my God, art He who beholdeth all things. And with Thee to behold is to work. So Thou workest all things. Therefore not unto us, O Lord, not unto us, but unto Thy great Name, which is Θεός, I will sing glory for ever. For I have naught save that Thou givest, nor could I keep that Thou hast given didst not Thou Thyself preserve it. Thus Thou ministerest all things unto me. Thou art the Lord, powerful and pitiful, who givest all; Thou art the Minister who administerest all; Thou art the Provider, and He that taketh thought for us, and our Preserver. And all these things Thou workest with one simplest glance of Thine, Thou who art blessed for evermore.

CHAPTER VI. OF SEEING FACE TO FACE

O Lord my God, the longer I look upon Thy face the more keenly dost Thou seem to turn the glance of Thine eyes upon me! Thy gaze causeth me to consider how this image of Thy face is thus perceptibly painted, since a face cannot be painted without colour, nor can colour exist without quantity. But I perceive, not with my fleshly eyes, which look on this icon of Thee, but with the eyes of my mind and understanding, the invisible truth of Thy face, which therein is signified, under a shadow and limitation. Thy true face is freed from any limitation, it hath neither quantity nor quality, nor is it of time or place, for it is the Absolute Form, the Face of faces.

When, therefore, I meditate on how that face is truth, and the most adequate measure of all faces, I am brought into a state of great wonder. For that face which is the true type of all faces hath not quantity. Wherefore, it is neither greater nor less than others, and yet 'tis not equal to any other; since it hath not quantity, but 'tis absolute, and exalted above all. It is, therefore, the Truth, which is equality, freed from all quantity. Thus, then Lord, I comprehend Thy face to precede every face that may be formed, and to be the pattern and true type of all faces, and all faces to be images of Thy face, which may not be limited or shared. Each face, then, that can look upon Thy face beholdeth naught other or differing from itself, because it beholdeth its own true type. And the pattern truth cannot be other or differing, but those attributes are found in the image just by reason that it is not the very pattern.

Thus, then, while I look on this pictured face, whether from the east or from the west or south, it seemeth in like manner itself to look on me, and, after the same fashion, according as I move my face, that face seemeth turned toward me. Even so is Thy face turned toward all faces that look upon Thee. Thy glance, Lord, is Thy face. He, then, who looketh on Thee with loving face will find Thy face looking on himself with love, and the more he shall study to look on Thee with greater love, by so much shall he find Thy face more loving. He who looketh on Thee in wrath shall in like manner find Thy face wrathful. He who looketh on Thee with joy shall find Thy face joyful, after the same sort as is his own who looketh on Thee. 'Tis as when the eye of flesh, looking through a red glass, thinketh that it seeth all things red, or, looking through a green glass, all things green. Even so the eye of the mind, muffled up in limitation and passivity, judgeth Thee, the mind's object, according unto the nature of its limitation and passivity.

Man can only judge with human judgment. When a man attributeth a face unto Thee, he doth not seek it beyond the human species, because his judgment, bound up with human nature, in judging transcendeth not its limitation and passivity. In like manner, if a lion were to attribute a face unto Thee, he would think of it as a lion's; an ox, as an ox's, and an eagle as an eagle's.

O Lord, how marvellous is Thy face, which a young man, if he strove to imagine it, would conceive as a youth's; a full-grown man, as manly; an aged man, as an aged man's! Who could imagine this sole pattern, most true and most adequate, of all faces—of all even as of each—this pattern so very perfectly of each as if it were of none other? He would need to go beyond all forms of faces that may be formed, and all figures. And how could he imagine a face when he must go beyond all faces, and all likenesses and figures of all faces, and all concepts which can be formed of a face, and all colour, adornment, and beauty of all faces? Wherefore he that goeth forward to behold Thy face, so long as he formeth any concept thereof, is far from Thy face. For all concept of a face falleth short, Lord, of Thy face, and all beauty which can be conceived is less than the beauty of Thy face; every face hath beauty yet none is beauty's self, but Thy face, Lord, hath beauty and this having is being. 'Tis therefore Absolute Beauty itself, which is the form that giveth being to every beautiful form. O face exceeding comely, whose beauty all things to whom it is granted to behold it, suffice not to admire!

In all faces is seen the Face of faces, veiled, and in a riddle; howbeit unveiled it is not seen, until above all faces a man enter into a certain secret and mystic silence where there is no knowledge or concept of a face. This mist, cloud, darkness or ignorance into which he that seeketh Thy face entereth when he goeth beyond all knowledge or concept, is the state below which Thy face cannot be found except veiled; but that very darkness revealeth Thy face to be there, beyond all veils. 'Tis as when our eye seeketh to look on the light of the sun which is its face; first it beholdeth it veiled in the stars, and in colours and in all things that share its light. But when it striveth to behold the light unveiled it goeth beyond all visible light, because all this is less than that which it seeketh. A man seeking to see a light beyond his seeing knoweth that, so long as he seeth aught, it is not that which he seeketh. Wherefore it behoveth him to go beyond all visible light. For him, then, who must go beyond all light, the place he entereth must needs lack visible light, and is thus, so to speak, darkness to the eye. And while he is in that darkness which is a mist, if he then know himself to be in a mist, he knoweth that he hath drawn nigh the face of the sun; for that mist in his eye proceedeth from the exceeding bright shining of the sun. Wherefore, the denser he knoweth the mist to be, by so much the more truly doth he attain in the mist unto the light invisible. I perceive that 'tis thus and not otherwise, Lord, that the light inaccessible, the beauty and radiance of Thy face, may, unveiled, be approached.

CHAPTER VIII. THAT THE GAZE OF GOD IS ITSELF THE LOVING, EFFECTING, READING, AND POSSESSING OF ALL THINGS IN ITSELF

My heart is not at rest, Lord, because Thy love hath inflamed it with so great desire that it can only rest in Thee. I began to pray the Lord's Prayer, and Thou didst inspire me to consider in what manner Thou art our Father. For Thy love is Thy regard, Thy fatherhood is Thy regard, which embraceth us all in fatherly wise: for we say: Our Father. For Thou art the Father of the whole world, and of each individual. Each saith Our Father, and because of it Thy fatherly love comprehendeth each and all of Thy sons. For a father so loveth all his sons as he doth each one, because he is as much the father of all as he is of each one. He so loveth each of his sons that each may imagine himself to be favoured beyond all.

If, then, Thou art a Father, and our Father, we are Thy sons. But paternal love precedeth filial. As long as we Thy sons look upon Thee as do sons, Thou ceasest not to look upon us as doth a father. Therefore Thou wilt be our fatherly Providence, having fatherly care for us. Thy regard is providence. But if we Thy sons reject Thee our Father, we cease to be Thy sons, nor are we thenceforth free sons nor our own masters; but separating ourselves from Thee, we go into a far country, and then endure grievous slavery under a prince that is Thine adversary, O God. But Thou our Father, who hast granted us freedom because we are Thy sons and Thou art very Liberty, dost permit us to depart, and to squander our liberty and our noblest substance, after the corrupt desires of our senses. Yet for all that Thou dost not leave us utterly, but art ever at our side beseeching us, and Thou speakest within us, calling us back to return unto Thee, ever ready to behold us again with Thy fatherly eye as aforetime, if we return, if we turn again unto Thee. O pitiful God, look on me, who, remorseful, now return from my wretched slavery, from the slime and filth of the swine, where I perished with hunger, and in Thy house would seek to be fed after any wise. Feed me with Thy gaze, O Lord, and teach me how Thy gaze regardeth every sight that seeth, and all that may be seen, and each act of seeing, and every power of seeing, or of being seen, and all the seeing which thence resulteth. For with Thee to see is to cause; Thou seest all things who causest all things.

Teach me, O Lord, how at one glance Thou discernest both all together and each in particular. When I open a book to read, I see the whole page confusedly, and, if I wish to distinguish separate letters, syllables, and words, I must needs turn my particular attention to each individual thing in succession. I can only read one letter in turn after another, and one word after another, and one passage after another. But Thou, Lord, dost see and read the whole page together, in an instant. If two of us read the same thing, one more quickly, the other more slowly, Thou readest with us both, and dost appear to read in time, since Thou readest with them that read; yet dost Thou see and read it all together, above and beyond time. For with Thee to see is to read. Thou from eternity hast seen and read, together and once and for all, all written books, and those that can be written, regardless of time; and, in addition, Thou dost read those same books one after another with all who read them. Nor dost Thou read one thing in eternity and another with them that read in time but the same; Thou behavest Thyself in the same way, since Thou changest not, being a fixed eternity. Yet eternity, because it is bound up with time, seemeth to be moved with time, albeit motion in eternity is rest.

Lord, Thou seest and hast eyes. Thou art an Eye, since with Thee having is being, wherefore in Thyself Thou dost observe all things. If in me my seeing were an eye, as 'tis in Thee, my God, then in myself I should see all things, since the eye is like a mirror. And a mirror, however small it be, beholdeth in itself the image of a great mountain, and of all that existeth on the surface of that mountain, and so the species of all things are contained in the mirror of the eye. Notwithstanding this, our sight, through the mirror of the eye, can only see that particular object toward which it is turned, because its power can only be determined in a particular manner by the object, so that it seeth not all things contained in the mirror of the eye. But Thy sight, being an eye or living mirror, seeth all things in itself. Nay more, because it is the cause of all things visible, it embraceth and seeth all things in the cause and reason of all, that is, in itself.

Thine eye, Lord, reacheth to all things without turning. When our eye turneth itself toward an object 'tis because our sight seeth but through a finite angle. But the angle of Thine eye, O God, is not limited, but is infinite, being the angle of a circle, nay, of an infinite sphere also, since Thy sight is an eye of sphericity and of infinite perfection. Wherefore it seeth at one and the same time all things around and above and below.

O how marvellous is Thy glance, my God, which is Θεός unto all that examine it! how fair and lovely is it unto all that love Thee! How dread is it unto all them that have abandoned Thee, O Lord my God! For 'tis with Thy glance, Lord, that Thou quickenest

every spirit, and makest glad every saint, and puttest to flight
every sorrow. Look then on me in mercy, and my soul is healed!

CHAPTER X. HOW GOD IS SEEN BEYOND THE COINCIDENCE
OF CONTRADICTORIES AND HOW SEEING IS BEING

I stand before this image of Thy face, my God, and while I
look upon it with the eyes of sense, I strive with my inner eyes to
behold the truth which is figured forth in this picture, and it
seemeth to me, Lord, that Thy glance speaketh. For with Thee
speech and sight are one, since in reality they are not different in
Thee, who art Very Absolute Simplicity. Thence I prove clearly
that Thou seest at the same time all things and each thing.

When I preach, I speak alike and at the same time to the whole
congregation in church, and to the individuals present in church;
I preach one sermon only, and in that one sermon I speak to individuals. And what the church is to me that, Lord, the whole world
is to Thee, with the individual creatures which exist or can exist.
Then, if Thou speakest to individuals, Thou seest those things to
which Thou speakest. Thou, Lord, who art the sovran comfort
of them that hope in Thee, inspirest me to praise Thee from myself. For Thou hast given me a face according as Thou didst will,
and it is seen by all to whom I preach, individually and at the same
time. Thus my one face is seen by individuals, and my one speech
is wholly heard by individuals. I, however, cannot separately hear
all who speak together, but I must hear one after another; nor can
I separately see all at once, but one after another. But if such a faculty were in me as that to be heard were one with hearing, and to
be seen with seeing, and in like manner to speak with hearing
(even as it is with Thee, Lord, who art the sovran Power), then
indeed I could hear and see all and each at one and the same time.
And just as I could speak to individuals simultaneously, so, in the
same instant in which I were speaking, I could see and hear the
answers of all and each.

Whence I begin, Lord, to behold Thee in the door of the coincidence of opposites, which the angel guardeth that is set over the entrance into Paradise. For Thou art there where speech, sight, hearing, taste, touch, reason, knowledge and understanding are the same and where seeing is one with being seen, and hearing with being heard, and tasting with being tasted, and touching with being touched, and speaking with hearing, and creating with speaking.

If I were to see as I am seen I should not be a creature. And if Thou, God, didst not see as Thou art seen Thou wouldest not be God Almighty. Thou art to be seen of all creatures, and Thou seest all; in that Thou seest all, Thou art seen of all; for otherwise creatures could not exist, since they exist by Thy seeing. If they saw not Thee who seest them, they would not receive from Thee being; the being of the creature is Thy seeing and the being seen of Thee alike. Thou speakest by Thy Word to all things that are, and callest into being those that are not: Thou callest them to hear Thee, and when they hear Thee then they are. When Thou speakest Thou speakest unto all, and all things hear Thee to which Thou speakest. Thou speakest to the earth and callest it to human nature, and the earth heareth Thee and by this its hearing man is made. Thou speakest to that which is nothing as though it were something, and Thou callest nothing to be something, and that which is nothing hearest Thee because that which was nothing becometh something.

O infinite Power, Thy concept is Thy speech! Thou conceivest the heaven, and it existeth as Thou conceivest it. Thou conceivest the earth, and it existeth as Thou conceivest it; while Thou conceivest, Thou dost see and speak and work, and do all else that can be named. Marvellous art Thou, my God, Thou conceivest once, Thou speakest once! How, then, do not all things come into being simultaneously, but many of them successively? How do such diverse things spring from one only concept? Thou dost enlighten me while I am on the threshold of the door, showing me that Thy concept is pure and simple eternity itself. 'Tis impossible that aught should be made after eternity pure and simple. For infinite duration, which is eternity's self, includeth all succession, and all which seemeth to us to be in succession existeth not posterior to Thy concept, which is eternity. For Thy one and only concept, which is also Thy Word, enfoldeth all and each, while Thine eternal Word cannot be manifold, nor diverse, nor changeable, nor mutable, because it is simple eternity.

Thus, Lord, I perceive that naught existeth posterior to Thy concept, but that all things exist because Thou dost conceive them. Thou conceivest in eternity, but in eternity succession is without succession, 'tis eternity's self, 'tis Thy very Word, O Lord God. Thou hast no sooner conceived aught that appeareth to us in time than it is. For in eternity in which Thou conceivest, all succession in time coincideth in the same "now" of eternity. There is no past nor future where future and past are one with present. The reason why things in this world exist as earlier and later is that Thou didst not earlier conceive such things to exist: hadst Thou earlier conceived them they would have existed earlier. But he in whose thought earlier and later can occur, in such a way that he conceives one thing first and then another, is not almighty. Thus, because Thou art God Almighty, Thou dwellest within the wall of Paradise, and this wall is that coincidence where later is one with earlier, where the end is one with the beginning, where Alpha and Omega are the same.

So then, things alway exist because Thou biddest them exist, and they so not exist earlier because Thou dost not bid them earlier. When I read that Adam existed so many years ago, and that to-day such an one is born, it seemeth impossible that Adam existed then because Thou didst then will it, and likewise that the other is born to-day because Thou hast now willed it, and that nevertheless Thou didst not earlier will Adam to exist than the one born to-day. But that which seemeth impossible is necessity itself, for "now" and "then" are posterior to Thy Word. This is why for him that approacheth Thee, they meet in the wall surrounding the place where Thou abidest in coincidence. For "now" and "then" coincide in the circle of the wall of Paradise. But, O my God, the Absolute and Eternal, it is beyond the Present and the Past that Thou dost exist and utter speech!

CHAPTER XI. HOW IN GOD IS SEEN SUCCESSION
WITHOUT SUCCESSION

I experience Thy goodness, my God, which not only doth not condemn me, a miserable sinner, but doth sweetly feed me with a certain desire. Thou hast suggested to me an acceptable comparison touching the unity of Thy mental word or concept, and its variation in things seen in succession. The simple concept of a most perfect clock leads me on so that I become the more delectably rapt in the vision of Thy concept and word. For the simple concept of a clock enfoldeth all succession in time. Suppose, then, a clock to be a concept though we hear the striking of the sixth hour before the seventh, yet the seventh is only heard when the concept biddeth. Neither is the sixth hour earlier in the concept than the seventh or eighth, but in the one simple concept of the clock no hour is earlier or later than another, although the clock never striketh the hour save when the concept biddeth. 'Tis true to say, when we hear six o'clock strike, that the sixth hour striketh then because the concept of the master so willeth. Since in the thought of God the clock is a concept, 'tis perceived in some degree how that which is succession in the clock existeth without succession in the word or concept, and how in this simplest concept are enfolded all motions and sounds and whatsoever we find in succession. Naught of that which appeareth in succession departeth in any way from the concept, but 'tis the unfolding of the concept, seeing that the concept giveth being to each: naught in consequence hath existed earlier than it appeared, because it was not earlier conceived that it should exist. Let then the concept of the clock represent eternity's self; then motion in the clock representeth succession. Eternity, therefore, both enfoldeth and unfoldeth succession, since the concept of the clock, which is eternity, doth alike enfold and unfold all things.

Blessed be Thou, O Lord my God, who dost feed and nourish me with the milk of comparisons; until Thou shalt give me more solid food, lead me, Lord God, by these paths unto Thee! For if Thou lead me not, I cannot continue in the way, by reason of the frailty of my corruptible nature, and of the earthen vessel that I bear about with me. Trusting in Thine aid, Lord, I return again to find Thee beyond the wall of the coincidence of enfolding and unfolding, and as I go in and go out by this door of Thy word and Thy concept, I find sweetest nourishment. When I find Thee as the power that unfoldeth, I go out: when I find Thee as the power that alike enfoldeth and unfoldeth, I go in and go out alike. I go in, passing from the creatures to Thee, their Creator, from effects to the Cause; I go out, passing from Thee, the Creator, to the creature, from Cause to effects. I go in and go out simultaneously when I perceive how going out is one with going in, and going in with going out. In this manner one that reckoneth doth alike enfold and unfold, for he unfoldeth the power of unity, and enfoldeth number in unity. For the creature, to go forth from Thee is to enter into the creature, and to unfold is to enfold. When I behold Thee, my God, in Paradise, girt by that wall of the coincidence of opposites, I see that Thou dost neither enfold nor unfold, whether separately or together. For disjunction and conjunction alike are that wall of coincidence, beyond which Thou existest, set free from all that can be spoken or thought.

CHAPTER XIII. THAT GOD IS SEEN TO BE ABSOLUTE INFINITY

O Lord my God, the Helper of them that seek Thee, I behold Thee in the entrance of Paradise, and I know not what I see, for I see naught visible. This alone I know, that I know not what I

see, and never can know. And I know not how to name Thee because I know not what Thou art, and did anyone say unto me that
Thou wert called by this name or that, by the very fact that he
named it, I should know that it was not Thy name. For the wall
beyond which I see Thee is the end of all manner of signification
in names. If anyone should set forth any concept by which Thou
couldst be conceived, I know that that concept is not a concept of
Thee, for every concept is ended in the wall of Paradise. And if
anyone should set forth any likeness, and say that Thou wert to
be imagined as resembling it, I know in like manner that that is no
likeness of Thee. So too, if any were to tell of the understanding
of Thee, wishing to supply a means whereby Thou mightest be
understood, this man is yet far from Thee. For Thou art separated
by an exceeding high wall from all these. The high wall separates
Thee from all that can possibly be said or thought of Thee, for-
asmuch as Thou art Absolute above all the concepts which any
man can frame.

Thus, while I am borne to loftiest heights, I behold Thee as infinity. By reason of this, Thou mayest not be attained, or comprehended, or named, or multiplied, or beheld. He that approacheth
Thee must needs ascend above every limit and end and finite
thing. But how shall he attain unto Thee who art the End toward
whom he striveth, if he must ascend above the end? He who
ascendeth above the end, doth he not enter in to what is undefined
and confused, and thus, in regard to the intellect, into ignorance
and obscurity, which pertain to intellectual confusion? It behoveth, then, the intellect to become ignorant and to abide in
darkness if it would fain see Thee. But what, O my God, is this intellectual ignorance? Is it not an instructed ignorance? Thou,
God, who art infinity, canst only be approached by him whose intellect is in ignorance, to wit, by him who knows himself to be
ignorant of Thee.

How can the intellect grasp Thee, who art infinity? The intellect knoweth that it is ignorant, and that Thou canst not be

grasped because Thou art infinity. For to understand infinity is to comprehend the incomprehensible. The intellect knoweth that it is ignorant of Thee, because it knoweth Thou canst not be known, unless the unknowable could be known, and the invisible beheld, and the inaccessible attained. Thou, my God, art Very Absolute Infinity, which I perceive to be an end without an end, but I am unable to grasp how without an end an end could be an end. Thou, God, art the End of Thine own self, for Thou art whatever Thou hast; if Thou hast an end, Thou art an End. Thou art therefore an infinite End, because Thou art the End of Thine own self. Since Thine end is Thine essence, the essence of the end is not determined or ended in any place other than the end, but in itself. The end, then, which is its own end, is infinite, and every end which is not its own end is a finite end. Thou, Lord who art the End ending all things art the End whereof there is no end, and thus an end without an end, or infinite. This eludeth all reason, because it implieth a contradiction. Thus, when I assert the existence of an end without an end, I admit darkness to be light, ignorance to be knowledge, and the impossible to be a necessity. Since we admit the existence of an end of the finite, we needs must admit the infinite, or the ultimate end, or the end without an end. Now we cannot but admit the existence of finite beings, wherefore we cannot but admit the infinite. Thus we admit the coincidence of contradictories, above which is the infinite.

Howbeit, this coincidence is a contradiction without contradiction, even as an end without an end. And Thou, Lord, sayest unto me that, just as otherness in unity is without otherness because it is unity even so, in infinity, contradiction is without contradiction, because it is infinity. Infinity is simplicity itself, contradiction existeth not without because it is infinity. Infinity is simplicity itself, contradiction existeth not without becoming other. Yet in simplicity otherness existeth without becoming other because it is simplicity itself, seeing that all that is said of absolute simplicity coincideth therewith, because therein having is being. Therein the opposition of opposites is an opposition without opposition, just as the end of things finite is an end without an end. Thou, then, O God, art the Opposition of opposites, because Thou art infinite, and because Thou art infinite Thou art infinity itself. And in infinity the opposition of opposites existeth without opposition.

O Lord my God, Strength of the weak, I see Thee to be infinity itself, wherefore naught is alien to Thee, naught differing from Thee, naught opposed to Thee. For the infinite brooketh not otherness from itself, since, being infinity, naught existeth outside it: absolute infinity includeth and containeth all things. If infinity could ever exist, and aught else exist outside it, then neither infinity nor aught else could exist. Infinity cannot be greater or less; naught, therefore, existeth outside it. Did infinity not include in itself all being, it were not infinity. If it were not infinity, then neither would the finite exist, nor aught alien or different, since these cannot exist without otherness of ends and limits. If the infinite be taken away, naught remaineth. Infinity, accordingly, existeth, and enfoldeth all things, and naught can exist outside it, hence naught is alien to it or differing from it. Thus infinity is alike all things and no one of them all. No name can suit infinity, for every name can have it contrary, but naught can be contrary to infinity, which is unnameable. Neither is infinity a whole, whereunto a part is opposed, nor can it be a part; 'tis neither great nor small, nor any of all those things that can be named in heaven or earth; above all these it existeth, infinity. Infinity is neither greater nor less than anything, nor equal thereunto.

But while I consider infinity, how it is neither greater nor less than any given thing, I declare it to be the measure of all things, just because it is neither greater nor less. Thus I conceive it as equality of being. Yet such equality is infinity, and therefore it is not equality after the style in which inequality is opposed to equality, but therein inequality is equality: for in infinity inequality existeth without inequality because it is infinity; so too in infinity equality is infinity. Infinite equality is an end without end;

whence, albeit it be not greater nor less, 'tis yet not on that account equality in the manner in which limited equality is understood; nay, 'tis infinite equality, which admitteth not greater or less. And so 'tis not more equal to one thing than to another, but is as equal to one as to all, and to all as to none. For the infinite is not liable to limitation, but abideth absolute: if aught could be limited in infinity, 'twould not be infinite. Hence it may not be limited to equality with the finite, albeit 'tis not unequal to anything. For how could inequality suit with the infinite, when neither greater nor less doth so? The infinite, then, with regard to any given thing, is neither greater, nor less, nor unequal. Nor yet, by reason of this, is it equal to the finite, seeing that, [considered] in itself, it is above all that is finite. The infinite, then, is utterly absolute, and illimitable.

O how exalted art Thou, Lord, above all things, and humble withal, since Thou art in all! If infinity could be limited to anything that can be named, such as a line, or surface, or species, it would draw unto itself that whereto it was limited, and this implieth that the infinite would be limitable, since, though not limited, it would draw unto [itself a limit]. If I should say that the infinite is limited to a line, as when I speak of an infinite line, then the line is drawn unto the infinite, for a line ceaseth to be a line when it hath no quantity nor end. An infinite line is not a line, but a line at infinity is infinity. Just as naught can be added to the infinite, even so the infinite cannot be limited unto anything so as to become aught other than infinite. Infinite goodness is not goodness, but infinity; infinite quantity is not quantity, but infinity, and so with the rest.

Thou art the great God, of whose greatness there is no end, and thus I perceive Thee to be the immeasurable measure of all things, even as the infinite end of all. Wherefore, Lord, being infinite, Thou art without beginning and end; Thou art beginning without beginning and end without end; Thou art beginning without end and end without beginning; Thou art equally beginning as end and end as beginning, yet neither beginning nor end, but above beginning and end, absolute infinity itself, blessed for ever!

CHAPTER XIV. HOW GOD ENFOLDETH ALL THINGS
WITHOUT OTHERNESS

I see, Lord, through Thine infinite mercy, that Thou art infinity encompassing all things. Naught existeth outside Thee, but all things in Thee are not other than Thee. Thou dost teach me, Lord, how otherness, which is not in Thee, is not even in itself, nor can it be. Nor doth otherness, being not in Thee, make one creature to be different from another, albeit one be not another; the sky is not the earth, though 'tis true that sky is sky and earth is earth. If, then, I seek for otherness, which is neither in Thee nor yet outside Thee, where shall I find it? And if it existeth not, how cometh it that the earth is a different creature from the sky? for without otherness this cannot be conceived. But Thou, Lord, dost speak in me and say that there is no positive principle of otherness, and thus it existeth not: for how could otherness exist without a principle, unless it itself were a principle and infinity? Now otherness cannot be the principle of being, for otherness taketh its name from not-being, for because one thing is not another it is called other. Otherness, therefore, cannot be the principle of being, because it taketh its name from not-being, nor hath it the principle of being, since it ariseth from not-being. Otherness, then, is not anything, but the reason wherefore the sky is not the earth is because the sky is not infinity's self, which encompasseth all being. Whence, since infinity is absolute infinity, it resulteth that one thing cannot be another.

For example, the being of Socrates encompasseth all Socratic being, and in Socratic being pure and simple there is no otherness nor diversity. The being of Socrates is the individual unity of all those things that are in Socrates, in such a way that in that one being is enfolded the being of all those things which are in

Socrates, to wit, in that individual simplicity wherein naught is found other or diverse. But in that same single being all things which have the Socratic being exist and are unfolded, and outside it they neither exist nor can exist. Howbeit, in this onefold being, when all is said, the eye is not the ear and the head is not the heart, and sight is not hearing, and sense is not reason. Nor doth this result from any principle of otherness, but, granted the Socratic being pure and simple, it resulteth that the head is not the foot because the head is not that most simple Socratic being itself and hence its being doth not contain the whole Socratic being. Thus I perceive—Thou, Lord, enlightening me—that, because Socratic being pure and simple is utterly incommunicable, and not to be limited to the being of any one member—the being of any one member is not the being of any other, but that Socratic being pure and simple is the being of all the members of Socrates, wherein all variety and otherness of being that happeneth in the members is unity pure and simple, even as plurality of forms of parts is unity in the form of the whole.

Thus in some manner, O God, is it with Thy Being, which is absolutely infinity, in relation to all things which exist. But I say absolutely: as the absolute form of being of all limited forms. The hand of Socrates, being separated from Socrates, as after amputation, is no longer the hand of Socrates; yet it still retaineth some kind of being as a corpse. And the reason of this is that the form of Socrates which giveth being doth not give being pure and simple, but a limited being, to wit, the Socratic. From this the being of the hand may be separated, and may yet none the less remain under another form; but if once the hand were separated from the being that is entirely unlimited, to wit, from the infinite and absolute, then it would utterly cease to exist, because it would be cut off from all being.

I give Thee thanks, O Lord my God, who dost bountifully reveal Thyself unto me, in so far as I can receive it, showing how Thou art infinity's self, enfolding the being of all in its most simple power; and this were not infinity were it not infinitely united. For power united is stronger. Accordingly, that power which is united in the highest degree is infinite and almighty. Thou art God Almighty, because Thou art absolute simplicity, which is absolute infinity.

CHAPTER XVI. HOW THAT, UNLESS GOD WERE INFINITE,
HE WOULD NOT BE THE END OF DESIRE

Fire is ever aglow, so likewise is that yearning love which is directed toward Thee, O God, who art the form of all that is desirable, and that truth which in every desire is desired. In that I have begun to taste, of Thy honeysweet giving, Thy sweetness beyond understanding—which doth by so much the more please me as it appeareth more limitless—I perceive that the reason wherefore Thou, O God, art unknown to all creatures is that they may have in this divine ignorance a greater rest, as in a treasure beyond reckoning, and inexhaustible. For he who findeth a treasure that he knoweth to be utterly beyond reckoning and unlimited is moved by far greater joy than he who findeth one that may be counted, and that is limited. Hence this divine ignorance of Thy greatness is the more desirable nourishment for my intellect, chiefly when I find such a treasure in my field in such manner that the treasure is mine own.

O Fount of riches, Thou willest to be held in my possession, and yet to abide incomprehensible and infinite, because Thou art the treasury of delights whereof no man can desire an end! How should desire covet not-being? For whether the will covet being or not-being, desire itself cannot rest, but is borne on into infinity.

Thou dost come down, Lord, that Thou mayest be comprehended, and yet Thou abidest beyond reckoning, and infinite; and unless Thou didst abide infinite, Thou wouldest not be the end of desire. Wherefore, Thou art infinite that Thou mayest be the end of all desire.

Now, intellectual desire is not turned toward that which can be greater or more desirable. But all on this side infinity may be greater. The end of desire, therefore, is infinite. Thus Thou, O God, art very infinity, for which alone I yearn in every desire, but to the knowledge of which infinity I cannot approach more nearly than that I know it to be infinite. Wherefore, the more I understand that Thou, my God, art not to be understood, by so much the more I attain Thee, because the more I attain the end of my desire. Accordingly I reject as a delusion any idea occurring to me which seeketh to show Thee as comprehensible. My yearning, bright with Thee, leadeth me unto Thee; it spurneth all that is finite and comprehensible, for in these it cannot rest, being led by Thee to Thee. And Thou art beginning without beginning, and end without end. Wherefore my desire is led by the eternal beginning, from whom it cometh to be desire, unto the end without end, and He is infinite. If then, I, a poor little man, could not be content with Thee, my God, did I know Thee to be comprehensible, 'tis because I am led by Thee to Thee, who art incomprehensible and infinite.

I behold Thee, O Lord my God, in a kind of mental trance, for if sight be not sated with seeing, nor the ear with hearing, then much less is the intellect with understanding. Accordingly, that which sateth the intellect, or that is the end thereof, is not that which it understandeth; neither can that sate it which it no whit understandeth, but that alone which it understandeth by not understanding. For the intelligible which it knoweth doth not sate it, nor the intelligible whereof it is utterly ignorant, but only the intelligible which it knoweth to be so intelligible that it can never be fully understood—'tis this alone can sate it. Even so a man's insatiable hunger cannot be appeased by partaking of scanty food, or by food that is out of his reach, but only by food that is within his reach, and which, though it be continuously partaken of, can yet never be utterly consumed, since it is such that by eating 'tis not diminished, being infinite.

CHAPTER XVII. HOW GOD, UNLESS HE WERE ONE AND THREE, COULD NOT BE PERFECTLY SEEN

Thou hast shown Thyself unto me, Lord, as in the highest degree loveable, for Thou art infinitely loveable, my God! Hence Thou couldst never be loved by any in the degree that Thou art loveable, save by an infinite lover. Unless there were an infinite lover, Thou wert not infinitely loveable, for Thy loveableness, to wit, the power of being infinitely loved, existeth because there is a power of loving infinitely. And from these two powers ariseth an infinite bond of love, between the infinite lover and the infinitely loveable, and this bond may not be multiplied. Wherefore, Thou, my God, who art Love, art Love that loveth, and Love that is loveable and Love that is the bond between these twain. I perceive in Thee, my God, love that loveth and love that is loveable; and by the very fact that I perceive in Thee these twain, I perceive the bond between them. And this is naught other than that which I behold in Thine absolute unity, wherein I perceive unity that uniteth, unity that may be united, and the union of those twain. But whatsoever I perceive in Thee, that Thou art, my God.

Thou art, then, that infinite love, which cannot seem to me natural and perfect love without a lover, and one loveable, and a bond between them. For how can I conceive an entirely perfect and natural love without a lover, one loveable, and the union of both? For from limited love I learn that 'tis of the essence of perfect love that love be loving, and loveable, and the union of both; now that which is of the essence of a perfect love in limitation cannot be lacking in absolute love, whence limited love draweth whatsoever it hath of perfection. The simpler love is, the more perfect it is, and Thou, my God, art love the most entirely perfect and simple. Thus Thou art the very essence, most perfect, most simple, most natural, of love. Hence in Thee, who art love, the lover is not one thing, and the loveable another, and the bond between them a third, but they are one and the same, even Thou Thyself, my God. Since, then, in Thee the loveable is one with the lover, and being loved with loving, this bond of coincidence is an essential bond. For there is naught in Thee that is not Thy very essence. Those constituents, then, which appear unto me to be three, to wit, the lover, the loveable, and the bond, are that absolute and most simple essence itself. Thus they are not three, but one.

That Thine essence, my God, which seemeth to me to be most simple and, so to speak, most one, is not most natural and most perfect without these three constituents aforenamed. Thus the essence is triune, and yet there are not three essences therein, since it is most simple. Wherefore the plurality of these three afore-named is alike plurality and unity, and their unity alike unity and plurality. Their plurality is plurality without a plural number, for a plural number cannot be unity pure and simple, because it is a plural number. There is no numerical distinction between the three, for plural number is essential to distinction, one number being essentially distinct from another. And because this unity is triune, 'tis not the unity of a singular number, for the unity of a singular number is not triune. O most wondrous God, Thou art neither of singular number not yet of plural, but art above all plurality or singularity, One in Three and Three in One! I per-ceive, then, that in the wall of Paradise, where Thou, my God, dwellest, plurality is one with singularity, and that Thine abode is very far removed beyond them.

Teach me, Lord, how I can conceive that to be possible which I perceive to be necessary! For I am met by the impossibility that the plurality of three elements, without which I cannot conceive Thee as perfect and natural love, should be a plurality without number. When any saith one, one, one, he saith one thrice; he saith not three, but one, and that one thrice. Yet he cannot say it thrice without the number three, although he name not three. When he saith one thrice, he repeateth the same without numbering it, for to number is to make the one other, but to repeat one and the same thing thrice over is to make plural without number. Whence the plurality that I behold in Thee, my God, is an otherness without otherness, because it is an otherness which is identity. For, although I perceive that the lover is not the loveable, and that the bond between them is neither the one nor the other, I do not perceive it in the sense that the lover is one thing and the loveable another; but I perceive that the distinction between lover and loveable is beyond the wall of the coincidence of unity and otherness. This distinction, which is beyond the wall where distinguishable and indistinguishable are one, precedeth all otherness and diversity that can be understood. The wall is a barrier to the power of every intellect, albeit the eye penetrate beyond it into Paradise. But what it there seeth it cannot tell nor understand, for its love is a treasure, secret and hidden, which, when found, remaineth hidden, since 'tis found within the wall of the coincidence of the hidden and the manifest.

But I cannot withdraw me from the sweetness of the vision before that I have in some manner brought home to myself the revelation of the distinction between the lover, the loveable, and the bond between them. For one may, it seemeth, by a figure, win some slight foretaste of that sweetest food. Thou, Lord, grantest me to see in Thee love, because I see myself as lover. And seeing that I love myself I see myself as loveable, and myself to be the most natural bond between the twain: I am lover, I am loveable, I am bond. Accordingly, that love without which none of these three constituents could exist, is one. 'Tis the same, one I who am lover, and who am loveable, and who am the bond arising from the love wherewith I love myself: I am one, and not three. Suppose, then, that my love were my essence, as 'tis in my God—then in the unity of my essence there would exist the unity of the three constituents aforesaid, and in their trinity, the unity of my essence: all would exist in limitation in my essence, after the manner in which I perceive them to exist truly and absolutely in Thee. Yet the love that loveth would not be the love that is loveable, nor the bond between them: this I learn by the following practice.

The active love which I extend to an object outside myself, as to something loveable outside my own essence, is followed by a bond whereby I am attached to that object, as far as in me lieth: the object is not attached to me by the same bond, since perchance it loveth me not. Whence, albeit I so love it that my active love overfloweth itself, that active love of mine doth yet not draw out the love of me as loveable; for I do not become loveable in the other's sight, he careth not for me, albeit I love him much: 'tis as when a son sometimes careth not for his mother who loveth him most tenderly. And so I learn by experience that love that loveth is not love that is loveable, nor their bond, but I see that the lover is to be distinguished from the loveable and from their bond. This distinction, howbeit, is not of the essence of love, since I cannot love either myself or any being other than myself without love: thus love is of the essence of the three. Thus I perceive than the essence of these three constituents aforesaid is entirely onefold, albeit they are distinct one from the other.

I have set forth, Lord, by a comparison some kind of foretaste of Thy nature. Yet in mercy forgive me that I strive to image forth the unimaginable savour of Thy sweetness. If the sweetness of some fruit unknown may not be pictured through any painting or image, or described in any words, who am I, a miserable sinner, who strives to show Thee, that art beyond showing, and to image Thee, the invisible, as visible, and who makes bold to render delectable that Thine infinite and all-ineffable sweetness? Never yet have I merited to taste therof, and the words whereby I set it forth do rather minish than magnify it. But so great is Thy goodness, my God, that Thou permittest even the blind to speak of the light, and to herald the praises of Him of whom they neither know nor can know aught save it be revealed unto them.

Revelation, howbeit, reacheth not unto taste, the ear of faith reacheth not unto the sweetness of this foretaste. Yet, Lord, Thou hast revealed unto me that ear hath not heard, nor hath it entered into the heart of man, that infinity of Thy sweetness, which Thou hast prepared for them that love Thee. This Thy great Apostle Paul revealed unto us, who was rapt, beyond the wall of coincidence, into Paradise, where alone Thou mayest be seen unveiled, O Thou Fount of delights! I have endeavoured to submit me to be rapt, trusting in Thine infinite goodness, that I might behold Thee to be invisible, and the vision revealed to be beyond revealing. Thou knowest how far I have come, I know not: but Thy grace is sufficient for me, whereby Thou assurest me that Thou art incomprehensible, and dost uplift me to a firm hope that, with Thee for guide, I shall come to the fruition of Thee.

CHAPTER XVIII. HOW GOD, UNLESS HE WERE A TRINITY, COULD NOT BE BLISS

Would, Lord, that all who by Thy gift have received eyes of the mind would open them, and would see with me how Thou art a jealous God! For Thou, Love that lovest, canst hate nothing; for 'tis in Thee, O loveable God, that all things loveable are enfolded, and Thou lovest each of them. They would thus see with me the alliance or bond whereby Thou art united unto all.

Thou lovest, Lord, and lovest alike all in general and each in particular, Thou spreadest Thy love over all. Yet many love not Thee, but prefer something other than Thyself to Thee. If loveable love were not distinct from active love, Thou wouldst be seen so loveable by all that they could not love aught beside Thee, and all reasoning spirits would be constrained to love Thee. But Thou art so magnanimous, my God, that Thou willest reasoning spirits to be free to love Thee or not. Wherefore it followeth not on Thy loving that Thou art loved. Thou therefore, my God, art united by a bond of love to all, because Thou spreadest Thy love over every creature of Thine. But not every reasoning spirit is united unto Thee, because it directeth its love, not toward Thy loveableness, but toward some other thing whereunto it is united and bound. Thou hast espoused unto Thyself, by Thine active love, every reasoning soul; but every spouse loveth not Thee, her Betrothed, but too often some other unto whom she cleaveth. But how, my God, could Thy spouse, the human soul, attain her end if Thou wert not loveable, that thus, by loving Thee, the loveable, she might attain to be knit unto Thee, and unto most blissful union?

Who, then, can deny that Thou, God, art triune, when he perceiveth that, wert Thou not Three and One, Thou couldst not be either a magnanimous, or a natural and perfect God, and that the spirit could not enjoy free will, nor attain to fruition of Thee and to its own bliss? 'Tis because Thou art an intellect that understandeth and an intellect that is understood and again the bond between them, that the created intellect can attain in Thee, its intelligible God, union and bliss. In like manner, 'tis because Thou art loveable love, that the created will, by loving, can attain in Thee, its loveable God, union and bliss. For he that receiveth Thee, O God, Thou light that may be received by the reason, might attain unto so close a union with Thee as that of a son with his father.

I perceive, Lord, by Thine enlightening, that the reasoning nature can only attain union with Thee because Thou art loveable and canst be apprehended. Wherefore, human nature cannot be united unto Thee as a loving God (for in this aspect Thou art not its object), but it can be united unto Thee as its loveable God, since the loveable is the lover's object. Thus in like manner the intelligible is the object of the intellect, and this object we call truth. Wherefore, since Thou, my God, art the truth intelligible, the created intellect can be united unto Thee. And thus I perceive that the reasoning human nature can be united only unto Thy divine and intelligible and loveable nature, and that man, taking hold on Thee, a God that may be received, passeth into a bond which, by reason of its being so closely knit, may be given the name of sonship, since sonship is the most close-knit bond we know.

If this bond of union be the closest possible, it will of necessity result that, since Thou, the loveable God, canst not more be loved by man, this bond will attain to the most perfect sonship in that sonship which is perfection, embracing all possible sonships, whereby all sons attain final bliss and perfection. In this most exalted Son, sonship is as art in a master or light in the sun. In the rest, 'tis as art in disciples or light in the stars.

CHAPTER XIX. HOW JESUS IS THE UNION OF GOD AND MAN

I render unto Thee thanks unspeakable, O God, light and life of my soul. For I now perceive the faith which, by the teaching of the Apostles, the Catholic Church holdeth, to wit, how Thou, a loving God, dost beget of Thyself a loveable God, and how Thou, the loveable God begotten, art the absolute mediator. For 'tis through Thee that all existeth which doth exist or can exist, since Thou, the loving or willing God, enfoldest them all in Thee, the loveable God. For all that Thou, O God, willest or conceivest is enfolded in Thee, the loveable God. Naught can exist except Thou will it to be. Wherefore all things have their cause or reason for being in Thy loveable concept, and the sole cause of them all is that it so pleaseth Thee; naught pleaseth a lover, as a lover, save the loveable. Thou, O loveable God, art the Son of God the loving Father, since in Thee is all the Father's delight. Thus all creatable being is enfolded in Thee, the loveable God.

Thou too, O loving God—since from Thee cometh the loveable God, as a son from a father—art the Father of all beings by reason that Thou art God, the loving Father of the loveable God Thy Son. For Thy concept is a Son, in whom are all things, and

Thine union and Thy concept is act and operation arising there-from—the act and operation wherein existeth the actuality and unfolding of all things. As therefore of Thee, the loving God, there is begotten the loveable God, and this generation is a concept, even so there proceedeth from Thee, the loving God, and from Thy concept, the loveable God begotten of Thee, Thine act and concept, to wit, the bond knitting together and the God uniting Thee and Thy concept, even as the act of loving uniteth in love the lover and the beloved. And this bond is called Spirit; for spirit is like motion, proceeding from that which moveth and that which is moved. Thus motion is the unfolding of the concept of him that moveth. Wherefore in Thee, God the Holy Spirit, all things are unfolded, even as they are conceived in Thee, God the Son.

I perceive, then—Thou, God, enlightening me—how all things of God the Father are in Thee, God the Son, as in His reason, concept, cause, or exemplar, and how the Son mediateth all things because He is the reason. For 'tis by means of reason and wisdom that Thou, God the Father, workest all things, and the spirit or motion giveth effect unto the concept of reason, as we learn from the craftsman, who, by the motive power in his hands, giveth effect unto the coffer which he hath in his mind. Thus, my God, I perceive how Thy Son mediateth the union of all things, that all may find rest in Thee by the mediation of Thy Son. And I see that blessed Jesus, Son of Man, is most closely united unto Thy Son, and that the son of man could not be united unto Thee, God the Father, save by mediation of Thy Son, the absolute mediator.

Who would not be ravished to the highest in the attentive consideration of these things? Thou, my God, disclosest unto me, a poor wretch, this so great secret that I may perceive that man cannot apprehend Thee, the Father, save in Thy Son, who may be apprehended and who is the mediator, and that to apprehend Thee is to be united unto Thee. Man, then, can be united unto

Thee through Thy Son, who is the means of union; and human nature most closely knit unto Thee, in whatsoever man it be, cannot be more united unto the intermediary than it is, for without an intermediary it cannot be united unto Thee. Thus it is united in the closest degree unto the intermediary, yet it doth not become the intermediary: wherefore, albeit it cannot become the intermediary (since it cannot be united unto Thee without an intermediary), 'tis yet so joined unto the absolute intermediary that naught can mediate between it and Thy Son, the absolute mediator. For if aught could mediate between human nature and the absolute mediator, human nature would not then be united unto Thee in the closest degree.

O good Jesu, I perceive that in Thee human nature is linked most closely unto God the Father, by that most exalted union through which it is linked unto God the Son, the absolute mediator. Since Thou art Son of Man, human sonship is in the highest degree united in Thee, Jesu, unto the divine sonship, so that Thou art rightly called Son of God and Son of Man, for in Thee naught mediateth between those twain. In that absolute sonship, which is the Son of God, is enfolded all sonship, and thereunto Thy human sonship, Jesu, is supremely united. Accordingly, Thy human sonship subsisteth in the divine, not only as enfolded therein, but as that which is attracted in that which attracteth, and that which is united in that which uniteth, and that which is substantiated in that which giveth substance. Thus in Thee, Jesu, there can be no possible separation between Son of Man and Son of God. Possibility of separation ariseth from the fact that an union is not of the closest, but, where an union is of the closest possible, there no intermediary can exist. Separation, then, can have no place where naught can mediate between the things united. But where that which is united subsisteth not in that which uniteth, the union is not the closest possible; for 'tis a closer union where the united subsisteth in the uniter than where it subsisteth separately, separation being a withdrawal from perfect union.

Thus in Thee, my Jesu, I see how the human sonship whereby Thou art Son of Man subsisteth in the divine sonship whereby Thou art Son of God, as in the most perfect union that which is united subsisteth in that which uniteth. Glory be to Thee, O God, throughout all ages!

CHAPTER XX. HOW JESUS IS UNDERSTOOD TO BE THE UNION
OF THE DIVINE NATURE AND THE HUMAN NATURE

Thou showest me, O Light unfailing, that the perfect union whereby human nature is united through my Jesus with Thy divine nature is not in any wise like unto infinite union. The union whereby Thou, God the Father, art united unto God Thy Son is God the Holy Spirit, and thus 'tis an infinite union, seeing that it attaineth unto absolute and essential identity. 'Tis not so when human nature is united unto the divine, for human nature cannot pass over into essential union with the divine, even as the finite cannot be infinitely united unto the infinite, because it would pass into identity with the infinite, and thus would cease to be finite when the infinite were verified in it. Wherefore this union, whereby human nature is united unto the divine nature, is naught else than the attraction in the highest degree of the human nature unto the divine, in such wise that human nature, as such, could not be attracted to greater heights. This union, then, of human nature, as such, with the divine is the greatest, in the sense of being the greatest possible, but it is not purely and simply the greatest, and infinite, as is the divine union.

Thus through the bounty of Thy grace I see in Thee, Jesu, Son of Man, the Son of God, and in the Son of God, the Father. Now, in Thee the Son of Man I see the Son of God, because Thou art both of these alike, and in Thy finite nature which is attracted I perceive the infinite nature which attracteth; in the absolute Son I behold the absolute Father, for the Son cannot be seen as Son unless the Father be seen. I behold in Thee, Jesu, the divine sonship which is the truth of all sonship, and equally with it the highest human sonship which is the most approximate image of the absolute sonship. Just as the image, between which and the exemplar no more perfect image can be interposed, hath an existence nearest in truth to the object whereof it is the image, even so I perceive Thy human nature subsisting in the divine nature.

Accordingly, I see in Thy human nature all that I see in the divine, but I see that in Thy human nature those attributes exist in human guise which in the divine nature are divine truth itself. That which I see to exist in human guise in Thee, Jesu, is a likeness unto the divine nature, but the likeness is united unto the exemplar without a medium, in such wise that no greater likeness can exist or be imagined. In Thy human or rational nature I see the rational human spirit most closely united unto the divine Spirit, which is absolute reason, and so the human intelligence and all things in Thine intelligence, Jesu, united unto the divine intelligence. For Thou, Jesu, as God, dost understand all, and to understand in this sense is to be all. As Man, Thou understandest all, and to understand in this sense is to be a likeness of all. For man only comprehendeth things by a likeness; a stone existeth not in human understanding as in its proper cause or nature, but as in its specific idea and likeness. Thus in Thee, Jesu, human intelligence is united unto the divine intelligence itself, even as a most perfect image unto the truth of its pattern. If I consider the ideal form of the coffer in the craftsman's mind and the species of coffer made by that master most perfectly carrying out his idea, I learn how the ideal form is the truth of the species, and that only in this one master is it united unto it as truth is unto the image. So in Thee, Jesu, Master of masters, I see that the absolute idea of all things, and with it what resembles it in species, are united in the highest degree.

I see Thee, good Jesu, within the wall of Paradise, since Thine intelligence is alike truth and image, and Thou art alike God and creature, alike infinite and finite. And 'tis not possible that Thou shouldst be seen this side of the wall, for Thou art the bond between the divine nature that createth and the human nature that is created.

Howbeit, between Thy human intellect and that of any other man soever I perceive a difference: for no one man knoweth all things that may be known by man, since no man's intellect is so joined unto the exemplar of all things, as the image unto the truth, but that it could not be more nearly joined, and more actually set therein, and so it doth not understand so much but that it could understand yet more, had it access unto the exemplar of things whence every thing actually existent deriveth its actuality. But Thine intellect actually understandeth all that may be apprehended of men, because in Thee human nature is in full perfection, and most entirely joined unto its exemplar. By means of this union, Thy human intelligence exceedeth all created intelligence in perfection of understanding. Wherefore, all rational spirits are far beneath Thee, and Thou, Jesu, art the Master and Light of them all, and Thou art perfection, and the fullness of all things, and by Thee they attain unto absolute truth, as by their mediator. For Thou art alike the way unto truth, and the truth itself; Thou art alike the way unto the life of the intellect and that life itself; Thou art alike the fragrance of the food of joy and the taste that maketh joyful. Be Thou, then, most sweet Jesu, blessed for ever!

CHAPTER XXI. THAT BLISS IS NOT POSSIBLE WITHOUT JESUS

O Jesu, Thou end of the universe, in whom resteth as in the final degree of perfection, every creature, Thou art utterly unknown to the wise of this world. For of Thee we affirm many antitheses that are yet most true, since Thou art alike Creator and creature, alike He that attracteth and He that is attracted, alike finite and infinite. They pronounce it folly to believe this possible, and because of it they flee from Thy Name, and do not receive Thy light whereby Thou hast illumined us. But, esteeming themselves wise, they remain for ever foolish, and ignorant, and blind. Yet if they would believe that Thou art Christ, God and Man, and would receive and handle the words of the Gospel as being those of so great a Master, then at last they would see most clearly that, in comparison with that light there hidden in the simplicity of Thy words, all things else are naught but thickest shadows, and ignorance. Thus 'tis only humble believers who attain unto this most gracious and life-giving revelation. There is hidden in Thy most holy Gospel, which is heavenly food, as there was in the manna, sweetness to satisfy all desire, which can only be tasted by him that believeth and eateth. If any believeth and receiveth it, he shall prove and find the truth, because Thou didst come down from heaven and Thou alone art the Master of truth.

O good Jesu, Thou art the Tree of Life, in the Paradise of delights, and none may feed upon that desirable life save from Thy fruit. Thou art, O Jesu, the food forbidden to all sons of Adam who, expelled from Paradise, seek their sustenance from the earth whereon they toil. Wherefore it behoveth every man to put off the old man of presumption and to put on the new man of humility, which is after Thy pattern, if he hope to taste the food of life within the Paradise of delights. The nature of the new and of the old Adam is one, but in the old Adam it is animal; in Thee, the new Adam, it is spiritual, for in Thee, Jesu, it is united unto God, who is Spirit. Wherefore, every man must needs be united in one spirit unto Thee, Jesu, even as he is by the human nature that is common to himself and to Thee, to the end that thus in his own nature, which Thou, Jesu, dost share, he may be able to draw near unto God the Father, who is in Paradise. Now to behold God the Father, and Thee, Jesu, His Son, is to be in Paradise, and is glory everlasting. For he that stayeth outside Paradise cannot have such a vision, since neither God the Father nor Thou, Jesu, are to be found outside Paradise.

Every man, then, hath attained bliss who is united unto Thee, Jesu, as a limb unto the head. None can come unto the Father unless he be drawn by the Father. The Father drew Thy humanity, Jesu, by His Son, and by Thee, Jesu, the Father draweth all men. Just as Thy humanity, Jesu, is united unto the Son of God the Father, as unto the means whereby the Father drew it, even so the humanity of every man soever is united unto Thee, Jesu, as unto the one and only means whereby the Father draweth all men. Therefore without Thee, Jesu, 'tis impossible for any man to attain bliss. Thou art, Jesu, the revelation of the Father. For the Father is invisible to all, and visible only to Thee, His Son, and, after Thee, to him who through Thee and Thy revelation shall be found worthy to behold Him. Thou art, therefore, He that uniteth each of the blessed, and each of the blessed subsisteth in Thee, as that which is united in that which uniteth.

None of the wise men of this world can attain true bliss while he knoweth Thee not. None of the blessed can see the Father in Paradise save with Thee, Jesu. Antitheses are made true in the blessed, even as in Thee, Jesu, since he is united unto Thee in a rational, natural and single spirit. For every blissful spirit subsisteth in Thine, as that which is quickened in the lifegiver. Every blissful spirit beholdeth the invisible God and is united in Thee, Jesu, unto God the unapproachable and immortal. And thus in Thee the finite is united unto the infinite, and unto that which is beyond union, and the incomprehensible is possessed in an eternal fruition which is bliss most joyous and inexhaustible. Be merciful unto me, Jesu, be merciful, and grant me to behold Thee unveiled, and my soul is healed!

CHAPTER XXIII. HOW THAT WHEN JESUS DIED HIS UNION
WITH LIFE PERSISTED

O Jesu, the mind's most delectable food, when I look upon Thee within the wall of Paradise, how marvellous dost Thou appear unto me! For Thou art the Word of God humanified, and Thou art man deified. Yet art not Thou as it were compounded of God and man. Between component parts some proportion is necessary, without which there can be no composition, but there is no proportion between the finite and infinite. Nor art Thou the coincidence of the creature and Creator, in the sense in which coincidence maketh one thing to be another. For human nature is not divine nor divine nature human. The divine nature is not mutable nor can it be changed into another nature, since it is eternity itself. Nor can any nature by reason of its union with the divine pass over into another nature: as is illustrated in the case of the image, when united unto its truth. For an image cannot be said to become other when thus united, but rather to withdraw itself from otherness, because it is united unto its own truth, which is unchangeableness itself.

Neither, most sweet Jesu, canst Thou be said to be of an intermediate nature, between divine and human, for between these twain it is not possible for any intermediate nature to be set, partaking of both. For the divine nature may not be shared, since it is entirely and absolutely onefold, nor in that wise wouldst Thou, blessed Jesu, be either God or man. But I see Thee, Lord Jesu, to be One Person beyond all understanding, because Thou art One Christ, in the same manner that I see Thy human soul to be one, albeit therein, as in any human soul, I see Thy human soul to be one, albeit therein, as in any human soul, I see there was a nature of the senses liable to corruption, subsisting in an intellectual and incorruptible nature.

The soul was not composite of corruptible and incorruptible, nor is the nature of the senses one with that of the intellect; but I perceive the intellectual soul to be united through the sentient faculty with the body, which it quickeneth. If a man's intellectual soul should stay from quickening the body without being separated from the body, that man would be dead, because life would cease: and yet his body would not be separated from life since the intellect is his life. 'Tis as when a man, who had attentively sought by means of his sight to discern someone approaching, becometh rapt in other thoughts and so withdraweth his attention from that pursuit, though his eyes are none the less directed toward it—that man's eye is not then separated from his mind, although it existeth in separation from the mind's discerning attention. But if that state of being rapt should not only cease quickening his discernment but should also cease quickening his senses, his eye would be dead because it would not be quickened. Howbeit, for all that, it would not be separated from the intellectual form, which is the form that giveth being, just as a withered hand remaineth united unto the form which maketh the whole body one.

There are men, so Saint Austin saith, who have skill to withdraw the lifegiving spirit from their body, and appear dead and without feeling. In such a case, the intellectual nature would remain united unto the body, because that body would not exist under another form than afore: nay more, it would not only have the same form and remain the same body, while the quickening power would not cease to exist, but it would remain in union with the intellectual nature, albeit that did not actually extend itself unto the body. I perceive a man in such a case as one truly dead because he lacketh the quickening life (death being the lack of that which quickeneth), and yet he would not be a dead body separated from its life, which is its soul.

'Tis thus, Jesu most merciful, that I look upon the absolute life, which is God, inseparably united unto Thy human intellect and thereby unto Thy body. For that union is such that none can be closer. Every union that can be disparted is far inferior to that than which none can be closer. Wherefore it never was true nor can it ever be that Thy divine nature was separated from Thy human nature, nor yet from Thy mind nor Thy body, the parts without which human nature cannot exist. Although it be most true that Thy soul did cease from quickening Thy body and that Thou didst truly undergo death, yet wast Thou never separated from true life. If that priest of whom Austin telleth had some kind of power of withdrawing from the body that which quickeneth, and attracting it into the soul—as if a candle illumining a room were a living thing, and should attract to the centre of its light the beams whereby it illumined the room, without being separated from the room, and this attraction were naught else than ceasing to shed forth those beams—what marvel, then, if Thou, Jesu, hadst the power (since Thou art the most free of living Lights), of assuming and of laying down Thy quickening soul? When Thou willedst to lay it down Thou didst suffer death, and when Thou willedst to resume it Thou didst rise again in Thine own might.

Now the intellectual nature, when it quickeneth or animateth the body, is called the human soul. And the soul is said to be removed when the human intellect ceaseth to quicken it. For when the intellect ceaseth from its function of quickening, and, with regard to that, separateth itself from the body, it is not therefore separated purely and simply.

These thoughts Thou inspirest, Jesu, that Thou mayest show Thyself unto me, most unworthy, in so far as I can receive it, and that I may contemplate how in Thee mortal human nature put on immortality, so that all men sharing that same human nature may in Thee attain to resurrection and divine life. What can be sweeter, what more delightsome, than to know that in Thee, Jesu, we find all things that be in our nature—in Thee, who alone canst do all things, and givest most liberally and upbraidest not? O ineffable lovingkindness and mercy! Thou, God, who art goodness' self, couldest not satisfy Thine infinite clemency and bounty unless Thou gavest us Thyself! Nor could this be done more beseemingly, more possibly, for us recipients than in Thy taking on Thee our nature, because we could not approach unto Thine. Thus Thou camest unto us, and art called Jesus, our Saviour ever blessed.

CHAPTER XXIV. HOW JESUS IS THE WORD OF LIFE

Of Thine own best and greatest gift, my Jesus, I contemplate Thee preaching words of life, and plentifully sowing the seed divine in the hearts of them that hear Thee. I see those depart from Thee who have not perceived the things that are of the Spirit. But I see the disciples remaining, who have already begun to taste the sweetness of the doctrine that quickeneth the soul. On behalf of all these, that prince and leader of all the Apostles, Peter, confessed how Thou, Jesu, haddest the words of life, and marvelled that seekers after life should depart from Thee. Paul in ecstasy heard from Thee, Jesu, the words of life, and thereafter neither persecution, nor sword, nor bodily hunger could separate him from Thee. None could depart from Thee who had tasted the words of life. Who can separate a bear from honey after he hath once tasted the sweetness thereof? How great is the sweetness of truth which maketh life delightsome to the full! It surpasseth all bodily sweetness, for 'tis absolute sweetness, whence floweth all that is desired by every taste! What is stronger than love, whence all that is loveable hath that for which it is loved? If the bond of love in limitation be sometimes so strong that the fear of death cannot sever it, how strong is the bond when that love is tasted whence all love springeth? I wonder not that their cruel torments were accounted as naught by other of Thy soldiers, Jesu, to whom Thou hadst afforded a foretaste of Thyself, the Life. O Jesu my Love, Thou hast sowed the seed of life in the field of the faithful, and hast watered it by the witness of Thy blood, and hast shown by bodily death that truth is the life of the rational spirit; the seed grew in good soil and bore fruit.

Thou showest me, Lord, how my soul is the breath of life in regard to my body, whereinto it breatheth and infuseth life, but 'tis not life in regard to Thee, O God, but as it were a potentiality of life. Now, Thou canst not but grant our petitions if they be made in most expectant faith. And so Thou dost inspire me with the thought that there is a soul in the child which hath vegetative power in actual exercise, since the child groweth; he hath also a percipient power in actual exercise, since the child feeleth; he hath moreover an imaginative power, but not as yet in actual exercise; and a reasoning power, the exercise whereof is as yet still more remote; he hath, too, an intellectual power, but that is even more delayed in developing. Thus we find that one and the same soul hath the lower powers in actual exercise first, and afterward the higher, as if man were animal before he is spiritual.

In the same way, we find that a certain mineral power, which can also be called spirit, existeth in the bowels of the earth, and hath the power to become a mineral of stone, or hath the power to become salt, or, again, the power to become a metal, and that there are divers such spirits in that stones, salts and metals are diverse. Howbeit, there is but one spirit of the mineral of gold, which, being ever more and more refined through the influence of the sun or sky, is at last fashioned into gold of such a nature that it may not be corrupted by any element. And 'tis in it most chiefly that the heavenly incorruptible light shineth forth, for it much resembleth the sun's corporeal light. We find the same of the vegetative spirit and of the percipient spirit. The percipient spirit, in man, conformeth itself closely unto the motive and influential power of the heavens, under which influence it receiveth one increase after another, until it is set in perfect act. But as 'tis drawn out from the power of the body, its perfection ceaseth with the failing of the bodily perfection whereon it dependeth.

There is, finally, an intellectual spirit which, in the act of its perfection, is independent of the body, but is united thereunto by means of the percipient power; this spirit, being independent of the body, is not subject unto the influence of the heavenly bodies; 'tis independent of the percipient spirit, and thus of the motive power of the heavens. But, just as the motive forces of the heavenly bodies are subject unto the First Mover, so too is this moving force, which is the intellect. Howbeit, since 'tis united unto the body by means of the percipient power, it cometh not to perfection without the senses, since all that reacheth it from the world of sense doth so by the medium of the senses. Whence naught of this kind can exist in the intellect that hath not first existed in the senses, but the more the senses are pure and perfect, the imagination clear, the discursive reason in good state, the more the intellect in its intellectual operations is unhampered, and clear-sighted.

But the intellect feedeth on the Word of life, under whose influence it is established, like the motive forces of the orbs; howbeit in other fashion, as even the spirits which are subject unto the influences of the heavens come to perfection in divers ways. And the intellect is not perfected, save incidentally, by the percipient spirit, just as an image maketh not perfect, albeit it stirreth up an inquiry after the truth of the exemplar. The image of the Crucified, for example, doth not inspire devotion, but kindleth the memory that devotion may be inspired. Since the intellectual spirit is not constrained by the influence of the heavens, but is absolutely free, it cometh not to perfection unless it submit itself through faith unto the Word of God, like a free disciple, under no control, who is not perfected unless by faith he submit himself unto the word of a master: he needs must have confidence in the master and listen unto him. The intellect is perfected by the Word of God, and groweth, and becometh continually more receptive and apt, and liker unto the Word.

This perfection, which thus cometh from the Word whence it had being, is not a corruptible perfection, but Godlike. Like the perfection of gold, 'tis not corruptible, but of heavenly form. But it behoveth every intellect to submit itself by faith unto the Word of God, and to hear with closest attention that inward teaching of the supreme Master, and by hearing what the Lord saith in it, it shall be made perfect. 'Twas for this that Thou, Jesu, one and only Master, didst preach the necessity of faith for all approaching the fount of life, and didst show that the in-flowing of divine power was according unto the measure of faith.

Two things only hast Thou taught, O Saviour Christ—faith and love. By faith, the intellect hath access unto the Word; by love, 'tis united thereunto; the nearer it approacheth, the more it waxeth in power; the more it loveth, the more it stablisheth itself in its light. And the Word of God is within it, it needeth not to seek outside itself, since it will find Him within, and shall have access unto Him by faith. And by prayer it shall obtain a nearer approach unto Him, for the Word will increase faith by com-munication of His light.

I render Thee thanks, Jesu, that by Thy light I have come thus far. In Thy light I see the light of my life. I see how Thou, the Word, infusest life into all believers, and makest perfect all that love Thee. What teaching, good Jesu, was ever briefer and more effectual than Thine? Thou persuadest us but to believe, Thou biddest us but to love. What is easier than to believe in God? What is sweeter than to love Him? How pleasant is Thy yoke, how light is Thy burden, Thou one and only Teacher! To them that obey this teaching Thou dost promise all their desires, for Thou requirest naught difficult to a believer, and naught that a lover can refuse. Such are the promises that Thou makest unto Thy disciples, and they are entirely true, for Thou art the truth, who canst promise naught but truth. Nay more, 'tis naught other than Thyself that Thou dost promise, who art the perfection of all that may be made perfect. To Thee be praise, to Thee be glory, to Thee the rendering of thanks through endless ages! Amen.

CHAPTER XXV. HOW JESUS IS THE CONSUMMATION

What is it, Lord, that Thou conveyest to the spirit of the man whom Thou makest perfect? Is it not Thy good Spirit, who in His Being is consummately the power of all powers and the perfection of the perfect, since it is He that worketh all things? 'Tis as when the Sun's strength, descending on the spirit of growing things, moveth it toward perfection, so that by the right pleasant and natural mellowing of the heavenly heat it may become good fruit on a good tree: even so Thy Spirit, O God, cometh upon the intellectual spirit of a good man, and, by the heat of divine love, melloweth its latent power toward perfection, that it may become fruit most acceptable unto Him.

Lord, we find that Thy One Spirit, infinite in power, is received in one way by one, in whom It produceth the spirit of prophecy, and in another way by another, in whom It produceth skill in interpretation, and by yet another, to whom It teacheth knowledge, and so in divers ways in others. For His gifts are diverse, and they are perfections of the intellectual spirit, even as that same heat of the sun bringeth to perfection divers fruits on divers trees.

I perceive, Lord, that Thy Spirit cannot be lacking unto any spirit, because It is the Spirit of spirits, and motion of motions, and It filleth the whole world: but It directeth all such things as have not an intellectual spirit by means of intellectual nature which moveth the heavens and, by their motion, all things that exist thereunder. But the disposition and distribution of intellectual nature He reserved for Himself alone. For He hath espoused unto Himself this nature, wherein He chose to rest as in an house of abiding and in the heaven of truth: since 'tis intellectual nature alone that can grasp truth of itself.

Thou, Lord, who makest all things for Thine own sake, hast created this whole world for the sake of intellectual nature. Even so a painter mixeth divers colours that at length he may be able to paint himself, so that he may possess his own likeness, wherein his art may rest and take pleasure, and so that, his single self being not to be multiplied, he may at least be multiplied in the one way possible, to wit, in a likeness most resembling himself. But the Spirit maketh many figures, because the likeness of His infinite power can only be perfectly set forth in many, and they are all intellectual spirits, serviceable to every spirit. For, were they not innumerable, Thou, infinite God, couldst not be known in the best fashion. For every intellectual spirit perceiveth in Thee, my God, somewhat which must be revealed unto others in order that they may attain unto Thee, Their God, in the best possible fashion. Wherefore these spirits, full of love, reveal one unto another their secrets, and thereby the knowledge of the Beloved is increased, and yearning toward Him is aflame, and sweetness of joy.

Yet, O Lord God, Thou couldst not have brought Thy work to perfect consummation without Thy Son, Jesus, whom Thou hast anointed above His fellows, who is the Christ. In His intellect the perfection of creatable nature is at rest, for He is the final and entirely perfect Image of God who cannot be multiplied, and there can be but one such supreme Image. Howbeit, all other intellectual spirits are, through the medium of that Spirit, likenesses, and the more perfect the more they resemble. And all rest in that Spirit as in the final perfection of the Image of God, of whose Image they have attained the likeness, and some degree of perfection.

Wherefore of Thy giving, O my God, I possess this whole visible world and all the Scripture, and all ministering spirits to aid me to advance in knowledge of Thee. Yea, all things stir me up to turn unto Thee: all Scriptures strive only to set Thee forth, and all intellectual spirits exercise themselves only in seeking Thee and in revealing as much of Thee as they have found. Thou hast above all given me Jesus as Master, as the Way, the Truth, and the Life, so that absolutely nothing may be lacking unto me. Thou dost strengthen me by Thy Holy Spirit, through Him Thou dost inspire the choice of life, holy yearnings. Thou dost draw me, by a foretaste of the sweetness of the life in glory, to love Thee, O infinite Good! Thou dost ravish me above myself that I may foresee the glorious place whereunto Thou callest me. For Thou showest me many dainties most delectable, that allure me by their excellent savour: Thou grantest me to behold the treasury of riches, of life, of joy, of beauty. Thou uncoverest the fountain whence floweth all that is desirable alike in nature and in art. Thou keepest naught secret. Thou hidest not the channel of love, of peace, and of rest. All things dost Thou set before me, a miserable creature whom Thou didst create from nothing.

Why then do I delay, why do I not run, in the sweet smell of the unguents of my Christ? Why do I not enter into the joy of my Lord? What restraineth me? If ignorance of Thee, Lord, hath held me back, and the empty delight of the world of sense, they shall restrain me no longer. For I desire, Lord (since Thou grantest me so to desire) to leave the things of this world, because the world desireth to leave me. I hasten toward the goal, I have all but finished my course, I will be beforehand with it in taking farewell, I who pant for my crown. Draw me, Lord, for none can come unto Thee save he be drawn by Thee; grant that, thus drawn, I may be set free from this world and may be united unto Thee, the absolute God, in an eternity of glorious life. Amen.

CONCERNING CONCORD IN
RELIGIOUS BELIEF

IT IS NO DOUBT a source of surprise that a Cardinal of the Roman Church should have produced what many critics consider to be one of the finest and most practical treatises on the question of religious tolerance. Though Cusa was not the first Christian theologian to speculate on the question of religious pluralism—Minucius Felix in the third century, Peter Abelard in the twelfth, and later Raymund Lull and Roger Bacon advocated the idea of a universal religion for mankind, based on the elements of common faith—he nevertheless arrives at the finest expression of this conviction in his *De Pace Fidei*. Even the tolerance aimed at by the writers of the Enlightenment fell short of the ideals of the Cardinal. The *De Pace Fidei* was written soon after the fall of Constantinople in 1453, the terrible memory of which was still fresh in the mind of the author, probably in September of the same year. Certainly recollections of Cusa's visit to the God-guarded city on the Golden Horn as a member of the papal commission sixteen years before were in mind when he wrote of the catastrophe that now made more necessary than ever some sort of religious universalism.

There is a specific character of human societies throughout the thought of Nicholas of Cusa fundamental to the universal religion he intends to describe in *De Pace Fidei*, namely, the organic nature of society. His political and ecclesiastical theory is always based on internal harmony rather than imposed authority. In society men are bound together by common agreement in the natural law of reason, and the Church is analogously the union of the faithful in the love of Christ. Societies, encompassing as they do great multitudes of people "cannot subsist without great diversity." Nicholas always finds the analogy with the organic body most appropriate to express his meaning of social unity and organization. Within this framework no one element could adequately account for the entire social structure, and upon none was the unified body exclusively dependent. However, it was possible that a multiplicity of factors be indispensable to that particular form of organization. Consequently each part of society had a limited but necessary function which could be effectively accomplished only in conjunction with the other parts. However, the whole body and its end or goal was always foremost in Cusa's mind and superior to the individual components.

Nor was this an inflexible structure; rather, wherever necessary, for the good of the entire body, Cusa could compromise its individual elements and yet retain the ultimate *raison d'etre* of that society. From this point of view conciliarism was merely one particular form which this over-all view could engender, and probably the most immediately evident one; but others have not thereby been excluded. If it were not for this general concept of society, with all its toleration of variance and flexible harmony of coordinated processes, it would never have been possible for Cusa to have envisioned the universal Christendom of the *De Pace Fidei*. And in this respect he is totally medieval since to him this unified Christendom was still an attainable reality, and yet he is also free from the typical Scholastic provincialism and lack of toleration because no truly human social elements could be basically foreign to the forthcoming Christianity.

More immediately determining *De Pace Fidei* are Cusa's theories concerning all religions in general. The human mind naturally desires and inclines towards truth. On the strength of this hypothesis Nicholas concludes that all men have a knowledge, however indeterminate, of the infinite God, and that at the heart of the worship of all nations there is a recognition of God as the Maximum. The verity of this conclusion may be ascertained by an investigation of the nature of wisdom itself. To love wisdom, as the philosopher purports to do, presupposes the existence of an absolute wisdom. A contrariety of cults and rites does not deter from this essential fact of all religions; and therefore it is their particular manifestations and not the religions themselves that are in contradiction. Each religion presupposes this basic worship and knowledge of the unique God, and since this is essentially the same fact in each, Cusa's task rests more on charity rather than on polemics or dogmatics. Such conclusions are perfectly consistent with the philosophic principles of Cusa. And on the basis of this theory rest the initial beginnings of *De Pace Fidei*, not on the specifically Christian revelation and God's authority as one would normally expect. This characteristic of all religions is the common denominator on the basis of which Cusa intends to establish the harmony and unity of all religions.

But even this natural phenomenon does not fully explain the foundation upon which Cusa proposes to reconcile religious differences and animosity. In *De Pace Fidei* Cusa accounts for religious diversity also by the fact that God informed each nation with their own prophets, each of them truly revealing God's laws. In obeying their own religion every nation has been obedient to the Creator. God Himself is also partly responsible for the diversity of religious worship. The divine commands, brief and intelligible to all, have been revealed to all by God. The reader must be cautioned here because Nicholas has in no way denied the superiority of the Christian revelation, but he has only asserted that God has made known the minimal ordinances by which human life shall be governed. Here again is compelling evidence that all religions are basically in accord with each other since "the truth is but one . . . and the diversities ought now to give up their place to a single orthodox faith." To Cusa, therefore, rather than undermining the Christian faith, these conditions actually serve to facilitate the reception of Christianity by all nations.

In *De Pace Fidei* Nicholas of Cusa indicates three principal ideas through which Christianity will become acceptable to all nations, and upon which Christianity is exclusively dependent. These minimal requirements for the Catholic peace are Christ, the Trinity, and the Church. Upon these principles alone, and particularly the first two, rests the entire structure of *De Pace Fidei;* but, as is usual within the thought of Cusa, these principles acquire a specifically distinct meaning.

According to Nicholas of Cusa all knowledge is but preparation for faith in Christ. Depending solely upon human means we are forced to recognize the difficult situation of human knowledge, and with this realization the necessity of Christ becomes apparent, or at least friendly to the human mind. It is necessary to remember that in Cusa there is an unequivocal superiority of the intellect over the will, and it is therefore to be expected that the role of Christ be presented as one essentially of knowledge. In fact, the entire philosophic structure of Nicholas is conceived as the indoctrination by means of which we are able to fully grasp the ultimate significance of Christ. Christ is therefore the keystone binding together the diverse elements of his system, the most positive prevention against skepticism and without which the elaborate superstructure of this system lacks value and purpose. With Christ the doctrine of learned ignorance, rather than being destroyed, is fulfilled and achieves its purpose of freeing man's intellect of its finite boundaries.

Moreover, Christ is not merely a convenient supernatural solution extrinsically imposed; the fact of the matter is that faith in Christ is necessary for all knowledge. In faith all things are included, and understanding is nothing other than the unfolding of faith. It is therefore evident how thoroughly the complete system of Cusa is imbued with the Christian faith. But there is a similar faith that seldom has the explicit form we find in Christianity, and it is Cusa's intention to explicate the real and hidden meaning of that faith which is common to all men and to show how it is actually a faith in Christ.

The fundamental importance of Christ is to be found in His capacity as Mediator. The need of redeeming man from the state of original sin is not at all thereby diminished by this emphasis of Cusa, and, in fact, this restoration of human nature and its liberty of choices is presupposed. But even here, as in the case of faith, Nicholas immediately concentrates upon the importance of Christ in relation to the human intellect and knowledge. And by stressing the function of Christ as Mediator, an office ever remaining present and individual to each person throughout history and not merely an historical fact accomplished once and for all, Cusa thereby impresses the personal reality of Christianity as a vital and organic force throughout all ages.

A mediator is a means whereby two distinct realms or entities are related so as to allow free passage or communication from one to the other. Now, despite all his pantheistic traits, and his tendency to fuse and intermingle the natural with the supernatural, the thought of Cusa does recognize these as distinct "worlds." Only with great difficulty and admixture of much error can man's knowledge transcend from the limited natural world to that of infinite reality toward which it ultimately aspires. And by original sin man is even more thoroughly restricted to earthly knowledge. If, therefore, only such transcendent knowledge perfects man, Christ as the Mediator is necessary for human perfection since through this union of God-man all things, especially man, are related to God. This union absolute in itself, effectively bridges the gap between God and man, and, because human nature is a microcosm of the whole universe, Christ Himself, in addition to being absolute creative power, is the perfection of creation and the universe. To man in particular, the basic foundation of the Mediator, through His humanity, is to unite the human intellect to the divine reality and knowledge by means of which humanity subsists in the divine and achieves immortality. Hence, Christ as the "Humanization of the Word," having made this Word concretely attainable to man, represents not only the necessary restoration of man but is also the means whereby man attains perfection in the divine life and knowledge itself—"the plenitude of divinity and Grace." This mediatory function of Christ is important in the light of his previous philosophic principles, namely, God as the Maximum and in Him the coincidence of opposites, and through these principles we may better understand the importance placed on Christ as the Mediator by Cusa.

The second constitutive element of Christianity insisted upon by Nicholas of Cusa in *De Pace Fidei* is that of the Trinity. Two aspects of his doctrine have an important bearing on *De Pace Fidei:* the conception of the Trinity in itself and in its intelligibility from reason alone, and the Trinity in relation to the universe.

Nicholas of Cusa purports to demonstrate the necessity of a "triune" God, and it never occurs to him to refer to Scripture. The unspoken premise is always that God must be the Maximum—unity, eternity, infinity, etc. Considering God in Himself, and because there exists an observable diversity in nature, we therefore know that God must be absolute Unity because this is necessarily prior to diversity. Then in like manner observing inequality, we are brought to realize that God must be Equality of some sort and thereby implying distinctions. And finally, in noticing division in nature we may likewise conclude that there must be Connection in God. But since each of these absolute qualities must be eternal also, we are forced to recognize that there may be only one divine essence fully possessed by each.

The third and final element of *De Pace Fidei* is the role of
the Church, the role Cusa intended in this universally accepted
Christianity. Under this principle comes Nicholas' treatment
of justification, the sacraments and other constituents of the
visible Church, or his omission of these points. One is first im-
pressed by the fact that anything in *De Pace Fidei* related to
the Church is ostensibly consonant with his conciliarist principles, although Cusa's own practical activity had radically
altered his loyalty by this time. Nowhere do we see him con-
tradicting his previous theoretical position; in fact, it is possible to show how the implications of his "ecclesiology," if
it can be called that, are basically consistent with his earlier
position, although *De Pace Fidei* is a different approach to the
subject than *De Concordantia Catholica*.

In *De Pace Fidei* Cusa proposes that "all diversities of religion ought now to give up their place to a single orthodox
faith," but one which in no way entails the assertion of one
faith over another. Rather, Cusa's entire effort is to show how
all religions are ultimately grounded in the same faith and that
this common core of belief, regardless of its explicit formu-
lation, is actually faith in Christ. But there is also a further
importance of faith in the thought of Cusa, one more ortho-
doxly Christian. St. Paul, appropriately, assumes the leading
role in the dialogue and proposes to teach that "The salvation
of all souls does not come from good works, but from faith."
But this is not an indeterminate faith in an unseen God; on the
contrary, Cusa carefully establishes the necessity of faith in
the Christ Incarnate—Redeemer and Mediator. In Cusa's
mind, therefore, this religion of the future is not a vague,
meaningless compromise; instead he seeks to enliven every

element or principle he considers necessary with a real belief in and dependence upon Christ. Consequently, "the plenitude of divinity and grace lives in the spirit of Christ and it is in this plenitude that all those who will be saved receive the grace of salvation." If it is only through this grace that salvation is merited, then Cusa's foremost task was to instill into the heart of all nations the faith in Christ, and this does actually seem to have been his intention. Such is the faith, not dependent on any good works but from which meritorious deeds naturally emanate, which alone is at the foundation of this universal religion. Once he succeeded in implanting the basic faith of Christ he has little concern over its local manifestations amongst which he recognizes the probability of diversity. In the final consideration, Cusa's concept of the sacraments is reducible to a particular expression of faith which seems to be most universally applicable.

Concerning the less important elements of the visible Church Cusa is even more indeterminate and unwilling to enforce Catholic (western and Roman Christianity) customs on other cultures. Wherever possible, and if a greater good would result, uniformity of rites of worship, etc., is desirable. But as a practical psychologist, Cusa recognizes the importance of a concession in secondary matters once the basic faith has been received. And Christianity, divinely inspired and harboring the divine Word, is not dependent upon any particular rites or cult, but proposes to cut across and transcend this variety. A toleration of rites is therefore permissible if it is confirmed in the peace and love which is the law of faith. In fact, a diversity of modes of worship may at times be announced, rather encouraged, since it may be a means of augmenting devotion, zeal, and diligence. Nowhere does he become involved in the problem of authority in the Church, which may warrant the suspicion that his earlier ideas in theory had never really been relinquished. Cusa's idea of the Church always remained the "union of the faithful and loving in Christ." It was this faith and love, not the institutional Church, that was the message and Gospel preached by Christ, and the success or failure of the religion envisioned in *De Pace Fidei* will ultimately depend upon the strength of this bond of union.

DE PACE FIDEI

Due to the news of the atrocities which had recently been reported to have taken place in a most cruel fashion at Constantinople, at the hand of the king of the Turks, a certain individual, fired with the love of God, and since he had visited the aforementioned region, prayed with much weeping and besought the Creator of all that He might, out of compassion, alleviate the persecution that was raging there because of a difference of religious rites. It happened, perchance, from a long and serious meditation on this problem, that a vision appeared to this same zealous man. In this visitation it was made clear, by reason of the experience of a number of select individuals versed in the matter of religious pluralism throughout the world, how concord might be discovered and, through it, how lasting peace based on agreeable and truthful means might be established. Hence it is, so that this vision of those who were present might be made known, the author, in so far as he recalls, has clearly set it forth below. After, he was lifted up to a certain intellectual height where, as though in the company of those who had already departed from life, a discussion of this matter was held in the presence of these distinguished individuals, with the Almighty presiding. The King of Heaven and Earth then related that His messengers had brought news of the groans of those oppressed in the kingdom of this world, and that many, because of religion, were warring with one another, and that they were violently forcing others to either reject the faith to which they had so long adhered, or accept death. There were many reporters of these lamentations throughout the world, and these the King ordered to report to the entire assembly of the elect. Moreover, there were also seen here all of those whom the King Himself had, at the very beginning of the world, set in charge of all the provinces and sects of the earth. Their appearance was not anthropomorphic, but they appeared rather as intellectual agents.

Then one of the prominent individuals representing all of those assembled posed this query: "O Lord, King of the Universe, what does anyone possess that you have not bestowed upon him? It has pleased you to inspire the body of man, formed out of the slime of the earth, with a rational soul, so that in him the image of your ineffable excellence may shine forth. From one person a vast multitude has been increased so that it now inhabits the entire surface of the earth. And even though that spirit of the intellect, planted in the earth and hidden in the shadows, does not perceive the light and the beginning of its origin, nonetheless, everything else that you have created is a means by which, once being perceived by his senses, he is able from time to time to lift the eyes of his mind to you, the Creator of all things. He is thereby able to be reunited with you in sublime charity, and finally to return to his source with accomplishment.

"But you are aware, O Lord, that such a vast multitude cannot exist without a great deal of diversity, and that a large portion of this multitude is forced to live a life laden with woes and misery. They live, in many cases, subject to servility and umbrage to those who rule them. As a result, it happens that very few have sufficient leisure to enable them to proceed to a knowledge of themselves by using their own freedom of judgment. Burdened and preoccupied with the cares of the body they cannot seek you, the hidden God. It is because of this that you have provided certain leaders and overseers, whom we call prophets, for your people. A number of these, acting as your vicars and legates, have in your name formulated laws and divine cults, and instructed the uneducated in their meaning and practice. These regulations they have accepted just as if it was You yourself Who personally dictated them, and their credence was in you rather than in them. At various times you have sent various prophets and teachers, now to this nation, now to that nation. Yet human nature has this weakness, that after a long passage of time certain customs are gradually accepted and defended as immutable truths. Thus it happens that not a few dissensions grow out of the fact that some communities prefer their particular beliefs to those of other groups.

"Since you alone are all powerful, come to our aid in this matter. This rivalry comes about simply because each group seems to worship you in all that they appear to adore. No one really wants as his way of worship something that is common practice for all. To want what everyone else wants is imitation. In all those things that man seeks after, that alone is really sought which is the good, and that is You Yourself. What does the person who sees seek other than to see? He who exists, does he not endeavor to continue existing? You, therefore, who are the giver of life and of being, are that one who seems to be sought in the different rites, and who are designated with different names. For since you are Yourself an infinite power, you are something of those things that you have created, nor is any created being able to comprehend the idea of your infinity, since between the finite and the infinite there is no proportion. You can, however, O powerful God, even though you are invisible to all minds, show Yourself in any visible manner you want. Therefore, please do not conceal Yourself any longer. Be kind to us and reveal your face, and all people will be saved, who will desire all the more the artery of life, with a little foretaste of its sweetness. For no one really removes himself from you unless he is ignorant of you.

"If you would only deign to do this then the sword of envy and hatred would cease along with all other evils, and all would recognize that there is, in spite of many varieties of rites, but one religion. If, perchance, this diversity cannot be done away with, or its reduction would not be advisable, since in many cases a particular religion would actually be more vigilant in guarding what it considers to be the noblest way of manifesting its devotion to you as its King, at least just as you are God alone, so also let there be in the same manner one religion and one cult of divine worship. Therefore, O Lord, since your very anger is piety itself and your justice is mercy, be pleased with this suggestion and spare your weak creatures. We, therefore, who are your commissaries, whom you have made the custodians of your people, and, as you already know this situation, we humbly pray and beseech your majesty in the best way we know."

CHAPTER II

At this request of the archangel, since all of the heavenly body had made proper obeissance to the King, He who sat on the throne spoke forth saying that man had been entrusted to His special care, and in this capacity He had created him for His own fellowship. He pointed out that due to the fact that man walked according to the conditions of sensible life, which is nothing else than the world of the Prince of Darkness, his lower nature is detained in ignorance. In this way he acted at variance with the intellectual and interior man whose life is from the region of his origin. He then went on to say that He attempted to recall man to the right path by taking great care and diligence in sending various prophets who were, in comparison with others, His observers. Finally, when not even these prophets were able to sufficiently overcome the Prince of Ignorance, He sent His own Word through whom He created the world. The Word took on human nature so that in this way He could illuminate docile man in accordance with his free will. He wanted to see to it that man would have to walk according to his interior rather than his exterior nature, if he ever hoped to be brought to the sweetness of eternal life; and since the Word took on human nature and gave testimony of His truthfulness through His blood, He showed that man is capable of eternal life and that in attaining this his animal and sensible life is of no avail. He showed also that this eternal life is nothing other than the ultimate desire of the interior man, that is to say, the Truth which alone is sought after, and just as it is eternal it nourishes the mind eternally, and this Truth which feeds the mind is nothing other than the Word Itself, in which all things are contained, through which all things are set forth. This Word took on human nature so that every man, according to the choice of his own will and his own human nature, would not doubt that the everlasting food of Truth could be attained, and that man is also the Word. He added to this that since these things are so, "What is there that could take place and has not taken place?"

CHAPTER III

To that question of the King of Kings the Word made Flesh, Who held first place in this heavenly gathering, had this to say in behalf of all: "Father of Mercies, even though all of your works are most perfect and there is nothing that could be added to make them more complete, yet since in the very beginning you decreed that man must remain in possession of his free will, and since nothing remains unchanged in the sensible world and as from time to time opinions and conjectures change as well as language and interpretations, human nature demands frequent visitations so that the errors which many hold concerning the Word might be eliminated, and thus truth may continually shine forth. Since this Truth is one, and since it can be understood by every free mind, every diversity of religion can be reduced to one orthodox faith." This pleased the King, and summoning the angels who represented all nations and tongues, He ordered each one of them that they bring the most learned to the Word Incarnate. Very soon thereafter there appeared before the Word the more important men of this world, rapt as it were in ecstacy. The Word of God spoke to them in this way: "The Lord of Heaven and Earth has heard the groans of those who have been slaughtered and imprisoned and reduced to slavery, and who suffer because of diversity of religion. And because all of these, who either are the agents of this persecution or suffer the persecution, are motivated in no other way but that they believe that this is necessary for salvation and pleasing to the Creator, He is moved with pity towards His people and will try to reduce all diversity of religion to one that in the opinion of everyone is inviolable in its greater harmony. This task He has given to you chosen individuals by giving you, as assistants, angelic administrators from His own court who will guard you and direct you, and He has pointed out that Jerusalem should be the place most suitable for this."

CHAPTER IV

At this, one who is a little older than the others and, as it appeared, a Greek, making proper adoration, answered: "We give praise to our God whose mercy is above all His works, Who alone is able to bring it about that diversity of religion can be found in one concordant peace, Whose command we His creatures are not able to disobey. We beseech you that you instruct us how this unity of religion may be introduced by us, for a faith other than that which some nations have defended with their very blood will, as we see it, be accepted only with difficulty."

The Word answered: "You will find that it is not another faith but the very same faith which is everywhere presupposed. You who are now present, among those who speak your own language, are called wise, or at least philosophers or the lovers of wisdom."

"This is true," said the Greek, "If everyone loves wisdom, do they not presuppose the same wisdom?"

Everyone answered simultaneously that there was no doubt of this.

The Word then added: "There cannot be but one wisdom. If it were possible to have several wisdoms these would have to be from one; for before there is any plurality there must be a unity."

Greek: Certainly none of us would hesitate in this since there is one wisdom which all of us love, and because of which we are called philosophers, and even though many wise men participate in this, this wisdom remains in itself simple and undivided.

Word: You all agree, therefore, that there is but one most simple wisdom whose power is ineffable, and everyone discovers in explaining the power of this virtue that it is an ineffable and infinite force. Whenever the sight focuses itself on those things that are visible, whatever it sees it attempts to produce by reason of wisdom. The same is true of hearing, and whatever is perceived by the other senses—everything points to the fact that invisible wisdom excels all.

Greek: We who make a profession out of philosophy certainly do not love the sweetness of wisdom in any other way except insofar as we get a foretaste of it through what appeals to the senses. For who would not die to acquire this wisdom from which flows beauty, every sweetness of life, and everything that one can desire? What a great power of wisdom shines forth in the human makeup, in its members, in the coordination of its members, in the infused life and the harmony and motion of its organs, and finally, in the rational soul which is capable of so many marvellous acts, and which is, as it were, the stamp of wisdom. For in the reason eternal wisdom shines forth above all things as a mirror, approaching truth in its closest reflection, and what is even more marvellous than this, this splendor of wisdom by marvellous change enables the soul to move closer and closer to truth, until its living glow moves away from the shadow of the image and grows more in conformity with true wisdom. And even though this wisdom is never perfect, as it is, it can be perceived in another. And thus, that intellectual food might be everlasting and unfailing, we have an eternal and inexhaustible wisdom.

Word: Certainly you are advancing towards the goal we have in mind for all of you, even though you are designated in terms of different religions, yet you presuppose in all this diversity one religion which you call wisdom. But tell me, isn't all that can be expressed contained in one notion of wisdom?

CHAPTER V

The Italian answered: Certainly there is no Word outside of wisdom. The Word is the supreme wisdom and wisdom is in the Word, nor is there anything outside of it. Wisdom embraces everything that is infinite.

Word: If anyone would say that all things are in created wisdom, and if another person would say that all created things are in the Word, would they not say the same thing?

Italian: Even though there appears to be a difference in speech, yet they express the same idea, for the Word of creation, in whom all things were created, can be nothing other than His wisdom.

Word: What does this seem to you? Is this wisdom God Himself or is it a creature?

Italian: Since God as creator creates all things in wisdom, He is through necessity the wisdom of created wisdom. Wisdom must be prior to every creature, through which each creature is what it is.

Word: Thus it is that wisdom is everlasting, since it precedes every beginning and everything made.

Italian: No one can deny that what is understood precedes all beginning and is eternal.

Word: Therefore, it must be the beginning.

Italian: This is certainly true.

Word: It must also be completely uncompounded. Whatever is composite is already begun; component parts cannot exist after they have been brought together.

Italian: I admit this.

Word: Hence it is that wisdom is eternal.

Italian: This could not be otherwise.

Word: Nor is it possible that there be more than one eternal entity, since previous to all plurality there must be unity.

Italian: I don't think anyone would disagree in this.

Word: God, therefore, is wisdom, one, simple, everlasting, and the beginning of all things.

Italian: This has to be so.

Word: Then behold the fact that you as the philosophers of the various sects are in agreement, both insofar as you presuppose a belief in the religion of the one God and in so far as you profess to be the lovers of wisdom.

CHAPTER VI

Here the Arab answered: Nothing clearer or truer can be said.

Word: But just as you, since you are seekers after wisdom, profess absolute wisdom, do you think men active in intellect do not love wisdom?

Arab: I certainly think that all men seek wisdom, since wisdom is the life of the intellect, which cannot be preserved in existence by any nourishment other than the truth and the word of life, or its own intellectual bread-wisdom. Just as every existing thing seeks that without which it cannot live, so too does the intellectual life seek wisdom.

Word: All men, therefore, profess with you one absolute wisdom whose existence they profess; this is the One God.

Arab: Yes—no intelligent person could think otherwise.

Word: Then all who use their reason have one religion and cult which is at the bottom of all the diversity of rites.

Arab: You are wisdom because you are the Word of God. I

would ask those who worship many gods how they can reconcile this belief with that of the philosophers in One God. For at no time are philosophers found professing a belief other than that it is impossible for there to be a plurality of gods over whom one God is not exalted; He alone is the principle from which the others have what they possess; He is far greater than simply one amongst many.

Word: All who worship many gods presuppose a divinity. This divinity they adore in all the gods as participants in it. For just as there cannot be things white without presupposing the existence of whiteness, so without the presumption of divinity there can be no gods. So the worship of many gods admits divinity. When they teach a plurality of gods, they teach one antecedent principle of them all; as those who say there are many saints must say there is one Saint of saints, in whose participation all the others are saints. Never was there a race so backward which believed in a plurality of gods and did not admit some first cause, a principle or Creator of the universe.

Arab: I agree. For it is a contradiction that there be a multiplicity of first principles. The first principle cannot be caused because it would be caused of itself and would exist before its existence—this reason cannot accept; the principle, therefore, is eternal. Nor is it possible that there be many external principles, because before all plurality there is unity. Therefore, it is necessary that there be one principle and universal cause. Nor have I yet discovered any race which has slipped from the way of truth in this matter.

Word: If then all who venerate many gods would look at that which they presuppose, namely to the deity which is the cause of everything, and would bring this deity into open adoration as reason would dictate, since they already implicitly adore it in all whom they call gods, there no longer would be any argument.

Arab: Perhaps this point would not be difficult, but to remove the worship of gods will be. For these people certainly believe that help is given them through such veneration, and for this reason they are moved to these divinities for their own salvation.

Word: But if these people were informed about salvation in the way we have mentioned, they would seek salvation in Him who gave existence and who Himself is the saviour and infinite salvation, rather than in those who of themselves have nothing except what is given them by the Saviour Himself. Suppose a people, who reverenced gods, are held in common estimation as holy because they have lived like gods—to these they would turn as intercessors in some sickness or difficulty, or even pay someone the adoration of *dulia*, or reverence his memory as a friend of God or as an example to be followed: provided only that this people would give to God the worship of *latria*, their veneration would not contradict the true religion, and they would in this way be easily reconciled.

CHAPTER VII

Indian: What then of statues and images?

Word: Those images which lead to knowledge of God and which are permitted in the true cult of the One God, these are not condemned. But when they detract from the cult of *latria* due to one God, as though in these stones there were some divinity, then because they deceive and detract from the truth, they rightly should be done away with.

Indian: It is difficult to turn a people from long accustomed idolatry because of responses and answers given to their questions.

Word: Rarely are these answers made up differently by the priests who assert the divinity has thus answered. For once a question is proposed, whether by some art through which they gain information from the universe around them, or by some chance lot, they pretend an answer ascribed to the deity, as though this were the way heaven, Apollo, or the Sun ordered them to answer.

So it happens that many of their answers are ambiguous, in order the more easily to escape the charge of falsehood, or else completely false; and if sometimes the answers are true, it is simply a coincidence. When a priest is a talented guesser, he is a better divinator, and his answers are more likely to be true.

Indian: But it is certain that often some spirit of the image actually has given an answer.

Word: This is not the soul of any man, or Apollo, or Esculapius, or of anyone worshipped in place of God—it is the evil spirit, the enemy of man's salvation from the beginning, who has pretended that through human devices (though this is rare) he has been bound to this image and is forced to give answers, that he might thus practice his deceits; but after the falsehood was discovered, he ceased. So today "they have mouths but speak not." Afterwards, by actual experiment, this fallacy was discovered everywhere by intelligent men. Likewise it will not be difficult in the Orient to wipe away the error of idolatry for the invocation of the one God, so that they might conform to the other nations of the world.

Indian: Once these deceptions have been made clear, and the fact that due to such deceptions the Romans, Greeks, and Arabs wisely destroyed these images, it is to be hoped that the Indians will deal in similar fashion with their images, especially since they are an intelligent people and do not hesitate to admit the necessity of worship in the cult of One God. Even if together with this they would venerate idols in their own fashion, these idols would pertain to the adoration of the One God, and they would thus accept this peaceful conclusion. But it will be quite difficult to establish harmony everywhere about the Triune God; the concept of a Trinity without three will seem to all an impossibility. Further, if the trinity is in the divinity, then there will be a plurality in the deity. There is no plurality in an absolute deity, but only in the participants who are gods, not absolutely, but only by participation.

Word: God, as creator, is three-fold and one; as infinite, He is neither three-fold nor one, nor any name that can be offered. For the names which are attributed to God are taken from creatures, since in Himself He is ineffable and above everything which can be named. Therefore, since those who adore God should adore Him as the principle of the universe, in this universe there is found a multiplicity of parts, inequality and separation—the multiplicity of stars, trees, men, rocks, etc., is obvious—unity is the principle of multiplicity: therefore the principle of multiplicity must be eternal unity. There is found in the universe inequality in its parts, since nothing is similar to another; but inequality is a break down from the equality of unity; before an inequality, therefore, there is eternal equality. There is found further in the one universe a distinction or separation between its parts; but before every distinction there is a connection of unity and equality—and consequent to this connection comes separation or distinction; the connection, then, is eternal. Therefore, in one eternity there is unity, equality or union, and a oneness of unity and equality or a "nexus." So the principle of the universe is one and three-fold, since the thing caused derives its complexity from the cause and every caused thing finds in the principle its complexity, and in every caused thing there is found such a three-fold distinction in the unity of its essence. Therefore, the simplest principle of all will be three-fold and one.

CHAPTER VIII

Chaldean: Even if wise men could grasp a bit of this, still they would be far ahead of the common people. For, as I understand it, it is not true that there are three gods, but one, and this One God is a Trinity. Do you mean that this One is a Trinity in his power?

Word: God is the absolute power of all powers, because He is omnipotent. Since, therefore, there must be an absolute power, which is the divine essence, that power can no more be called three-fold than God can be called three-fold. But you would not thus understand power in that it is distinguished from reality, because in God power is reality itself; so too with absolute potency which is itself power. For it would not seem absurd to anyone if it would be said that divine omnipotence, which is God, has in itself a unity, which is being, equality, and a "nexus"; so with the result that the power of unity unifies or gives essence to everything which has existence (insofar as a thing exists, it is one: oneness and existence are interchangeable). The power of equality makes equal or informs everything which exists (insofar as thing is neither greater nor less than that which it is, it has equality; if it were greater or less it would not exist; without equality, therefore, there can be no existence), so the power of "nexus" brings together or joins. So omnipotence in the power of unity summons from non-existence, so that what was not becomes capable of sharing in its existence; in the power of equality it informs, in the power of the nexus it joins, as in the essence of love you see how loving joins loved one to lover. When man is called from non-existence through Omnipotence, first in order comes unity, then equality, then the nexus between them. For nothing can exist except it be one; first, then, it must be one. And since man is called from nonexistence, the unity of man comes first in order, then the equality of that unity or thing—for equality is the effect of the form in unity, for 'otherwiseness' does not produce equality, but only unity or identity—then from unity and equality comes love or the nexus between them. Unity and equality cannot be separated from each other. The nexus or love is so constituted that where there is unity there is equality, and no nexus exists except a nexus of unity of equality, so that the nexus is in unity and equality, equality is in the unity and the unity in equality, and unity and equality in the nexus; it is clear that in the Trinity there is no distinction of essence. For those things which differ in essence are so constituted that one can exist without the other. But because the Trinity is such that where there is unity there is equality of unity and vice-versa, and where there is unity and equality there is the nexus between them and vice-versa, so it is that not in essence but in relation are distinguished unity, equality, and the nexus. For a numerical distinction is an essential one. The concept of two differs essentially from that of three; where you have two you do not necessarily have three, and the notion of three does not follow from that of two. So the Trinity in God is not composite or numerical, but is simple unity. Those, therefore, who believe God to be One will not deny He is a Trinity when they understand that that Trinity is not different from simple unity, but is unity itself, so that were He not Trinity in Unity, He would not be the principle omnipotent to create the universe and the things in it. The more unified a power is the stronger it is; the more unified it is, the simpler it is: the more powerful, then, it is, the simpler it is. So since the divine essence is omnipotent, it is most simple and a Trinity; were He not a Trinity He would not be the principle which is at once the simplest, most powerful, and omnipotent.

Chaldean: I would think that no one could disagree with this reasoning. But the fact that God could have a Son and a partaker in His Deity is a point repudiated by the Arabians and many others with them.

Word: Some call the unity the Father, the equality the Son, and the nexus the Holy Spirit; these terms while not proper to them, conveniently signify the Trinity. For from the Father is the Son, and from the unity and equality of the Son is the love or Spirit. For the nature of the Father passes over into some equality of the Son. Therefore, love and the nexus results from unity and equality. Should simpler terms be sought, more apt ones would be unity, 'iddity,' and identity. For these terms seem more to explain the fecund simplicity of the essence. Observe that since in the essence of the rational soul there is a certain fecundity—the mind—wisdom, and love or will, in that the mind exercises the intellect or wisdom from which comes the will or love, it has this three-fold fecundity in the unity of the soul in the likeness of the uncreated Trinity. So every created thing produces an image of the creative power and has in its own way a fecundity in a close or distant likeness to the fecundity of that Trinity which is the creator of all. So the result is that not only does the creature have its being from the divine being, but a productive being in its own way three-fold from the productive being of the Three and One—without this productive being neither the world could exist nor could a creature exist in a way better than it could.

CHAPTER IX

Jew: Well have you explained the Blessed Trinity which cannot be denied. For a prophet opening this up to us briefly said he asked God how He who gave to others the productivity of generation could be Himself sterile. Although the Jews will not admit the Trinity because they think it a plurality, yet once they understand what is meant by productive simplicity, they will readily accept It.

Word: Also the Arabians and all wise men will understand that to deny the Trinity is to deny the divine productivity and creative power; and that to admit the Trinity is to deny plurality and equality of gods. For this productivity, the Trinity, makes it unnecessary that there be many gods who concur in creation, since one infinite productivity suffices to create everything creatable. The Arabians will much better be able to grasp the truth in this way rather in the way in which they assert that God has an essence and a soul and that He has a Verbum and a Spirit. For if God is said to have a soul, 'soul' can be understood only as the 'ratio' or Verbum which is God; for there is no other 'ratio' than the Verbum. And what then is the Holy Spirit but the love which is God? Of the most simple God nothing can be spoken which is not Himself. If it is true that God has a Verbum, it is true that the Verbum is God; if it is true that God has a Spirit, it is true that the Spirit is God. Of course the word 'has' is used improperly of God, because He is everything, so that what God has, He is. Therefore, the Arabians do not deny that God is a mind and from that mind generates a Verbum or Wisdom, and from these proceed a Spirit or Love. This is nothing but the Trinity explained above, and admitted by them, though many of them to not advert to the fact that they are confessing the Trinity. So in your prophets you Jews discover that by the Word of God and His Spirit the heavens were formed. Surely the manner in which the Jews and Arabians deny the Trinity must be rejected; whereas the way we have explained the Trinity should be embraced by all.

CHAPTER X

Scythian: No problem can be found in the adoration of the most simple Trinity which all who adore gods today venerate. For when wise men say that God is the Creator of both sexes and of love, they wish through this to explain in their own fashion the productive Trinity of the Creator. Others assert that the exalted God of Himself exercises intellect or reason; Him they call god of gods, and call Him creator since every created thing demands a cause and reason why it is one thing and not another. The infinite 'ratio' of all things, then, is God. This 'ratio' which is the 'logos' or Verbum, emanates from its source so that when the omnipotent Verbum produces it, there are created in actual existence what was present in the Verbum; so that if omnipotence should say, 'let there be light,' then light present in the Verbum comes into actual existence. The Verbum of God, then, is intellectual, and insofar as a thing is conceived in the intellect as existing, it exists in reality. Then they say that the Spirit of union proceeds in third order which joins everything to one that it might be unity as the unity of the universe. For they posit a soul of the world or Spirit which joins everything, through which every creature has participation in being part of the universe. But it is necessary that this Spirit in the principle be the principle itself, for love joins. Hence this Spirit whose power is diffused through the universe, God or charity, can be called love; so that the nexus, through which the parts are joined to one or the whole, without which perfection nothing could exist, must have God as its principle. So it can be seen that wise men have touched on the Trinity in Unity; when they hear the explanation we have heard, they will certainly rejoice.

Frenchman: One time I heard this argument discussed among scholars; eternity is either unproduced or produced, or neither unproduced nor produced. Note that the uncreated eternity is reasonably called the Father Almighty, the produced eternity called the Verbum or Son, the neither unproduced nor produced eternity called love or the Holy Spirit, because He proceeds from both. He is not unproduced because He is not the Father, nor produced because He is not the Son, but proceeds from them both. There is, then, one eternity, and that is three-fold and simple; one deity, one essence, one life, one power, one strength—yet all are three-fold. In this discussion things once obscure are now made clearer than light. And since there remain in the world so many disputes, some men saying that the Word was made flesh for the redemption of all, and others with different views, there rests on us the obligation to explain to all how we have in this difficulty achieved harmony.

Word: The Apostle Peter has undertaken the exposition of this part. Listen to him; he will explain to you everything you do not know.

Peter, coming among them, began as follows:

CHAPTER XI

Peter: These are the variations in the different views of the Incarnate Word. First, some say that the Word of God is not God. This has been treated sufficiently, for the Word of God cannot be but God. This Word is reason; for *logos* is the Greek word for reason. That God, who is the creator of all rational souls and spirits, has reason, is beyond doubt. This reason of God is only God, as has been said before, for in God possession and being are the same. For He from whom come all things embraces all things and is all in all, because He is the former of all; therefore, he is form of forms. The form of forms has within himself all formable forms. Therefore the Word, or reason, the infinite cause and measure of all that can exist, is God. Therefore, they who admit that the Word of God is incarnate or made man must admit that that man whom they call the Word of God is also God.

The Persian said: Peter, the Word of God is God. How could God, who is immutable, become not God but man and the creator a creature? Almost all of us, except for a few in Europe, deny this. If there are some among us who are called Christians, they agree with us that this is impossible, that what is infinite is finite and what is eternal is temporal.

Peter: I deny as vigorously as you that the eternal is temporal. But when all of you who follow the law of the Arabs say that Christ is the Word and God—and you say well—you must also admit that He is God.

Persian: We admit that He is the Word and the Spirit of God, for of all who live or have lived no one else had that excellentness of being Word and Spirit of God; but we do not admit therefore that He was God, for God has no co-sharer. Therefore, lest we have a plurality of gods, we deny that He is god but we admit that He is very close to God.

Peter: Do you believe there is human nature in Christ?

Persian: We believe it, and we declare that it was true human nature and remained so in Him.

Peter: Fine! Because this nature was human, it was not divine. And, therefore, in everything which you see in Christ, according to this human nature by which He was like to other men, you see not Christ as God but Christ as man.

Persian: That is correct.

Peter: No one disagrees with you on this point. Human nature was in Christ most perfectly; by it He was true man and also mortal, like other men; according to that nature He was not the Word of God. Now tell me: when you admit that He was the Word of God, what do you mean?

Persian: Not nature but grace; that is, He received the extraordinary grace of having God put His Word in Him.

Peter: Did not God in similar fashion put His Word in other prophets? For all of them spoke with the word of the Lord and were announcers of the Word of God.

Persian: That is true. But Christ was the greatest of the prophets; therefore it more befits Him to be called the Word of God than the other prophets. As an example, many letters can contain the word of a king in regard to particular dealings or in particular provinces; but only one letter has the word of the king that rules the whole kingdom, namely the letter that contains the laws and precepts which all are bound to obey.

Peter: You seem to have given a good example to show this, namely that the word of the king, written in various letters, does not change the letters into other natures, for their nature remains the same after the word was written in them as they were before. This is how you say that human nature remained in Christ.

Persian: That is what we say.

Peter: Alright. But note the difference between letters and the heir of the kingdom. In the heir of the king is properly the living and free and unlimited word of the king, but not at all in letters.

Persian: I admit that. If the king sends his heir into the kingdom, the heir carries the living and unlimited word of the king.

Peter: Is not the heir properly the word and not the messenger or commissariat or a letter or a missive? And are not all the words of letters and messengers in the word of the heir? And, although the heir is not the father but the son, he has the nature of the king, and by this equality is the heir.

Persian: I understand that. But a difficulty is that the king and his son are two, therefore, we do not admit that God has a Son. For the Son would be a different God from the Father, just as the son of a king is a different man than his father.

Peter: Your objection against the similitude is a good one, for it is not an exact one if you look at the persons. But if you remove the numerical diversity of the persons and look at the power which resides in the royal dignity of the Father and His heir, the Son, you see how that royal power is one in the Father and in the Son; in the Father as in one unbegotten, in the Son as in one begotten, or the living Word of the Father.

Persian: Continue.

Peter: Suppose, then, that there is such an absolute unbegotten and begotten royal power, and that such an unbegotten power summons to association in the connatural begotten succession one who is different by nature, so that a different nature in union with his own possesses the kingdom at the same time and undividedly. Do not the natural and gratuitous or adoptive successions concur in one heirship?

Persian: That is certain.

Peter: In the same fashion filiation and adoption are united in one succession to one kingship, but the succession by adoption exists not in itself but in the succession of filiation. For if an adoption, which succeeds not in itself, must succeed when there is filiation, then it follows that he who succeeds by nature does so not in himself but in the filiation. Therefore, if adoption, in order to succeed with filiation in the acquiring of a completely simple and indivisible heirship, gets succession not from itself but from filiation, the adoptive and the natural successor will not be different even though the nature of adoption or of nature are different. For if the adopted one were separated and not having the same hypostasis as the natural heir, how would they concur in the succession of an indivisible heirship? Therefore, in Christ it must be held that human nature is so united with the Word or divine nature that the human nature does not pass into the divine but clings so indissolubly with it that it is a distinct person not in itself but in divine nature; so that the human nature, summoned to succeed to eternal life with the divine nature, can acquire immortality in the divine nature.

CHAPTER XII

Persian: I understand that well. But clarify what you have said by another understandable similitude.

Peter: Precise similitudes cannot be given. But try this one: Is wisdom in itself an accident or substance?

Persian: In itself, a substance; as it occurs in another, an accident.

Peter: But all wisdom in all wise persons comes from that wisdom which exists by itself, since it is God.

Persian: This has been set forth.

Peter: Is not one man wiser than another?

Persian: Yes, indeed.

Peter: Therefore, he who is wiser is closer to wisdom per se, which is absolutely the greatest; he who is less wise, is farther from it.

Persian: Yes.

Peter: But no man is, according to human nature, so wise that he cannot be wiser, for between received wisdom, that is human wisdom, and wisdom-per-se, which is divine and the greatest and infinite, there is always an infinite distance.

Persian: That, too, is very clear.

Peter: It is similar in regard to absolute and received mastership, for in absolute mastership there is infinite art, in received mastership finite art. Suppose, then, that someone's intellect has such a mastership and such wisdom that it is not possible to have greater wisdom or greater mastership; in that case his intellect is most closely united with wisdom-per-se or mastership-per-se, so that that union could not be greater. Has not that intellect, by virtue of the greatest wisdom and the greatest mastership to which it is united, acquired divine power, and is not the human intellectual nature in a man who has such an intellect most immediately united to divine nature or eternal wisdom, to the Word or omnipotent art?

Persian: I grant all this. But this union, nonetheless, is one of grace.

Peter: When so great a union exists of an inferior nature to a divine one that it could not be greater, then it would be united to it also in personal union. For as long as an inferior nature is not elevated to personal and hypostatic union with the higher nature, it could be greater. Therefore, if it is the greatest, the inferior nature subsists by clinging to the higher one; and this occurs not by nature but by grace. This greatest grace, however, which cannot be greater, does not differ by nature but is united with it. Therefore, even if human nature is united with the divine by grace, nevertheless that grace, since it cannot be greater, most immediately terminates in nature.

Persian: In whatever way you say it, since human nature can be elevated by grace to union with the divine in any man, the man-Christ can no more be said to be God than any other man, even though he is the most holy of men.

Peter: If you see in Christ only the loftiest height which cannot be greater, and the greatest grace which cannot be greater, and the greatest holiness, and so on in respect to everything else, you would see that the height cannot be more than one, and similarly with respect to grace and holiness. After this you would see that all loftiness in every prophet, whatever degree it has, differs improportionally from that loftiness which cannot be greater, so that, granted any degree of loftiness, between it and the only highest one there can be an infinite number of degrees higher than the given one, and lower than the highest one. So, too, with regard to grace, holiness, prudence, wisdom, mastership, and everything.

Then you would see clearly that Christ can be the only one in whom nature is united in unity of person to the divine nature. This even the Arabs admit, although many do not think it through. For Arabs say that Christ alone is most lofty in this world and the next, and is the Word of God, and they who call Christ God and man say nothing else than that Christ alone is the greatest man and the Word of God.

Persian: It seems that, when that union which is necessary in the highest one is properly considered, that the Arabs can be brought to accept this belief, because by it the oneness of God, which they fight strongly to maintain, is not hurt but preserved. But tell me how it can be that human nature is personified not in itself but by being united with the divine.

Peter: Here is an example, but a farfetched one. A magnet draws iron upwards and by adhering to the metal of the magnet the nature of iron subsists not in its weighty nature—otherwise it would not hang in the air but would, according to its nature fall to the ground—but in virtue of the magnet the iron, by adhering to the magnet, subsists in the air and not by virtue of its own nature, according to which it could not be there. The reason why the nature of the iron is so inclined to the nature of the magnet is that the iron has in itself a likeness to this nature of the magnet, from which it is said to have its origin. In like manner, when human intellectual nature clings closely to divine intellectual nature from which it has received its existence, it clings to it inseparably as to the font of its life.

Persian: I understand.

Peter: The greater number of the Arabs admit that Christ raised the dead to life, and created flying beings from mud, and many other things which they expressly confess that Jesus Christ made like one having power; from which they can easily be led, since it cannot be denied that He did this in virtue of the divine nature to which His human nature was personally united. For the power of Christ, by which He ordered the doing of those things which the Arabs admit He did, could not have been according to human nature unless that human nature had been assumed in union with the divine nature, to the power of which it belongs to give such orders.

Persian: All this and more is affirmed of Christ by the Arabs, and they are written in the Koran. But it will be harder to bring the Jews to believe all this than other persons, because they admit nothing expressly of Christ.

Peter: They have all these statements relative to Christ in their scriptures, but, following the letter, they do not want to understand. But this resistance among the Jews will not hinder concord. For they are not numerous and they cannot by weapons disturb the whole world.

CHAPTER XIII

At this point the Syrian said: "Peter, I heard above that concord can be found in every sect from what is presupposed. Tell us how that statement can be verified in this point."

Peter: I shall tell you. But first tell me: Is not God alone eternal and immortal?

Syrian: I believe this, for everything besides God has a beginning. Hence, since it has a beginning, it will, in accordance with its nature, have an end.

Peter: Does not almost every religion—Jewish, Christian, Arabic, and most other men hold that the human mortal nature of every man will, after its temporal death, arise to eternal life?

Syrian: Yes.

Peter: All such persons, therefore, admit that human nature will be united to the divine and immortal one. For how could human nature pass on to immortality if it did not cling to it in an inseparable union?

Syrian: Belief of the resurrection necessarily presupposes this.

Peter: Therefore, if faith holds this, then human nature in some man is previously united to divine nature, in Him, who is the figure of all men and the loftiest Messias and Christus, insofar as the Arabs and Jews call him Christ. He, according to everyone the closest to God, will be in whom the nature of all men is priorily united to God. For that reason He is Saviour and mediator of all men, in whom human nature, which is one and by which all men are men, is united to the divine and immortal nature, so that in this way all men of the same nature receive resurrection from the dead.

Syrian: I understand that you insist that faith in the resurrection from the dead presupposes union of the divine and human natures, without which this faith would be impossible; and you say that this union is in Christ; wherefore faith presupposes Christ.

Peter: You've got it. Hence, except that all the promises made to the Jews are kept in the faith in the Messiah or mediator, by Whom alone the promises that concern eternal life could and can be fulfilled.

Syrian: What about other sects?

Peter: In the same way. For all men desire and expect eternal life only in their human nature, and they instituted purgation of souls and sacred rites so that they may, in better fashion, fit themselves for eternal life in their own nature; a man wishes only to be a man, not an angel or another nature; but he wishes to be a blessed man and to obtain eternal happiness. This happiness is nothing else than the enjoyment, that is union of human nature with its font, which flows its life, and this is divine immortal life. How could this be possible for a man unless it is conceded that the common nature of all men is elevated to such a union in some person, by whom as mediator, all men can acquire the ultimate of desires? And He is the way because He is the man by whom every man has access to God, Who is the goal of desires. Christ, therefore, is the One who is presupposed by all men who hope to acquire final happiness.

Syrian: This is very welcome. For if human intellect believes that it can acquire union with wisdom, where it can receive the eternal food for its life, it presupposes that the intellect of some lofty man has acquired that union and has received this loftiest mastership by which it similarly hopes it will at some time arrive at that wisdom. For if it did not believe it possible in some most lofty one of men, it would hope in vain, and since the hope of all men is that they will sometime acquire happiness—for which reason every religion exists—and since it cannot be deceived in this —for this hope is in everyone from a connate desire and to it every religion, which likewise is in common connate in everyone, aims —I see that this master and mediator, who holds the supremacy of human perfection and its principate, is presumed by everyone. But perhaps the Jews say that this prince of nature in whom all defects of all men are made up for, has not yet been born but will sometime be born.

Peter: It is enough that both Arabs and Christians, and others, who have given witness in their blood, testify, by what the prophets have said of Him, and by what He did above the powers of men when He was in the world, that He has come.

CHAPTER XIV

Spaniard: There will, perhaps, be another difficulty regarding the Messiah, whom the greater part of the world admits has come, since Christians and Arabs assert that He was born of the Virgin Mary, while others hold that this is impossible.

Peter: All who believe that Christ has come hold that He was born of a virgin. For, since He is the ultimate of the perfection of nature and alone most high, of what father must He be the son? For every father who begets in perfection of nature differs from the ultimateness of perfection in such a fashion that he cannot communicate to his son the ultimate perfection, than which a higher cannot be and which is not possible except for one man.

Only that Father can do this Who is Creator of nature. The most high person, therefore, has only Him for Father from Whom is all paternity. By divine power, therefore, was the most lofty One conceived in the womb of a virgin, and in this virgin there went together with virginity the most lofty fecundity. Hence, Christ was so born to us that He is almost joined to all men. For He has Him as Father from whom every father of a man has it that he is a father; and He has her as mother who is joined carnally to no man; so that thus each man may find by a most close connection in Christ his nature in its ultimate perfection.

Turk: There is still another not small difference, for Christians say that Christ was crucified by the Jews, but others deny this.

Peter: That some deny Christ's crucifixion, but say that He still lives and will come at the time of the Anti-Christ, is because they are ignorant of the mystery of death, and because He will come, as they say, they believe that He will come in mortal flesh, as if otherwise He could not conquer the Anti-Christ. And the denial of Christ's crucifixion by the Jews seems to come for their reverence for Christ, as though such men could not have had power over Christ. But notice that we ought to believe the many accounts of Him and the preaching of the Apostles who died for this truth, that is, that Christ did so die. The prophets, too, told of Christ: how He would die a shameful death, which was the death of the Cross. The reason is this: Christ came, sent by God the Father to preach the good news of the Kingdom of Heaven, and of that Kingdom He said things that could not be proved better than by the witness of His blood. Hence, that He might be most obedient to God the Father and might give all certainty to the truth which He announced, He died. He died a shameful death so that no man might refuse to receive this truth, in witness of which they would know that Christ voluntarily accepted death. For He preached the Kingdom of Heaven, telling how a man, capable of that Kingdom, might come to it. In comparison with that Kingdom this life in this world, which is so tenaciously longed for by all men, is to be regarded as nothing. And that they might know that truth is the life of that Kingdom, He gave the life of this world for truth, that thus He might preach the good tidings of the Kingdom of God and free the world from that ignorance which prefers this life to the life of the future. For this purpose He offered Himself in sacrifice for many, and was lifted up upon the Cross in the sight of all, that He might draw all to believe. He has made clear the message of the Gospel, and comforted the weak of heart. He gave Himself freely in the redemption of many, and all of this He did in the best possible manner, so that mankind would attain the faith of salvation, the hope of acquiring it, and the love necessary for fulfilling the Commandments of God. If, therefore, the Arabs would look to the result of Christ's death, and if they would consider the fact that Christ considered Himself as one sent by God to perform this self-immolation, and in so doing to fulfill the will of the Father, they would not deny the glory of the Cross of Christ. If they would consider that nothing was more glorious to Christ than to die out of a love of truth and obedience, even a most detestable death, they would not take away this great regard for the Cross of Christ, whereby He merited to be the greatest of men and the most exalted in the splendor of the Father. Finally, if Christ in His preaching proclaimed that man would obtain immortality after death, how could He have more perfectly given proof of this than by Himself undergoing death, and then rising again and appearing as one alive? The world was finally convinced of this when mankind heard the testimony of many witnesses that Christ had died openly on the Cross and had risen from the dead, and was living again. Those who saw this testified with their own death as witnesses to His Resurrection. This, therefore, was the most perfect way of spreading the Gospel, which Christ demonstrated in Himself. Who, therefore, believes that Christ fulfilled the will of the Father in a most perfect manner, must also make a public confession of all these things, without which this spreading of the Gospel would not have been most perfect. Consider the fact that the Kingdom of Heaven was hidden from everyone until the time of Christ. This is the Gospel of Christ, namely to announce this unknown Kingdom to all. For there was no faith, no hope of attaining the Kingdom of Heaven, nor could it have been loved by anyone when it was entirely unknown, nor was it possible that anyone could have obtained this Kingdom, since before this time human nature had not been elevated to a position where it could have been a consort with the divine nature. Christ, therefore, opened the Kingdom of Heaven in every way possible, but the Kingdom of Heaven can be entered by none until they leave the kingdom of this world through death. It is necessary, consequently, that all mortals lay aside mortality, that is, the ability for dying, and this cannot take place unless through death; then and then alone can one put on immortality. Christ, as a mortal man, if He had not died, would never have done away with mortality and, therefore, He would never have entered the Kingdom of Heaven, in which it is impossible for any mortal thing to exist. If, therefore, He who is the foremost and first born of all men had not opened the Kingdom of Heaven, our nature, united with God, would not have been introduced into this Kingdom. Thus it is that no mere human being could be found in this Kingdom, since our human nature united to God had not yet taken place. Everybody admits that the contrary of this is true if they give credence to the existence of this King, for all believe that the holy ones of their particular belief have ascended to happiness; therefore, the belief of all those who hold that their saints enjoy the happiness of heaven presupposes that Christ has died and ascended into heaven.

CHAPTER XV

German: Certainly everything that you say is well said, but I feel that in the matter of happiness not a few discrepancies will be encountered, for it is alleged that the Jews are promised in their law nothing but temporal things which consist in pleasures of the sense. The promises that are made to the Arabs from their law, which is written in their Koran, are nothing other than perpetual carnal pleasures. The Gospel, on the other hand, promises a sort of angelic reward in that men will become as angels, who are certainly not carnal.

Peter: What can possibly be thought of in this world, the desire of which does not decrease but rather continually increases?

German: All temporalities wither away, it is only things of the mind that perdure. These—eating, drinking, and everything that savors of luxury—even though they occasionally are pleasing, are also in themselves unreliable and the cause of displeasure. To know, to comprehend, and to look upon truth with the mind's eye, affords lasting pleasure, and the older a person becomes the more does the lack of these truths grieve him, and the more he acquires of them the greater is his desire for increasing them.

Peter: If, therefore, desire is perpetual and is, as it were, a continuing nourishment, it must be a kind of food for the intellectual life rather than something temporal and sensible, and, therefore, even though there is to be found in the law of the Koran a promise of Paradise, consisting of rivers of wine and honey and a great multitude of damsels, yet there are many even in this world who would not find pleasure in this, so how could they possibly be happy if they acquire in heaven those things that even here below are not the object of their desires? It says, for example, in the Koran, that many beautiful black damsels are to be found, who have large and white eyes. Now certainly no German in this world, even if he were given over to the vices of the flesh, would care for women of this description. Consequently, it ought to be clear that this has to be understood in a kind of allegorical way, for in another place the Koran forbids the presence of concubines in churches and synagogues, or do you suppose that the mosques are more holy places than Paradise? How could these things be prohibited in the mosques and at the same time be allowed in Paradise? In another place we read that heaven will contain all of those things that are required for a complete fulfillment of our pleasures. In this, what is said is tantamount to saying that all these other things will be found, for because these things are generally desired in this world it is presupposed that in the next world there will be an equal desire, and that then they will be found more exquisitely and abundantly, otherwise, without this simile, it would be impossible to explain that this life will be the completion of all desires. The author of the Koran did not wish to instruct the uneducated populace with a lot of hidden meanings, but only with terms that would seem desirable to their senses. He did this since the populace, not being able to really appreciate the things of the spirit, might possibly depreciate all the promises. The chief reason and the main concern of the author of the Koran was to turn the populace away from idolatry, and for this purpose he made these promises, as well as the other things that he wrote. On the other hand, he did not condemn the Gospel, rather he praised it and pointed out that the happiness that is promised in the Gospel is greater than any corporeal happiness. The more intelligent and wise know among themselves that this is true. Avicenna prefers the intellectual happiness of the vision or fruition of God, and incomparably the truth to the happiness, that is described in the law of Abraham, who was under this same law. The same can be said of other wise men. It must be admitted, therefore, that this happiness is beyond whatever can be written or said, since the fulfillment of every desire and the attainment of good is found in its origin, just as fulfillment of life is found in immortality.

German: What about the Jews who do not accept the promise of the Kingdom of Heaven, but rather place their trust only in temporal things.

Peter: The Jews have often undergone death in the observation of their law and its holiness, therefore, if they had not believed that they would secure happiness after death, since they prefer upholding the law to life itself, they would not have died. It is not part of Jewish belief that there is no eternal life, or that it is unattainable, otherwise none of them would have died for the law; rather the happiness that they expect they do not expect from the works of the law, since these works do not promise happiness, but they expect happiness from faith, which as we have already said before, presupposes a belief in Christ.

CHAPTER XVI

Tartar: I have certainly heard many things here that were previously not known to me. Many honest Tartars cherish the one God, as many admire the different rites of others and love the same God along with them, nevertheless, it is true that they ridicule certain of the Christians, and all of the Arabs and circumcised Jews, those who are signed with facial burns as well as those who are Baptised. Finally, in the matter of marriage, there is a great deal of diversity. Some have only one wife, others believe in a single marriage but maintain a number of concubines, while still others have a number of legitimate wives; with regard to sacrifices there are so many different opinions that they cannot be related. Among these various rites that have been mentioned, the sacrifice of the Christians, which involves the offering of bread and wine and which they say is the body and blood of Christ, and which, after they offer it to Him, they eat and drink, this appears the most abominable. They actually devour whom they love. How there could possibly be any kind of union in these things which vary from place to place and from time to time is something that I cannot comprehend. And yet, unless there is some kind of union, persecution will not cease. Diversity of religion produces division and enmities, hatreds and war.

Thereupon Paul, a teacher of the Gentiles, rose up, and by the authority of the Word, spoke the following:

Paul: It is necessary that we show that salvation of the soul is not obtained by works, but rather from faith, for Abraham, the father of the faith of all those who believe, whether Arab, Christian, or Jew, believed in God, and he was considered as being justified. The soul of the just will inherit life everlasting. Once this is admitted, these varieties of ritual will not be a cause of dissension, for as sensible signs of the truth of belief these things that have been instituted and received as signs are capable of change, not so the thing that is signed.

Tartar: Tell us how, then, does faith save?

Paul: If God should promise certain things because of His liberality and generosity, should not He, Who is able to provide all things and Who is truth, be believed?

Tartar: I'll have to admit that. No one can possibly be deceived who believes Him, and if he fails to believe Him he would not be worthy of obtaining any gift.

Paul: What, therefore, justifies him who obtains justice?

Tartar: Not merits, otherwise this would not be something gratuitous, but rather a debt.

Paul: Very well put, but because no living person can be justified through works in the sight of God, but only gratuitously, the Omnipotent gives whatsoever He will to whomsoever He will. Then, if anybody would be worthy to acquire a promise that was purely gratuitous, it is necessary that he believe in God. It is in this, therefore, that he is justified, because from this alone will he obtain the promise, because he believes in God and expects the Word of God to take place.

Tartar: After God has promised something it is certainly just that He keeps His promises. The person who believes Him is justified rather through the promise than through its faith.

Paul: God, Who promised the seed of Abraham, in which all were to be blessed, justified Abraham, that he might acquire the promise. But if Abraham had not believed in God he would have obtained neither justification nor the promise.

Tartar: I agree with that.

Paul: The faith, therefore, in Abraham was only this, that the fulfillment of the promises was just, because otherwise it would not have been just, nor fulfilled.

Tartar: What did God promise?

Paul: God promised Abraham that He would give him this one seed in the person of Isaac, in which seed all races would be blessed, and this promise actually took place. Since according to the ordinary laws of nature it was impossible for Sarah, his wife, to conceive or give birth, yet because he believed he acquired a son, Isaac. Later on God tempted Abraham, in that He asked him to offer and slay the boy Isaac, in whom His promise of the seed had been fulfilled. And Abraham obeyed God, believing no less in the future promise, even though it would involve the resuscitation of his dead son. When God discovered this faith in Abraham, then he was justified, and the promise was fulfilled in this one seed which descended from him through Isaac.

Tartar: What is this seed?

Paul: It is Christ, for all races have obtained in Him a divine blessing.

Tartar: What is this blessing?

Paul: The divine blessing is that final desire for happiness which we call eternal life, about which you have already heard.

Tartar: Do you desire, therefore, that God should promise us the blessing of eternal life in Christ?

Paul: That is what I wish. For if you believe in this same way you will be justified along with the faithful Abraham, and obtain the promise that was found in the seed of Abraham, Christ Jesus, and that promise is the divine blessing.

Tartar: Do you mean to say, therefore, that this faith alone justifies and enables us to attain of eternal life?

Paul: I do.

Tartar: How can you possibly get this idea across to the simple minded Tartars, so that they can understand that it is Christ in whom they can attain happiness?

Paul: You have already heard that not only Christians but also the Arabians profess that Christ is the very highest of all those who have ever been or ever will be in this world, and that He is the figure of all the races. If, therefore, the blessing of all races is found in one seed, how can it be any other than Christ?

Tartar: Could you give me some kind of proof for this statement?

Paul: As a proof I would rely on the combined testimony of the Arabs and the Christians, that the spirit that brings life to the dead is the spirit of Christ. If, then, the spirit of life is found alone in Christ, Who is able to vivify whom He wishes, He must also be the same spirit without Whom no one is able to raise the dead, and without Whom no spirit can live eternally. For the fullness of divinity and grace dwells in the spirit of Christ, and it is from this same fullness that all who are to be saved receive the grace of salvation.

Tartar: It is pleasing to hear this remark from you, O Teacher of the Nations, for this is in accordance with what has previously been discussed. I see that this belief is necessary for salvation, and that without it no one can be saved. However, I would like to ask now whether this belief is all that is necessary.

Paul: It is quite impossible to please God without faith. It is necessary, however, that this belief be, as it were, activated, for without works it remains dead.

Tartar: What, then, are these works?

Paul: If you believe in God, you will obey His Commandments. For how can you believe that God is really God unless you take care to keep His laws?

Tartar: It is certainly fitting that they should keep the Commandments of God. But it is a fact that the Jews claim that they have received His Commandments from Moses, the Arabs from Mohammed, the Christians through Jesus, and the other various nations venerate their own prophets, from whom they claim to have received the divine precepts. Since this is the case, how can they ever arrive at any concord?

Paul: I think that you will have to agree that the divine mandates are very brief and well known to all, and that they are the common heritage of all nations. In fact, the light that makes them so evident to all of us is created along with the creation of the rational soul. The voice of God speaks forth in all of us, urging that we love Him from Whom we have received our very being, and urging that golden rule, that we do not do unto others what we would not wish them to do to us. Love, therefore, is the fulfillment of divine legislation, and all other laws can be traced to this source.

Tartar: I have no doubt that both the faith of which you speak, as well as the law of mutual charity would be acceptable to the Tartars. However, the question of rites poses many problems. For example, the question of circumcision, a ritual that they ridicule, would hardly be acceptable.

Paul: The acceptance of circumcision is really not pertinent to the truth of salvation. In fact, circumcision does not save any individual, and certainly without it one may attain salvation. Yet whoever does not hold that circumcision is a requisite for reasons of health, but allows it to be performed on his foreskin so that he might be in conformity with Abraham and his followers, will certainly not be condemned for this action, as long as he holds to this basic faith which we are discussing. Thus, for example, Christ was circumcised, as well as many other Christians who lived after Him. The Ethiopians mentioned by St. James and others were not circumcised in the sense that they considered this a sacrament necessary for salvation. The real problem in this matter is how we may preserve peace among the various believers, if some are circumcised and some are not. The fact of the matter is that the great majority of the world's population is not circumcised, and I would contend that circumcision is not a matter of necessity. In my judgment, peace would be better preserved if the minority would conform to the majority with whom they are already united in basic belief. Yet, on the other hand, if for the purpose of maintaining peace the majority should conform to the will of the minority and receive circumcision, it should be done in an arbitrary fashion, so that tranquility might rest on a firmer basis because of this interchange of common practices. In this way, if some nations accept the basic beliefs of the Christians, and the Christians, on the other hand, allow themselves to be circumcised in order to maintain the peace, its foundation will be better secured. Nonetheless, I think there will be practical difficulties in this. It will suffice that there be unanimity in the matter of belief and the law of charity, and that toleration in the matter or ritual be allowed.

CHAPTER XVII

Armenian: Since you hold that Baptism is a matter of necessity among Christians, how do you propose to explain this?

Paul: Baptism is the sacrament of faith. Whoever believes that it is possible to obtain a certain justification will also believe that through Him there is a taking away of sins. The believer will manifest this in the cleansing that is signified in the Baptismal lotion. For Baptism is nothing other than a profession of his belief in a sacramental sign. He could hardly be called a believer who refused to profess, both verbally and according to the signs instituted by Christ for this purpose, his belief in Him. The idea of religious ablutions, or washings, is common to both the Jews and the Arabs; hence there would be no difficulty in accepting an ablution instituted by Christ as a manifestation of their belief.

Armenian: I can see how it is quite necessary to receive this sacrament, since it is required for salvation.

Paul: Faith is certainly a matter of necessity for adults, who can, nevertheless, be saved without the sacrament when it is impossible to receive it. When, however, they are in a position to receive the sacrament, we can hardly call them believers if they refuse to act as believers in rejecting the sacrament of regeneration.

Armenian: What about the case of children?

Paul: There will be no difficulty in coming to agreement on the matter of infant Baptism. If it was allowed that they undergo circumcision on the eighth day, this practise could be commuted to Baptism, and it could be an optional matter whether they wanted it to be included in the Baptismal rite.

CHAPTER XVIII

Bohemian: I can see that it is quite possible that we can reach agreement in everything that has been discussed up to this point, but I think that there will be a great deal of difficulty in the matter of sacrifices. I know that Christians, holding as they do that the oblation of the bread and wine is held to be the sacrament of the Eucharist, will not be inclined to compromise this belief just to please others. Certain other nations, since they do not hold to this idea of sacrifice, will present difficulties not easily overcome. The situation is further complicated by the fact that they consider the conversion of the bread and wine into the flesh and blood of Christ as something quite insane, especially the eating and drinking of these elements.

Paul: This sacrament of the Eucharist has no other significance than that, as a favor from Christ, we can obtain the nourishment of eternal life, just as in this life we are nourished on bread and wine. Since we believe that Christ is the food of our mind, then we believe also that we receive Him under the appearance of eating. And since it is necessary that we be of one mind in this belief, that we obtain the food of eternal life in Christ, why not demonstrate this by our belief in the sacrament of the Eucharist? It is to be hoped that all who believe will want to taste of this food, through faith, which will in fact, be the food of eternal life in the other world.

Bohemian: How are you going to persuade all these various peoples that the substance of the bread is changed into the body of Christ in the sacrament of the Eucharist?

Paul: Whoever really believes knows that the Word of God in Christ Jesus has transferred us from the misery of this world to adopted sons of God, and to the possession of everlasting life, because for God nothing is impossible. If we believe and hope in this, then we do not hesitate at all to believe that the Word of God, in arrangement with Christ, can change bread into flesh. If nature herself does this in the case of animal life, how should it be impossible to the Word, through which God has created the entire world? It is a matter of faith, then, that we believe this. For if it is impossible that we, as children of Adam, who are made of the slime of the earth, can be transformed in Christ Jesus, the Word of God, into the sons of an immortal God, and if we truly believe and hope in this, that we shall then be like Christ Jesus, the Word of God the Father, then it seems reasonable enough that we, in a similar fashion, give credence to the transubstantiation of bread into flesh and wine into blood through the same Word— the Word through Whom bread is bread, wine is wine, flesh is flesh, blood is blood, and through Whom in nature food is changed into the nourished.

Bohemian: I still find that this changing of the substance of the bread is a difficult thing to handle.

Paul: You will believe this more easily with faith, for this can only be touched upon with the mind. Our reason perceives that something exists, and not what it actually is; the substance pre-ceeds every accident. Hence it is that this substance has neither quality nor quantity, and it alone is changed so that it is no longer the substance of the bread but the substance of the flesh, and this changeover is one of a spiritual nature, which is the farthest re-moved from what is perceptible to the senses. Consequently, there is no increase in the quantity of the flesh, nor is it numerically multiplied. For this reason there is but one substance of flesh into which the substance of the bread has been changed, although bread be offered in many places, and there be many particles of bread used in the sacrifice.

Bohemian: As far as to the manner in which this sacrament is one of food for eternal life, and as to how, through it, we attain our inheritance as Sons of God in Jesus Christ, Who is the Son of God, I will accept quite willingly. I agree also as to how there is a similitude in this matter to the sacrament of the Eucharist, which is perceptible only to the mind and can be tasted and received through faith. But what will happen if this mystery is not accepted? For the unenlightened will shudder not only at having to believe this, but also will be opposed to taking for granted the other mysteries.

Paul: This sacrament, insofar as it is found in sensible things, arrived at through faith, is not a matter of necessity to the extent that, without it, there is no salvation, for it suffices for salvation to believe, and thus to eat the food of life. And, therefore, regarding its distribution, or to whom and how often it should be given to the faithful, this has not been set down as a matter of obligation, and hence it is that if anyone who believes and yet at the same time judges himself unworthy to approach the table of the great King, I would prefer that this humility be rather praised. Accordingly, with regard to the use and the rite of this sacrament, the Church authorities should be governed by expediency in complying with local conditions. Provided that the faith is preserved, a diversity of rites will not mitigate against a common law.

Englishman: What about the other sacraments, Matrimony, Orders, Confirmation, and Extreme Unction?

Paul: I feel that in this matter, due to the weakness of human nature, a great deal of latitude should be allowed, so long as it does not compromise eternal salvation. Any endeavor to impose exact conformity in everything is bound to disturb the peace. Yet I would hope that in the matter of matrimony and orders a certain agreement can be arrived at. In the question of matrimony it is a common practice among all nations that, following the law of nature, this union should be between one man and one woman. As for the priesthood, all religions have basically the same attitudes towards it. Harmony will be found in stressing these common elements, and the Christian religion will be approved insofar as in its observation it retains in both these sacraments that simplicity that in the estimate of others is most praiseworthy.

Englishman: What about fastings, ecclesiastical duties, abstinence in the matter of food and drink, formulae for prayers, and such matters?

Paul: Where it is impossible to maintain conformity, then, provided that faith and peace are preserved, the various nations should be permitted their own devotions and ceremonies. As a matter of fact, I think that this diversity would bring about an increase in devotion. For each individual nation will endeavor to make its own ritual more splendid, that they might surpass others and, in this way, they will achieve greater praise from both God and man.

After some time, when these matters had been duly considered by the wise men of the various nations, a number of books were produced, culled from among those who wrote on the observances of the ancients. These works were from among the most excellent authors, as for example Marcus Varro representing the Latins, and Eusebius representing the Greeks, who gathered together the varities of religion. After an examination of these and many others it was ascertained that this diversity was reducible to the worship of one God. It was discovered that from the very beginning there had been but one cult which was everywhere and continually observed in the veneration of the divine. Yet it happened that quite often, due to the simplicity of the people, they were led astray by the power of the Prince of Darkness, and were not aware of what they were doing.

Therefore, it was concluded from reason that in heaven a harmony is somehow permitted. And the King of Kings commanded that these wise men return, and that they lead the various nations to the unity of the true cult; and that in this endeavor they be led and assisted by the spiritual administrators, and finally, that with plenipotentiary power over all they assemble in Jerusalem, as in a common center, and that they accept in the name of all one common faith, and thus secure everlasting peace for themselves, so that the Creator of all men might be praised in peace and blessed for all ages.   Amen

CONCERNING EXPERIMENTS
IN WEIGHT

Cusa's little work on Weights or Balances, *De Staticis Experimentis*, forms the fourth and final book of the dialogue entitled the *Idiota* or the Layman. It was composed early in September of the year 1450 and both its style and compactness indicate the haste in which it was written. Reflected in the work are many of his cosmological conceptions that indicate a departure from the Aristotelian philosophy of quality to a more exact and mathematical account of physical phenomena. We see Cusa here at work in that experimental area that engenders the sort of predication and verification which is the lifeline of empirical science as we know it today. The influence of the dissenting Platonic movement of his time has already been expressed in Cusa's view of a universe and all it contains as an infinite harmony in which all things have their mathematical proportions. Accordingly, knowledge is always measurement and number is the first model of things in the mind of the Creator. He declares that there is no reason to suppose that change and decay occur only here on earth and not elsewhere in the universe. Indeed, he is close to the modern notion of cosmogenesis expounded by de Chardin in declaring that the corruption which is a particular feature of terrestrial being is by no means a real destruction, that is, a total and absolute loss of existence, but only a loss of that particular form of existence. Fundamentally, it constitutes a dissolution or resolution of a being into its constitutive elements and their reunification into something else, a process which he suggests probably takes place in the whole universe since the ontological structure of the world is everywhere the same. This he projects into the world of medicine, chemistry and musicology.

Readers will find his treatment of theories relating to specific gravity and quantitative analysis of interest for this period. It is particularly in this succinct treatment of medical problems that he displays an originality that is remarkable. His references to urinalysis is a departure from traditional medieval theories and recommendations for pulse determination were to await centuries for their modern counterparts in sphygmographs and spirometers.

DE STATICIS EXPERIMENTIS

Author: A Roman Orator often sought the company of an Citizen to hear the man's ideas which he always welcomed. Once when the Orator commended the balance-scale, the rule of justice, as an instrument necessary for the common good, the citizen replied:

Citizen: Although nothing in the world is absolutely precise yet experience demonstrates that the judgment of the balance-scale is one of the truest measurements we have; and so it is in demand everywhere. But please tell me, seeing different things of like volume cannot have the same weight, has anyone yet compiled a table of exact, experimentally verified differences of weights?

Orator: Not to my knowledge.

Citizen: I wish that someone would compile such a table; I would regard it more highly than many volumes of other books.

Orator: I feel no-one could do it any better than you, yourself, if you would undertake the task.

Citizen: Anyone could easily do it; but for my part I haven't the time.

Orator: Tell me what profit there would be in it and how to do it; and I'll see whether I, myself, or someone else whom I ask can do it.

Citizen: I think that by knowing the differences in the weights

241

of things we can more surely understand them and that many more probable conjectures can be made about things.

Orator: What you say is true; for I recall that a certain prophet says (Prov. 16: 11) weight and the balance are the judgments of the hand who created (Wisd. II, 17) all things in number, weight, and measure; who (Prov. 8: 28) weighed the oceans and the greatness of the Earth in a balance, as the wise man says.

Citizen: If therefore water from one source is not of the same weight as a like volume of water from another source, certainly a balance will better indicate the difference between the natures of the two than any other instrument.

Orator: That's right and Vitruvius, writing on architecture, tells us to choose for a dwelling a place which has light and airy waters and to avoid places where the waters are heavy and earthly.

Citizen: Just as waters from the same source seem to be of the same weight and nature so, too, waters from different sources seem to be of different weights and natures.

Orator: You say *seem to be* as though they are necessarily so.

Citizen: I confess that time may alter them though not perceptibly; for no doubt water has different weights at different seasons just as there is one weight of water near the source or head and another farther off. But their differences being scarcely noticeable are regarded as being of no account.

Orator: Do you think that what you say about water is also true of all other things?

Citizen: Yes, I do, because different things of the same volume never have the same weight. Therefore, if there is one weight for blood, another for urine, and for each of these one weight in a healthy man and another weight in a sick man, one in an old man, another in a young man, one in a German, another in an African. Wouldn't it be convenient for a physician to have a table of these differences?

Orator: I should say so; and, what is more, by having their weights noted down, one might make himself more respected.

Citizen: I think that a physician might make a more accurate judgment of urine by both weight and color than by color alone which may be misleading.

Orator: Yes, certainly.

Citizen: The same can be said of the roots of herbs, stocks, leaves, fruits, seeds, and juices having their own weights. Now if the weights of all herbs were noted down, with the different places they come from, the physician might better reach the nature of them all with the various phases of their origin, by their weight and smell, rather than by their taste which is misleading.

Orator: That is very true.

Citizen: Then by comparing the weights of the herbs to the weight of blood or urine he might know by the likeness or difference of the medicines what dose to prescribe, and he might make many startling prognoses and by static experiments more precisely conjecture whatever is known.

Orator: One wonders a good deal at the fact that even with so much painstaking research all men have been so neglectful of the designation of weights.

Citizen: If one had an hour glass filled with water and out of a straight, narrow hole in it allowed water to run into a basin while counting the pulse of a healthy young man to one hundred and if one did the same thing with a sick man, don't you think that there would be a great deal of difference between the weights of the two volumes of water?

Orator: Without a doubt.

Citizen: By the weight of water, therefore, one could arrive at the difference in pulse between a young man and a old man, a sick man and a sound man; consequently one could arrive at a better understanding of the disease since there must be one weight for one disease and another weight for another disease. And so there might be given a more perfect judgment by such an experimental difference of the pulses and weight of the urine than by merely the touch of one and the color of the other.

Orator: You are quite right.

Citizen: If furthermore one should observe particularly the frequency of breathing, using the above method, wouldn't one give a more precise judgment?

Orator: I believe he would.

Citizen: For if, while the water is running out of the hour glass, one could observe a child breathing one hundred times and do the same for an old man, it is not possible for the weights of the two volumes of water to be the same. The same holds true for different ages and complexions. If then a physician were correctly informed of the weight of the breathing of a healthy man or a child or a young man or the like, all of whom were sick with different illnesses, without a doubt by such an experiment he could more surely arrive at an understanding of health and sickness and so to the administration of remedies.

Orator: Yes, one could even conjecture about matters of time.

Citizen: You are so right. For if he should find in a young man a weight associated with an old, decrepit man, he might more certainly predict the time of his death. And he might make many other admirable conjectures. Moreover, in the case of fevers, if he would similarly register hot and cold paroxysms by the difference in the weights of volumes of water, couldn't he more truly determine the seriousness of the disease and the best remedy for it?

Orator: Certainly he could, for he would then have learned the volume of one quality over another, of heat over cold or vice versa; and according to the result he might apply a remedy.

Citizen: Furthermore, I would say that in different nations, regions, and times these things would be different, even though in the same age. Therefore, even though it might be difficult, yet it would be highly profitable for the differences in weights to be designated in accordance with all these circumstances.

Orator: What you say is true.

Citizen: On the other hand it seems to me that the weight of anything is to be considered as the average of the different weights of a thing in the average climate, I mean in different climates. Thus if we would consider the weight of a man as compared with some other living weight then we must consider a man not as inhabiting such a latitude as to be termed a northerner or a southerner, where there may be excess on both sides, but rather as inhabiting the average climate.

Orator: You are right. The ancients called that climate Dia Rhodon because it extends itself from the East to the West through the Rhodes Islands. But tell me, if you should seek the weight of a man in comparison to some other living creature, how would you go about it?

Citizen: I would put the man onto one side of the scale and the same weight of some other thing onto the other side of the scale to fix the exact weight of the man. Then I would put the man into water and weigh him again when he came out, noting the difference in the two weights. I would do the same with the other living creature, and by the difference in weights I would note that which I sought. Then I would look to the difference of the weight of the man and the other weight, out of the water, and according to this I would moderate the weight found and write it down.

Orator: I do not understand this moderation.

Citizen: I will demonstrate.

Author: Then the Citizen took a light piece of wood having a weight of three, and such that five would be the weight of an equivalent volume of water; he divided the wood into two unequal parts, one representing one third of the volume of the wood, the other, two thirds; he put them both into a deep flagon; and holding them down with a stick, he poured water on them; then pulling away the stick, he allowed the two pieces of wood to rise to the top of the water; and the larger piece reached the top before the smaller. Then he said:

Citizen: You see now that the difference in the motion is in proportion to this extent, that in light wood the greater the volume of the wood the more buoyancy there is in it.

Orator: I see that, and I am well pleased.

Citizen: That is what I mean; for that reason moderation should be made; for if a man should have more weight and be heavier than the other living creature, only for his great size, then he will necessarily sink faster into water than the other. Wherefore it is necessary that diminishing the moderation of the known difference be done proportionately according to the excess.

Orator: I understand now. But tell me, how does the water keep the wood from sinking?

Citizen: As a greater heaviness resists a lesser; for if you press a round piece of wood into wax and then pull it out again and fill the depression with water and then weigh both water and wood, you will find that if the weight of the wood exceeds the weight of the water then the wood will sink; if not, the wood will float; and a proportionate part of the wood will be above the water according to the extent to which the weight of the water exceeds the weight of the wood.

Orator: Why do you speak of a round piece of wood?

Citizen: Because if it were a broad piece, it would float more easily because it occupies more of the water; thus ships in shallow waters need broader bottoms.

Orator: Contrive in your original purpose, whether the weight of animals might be determined in another way.

Citizen: I think they might. First one should fill to the top a large vessel full of water and then pour that out into a still larger vessel and then weigh some man out of water. Then have the man step into the first vessel and pour over him from the second vessel enough water to fill the first vessel to the top. Finally, weigh the water which is left over. Proceed in like manner with another man, beast, or any other thing. By the difference in weights one can, by subtle inquiry, find what he is seeking.

Orator: You proceed with a great deal of subtlety and I have heard that in the same way the difference of metals has been found and that some have noted how much the fusion of an ounce of wax gathers of gold, silver, copper, and thus of all metals.

Citizen: Certainly he is much to be commended who by the fusion of wax understood the greatness, for he saw that if an ounce of gold filled the place of an ounce of wax that then it must weigh just as much as an ounce of wax and the same must be true with other metals; for it is most certain that there is one weight of gold and another of silver, and another of other things all having the same volume, and that something has one weight in air, another in water, another in oil or some other liquid. And if one had a table of these weights he would readily know how much more one metal weighs than the other in air and in water. Thus, given any volume of metal knowing its weight in air and in water, one would know of what metal and what mixture the volume is. And what I have said of air and water may also be said of oil or any other liquid with which the experiment may be conducted.

Orator: So, indeed, without mixing the volume of metal, or separation of the metals one could know the mixture; and this method would work with money to know how much copper there is in gold and silver.

Citizen: What you say is true and it would work in determining how far short of the truth the alchemist comes in his sophistic science.

Orator: If anyone would propose to write a book of weights he must, it seems, note the variety of every metal; for Hungarian gold is of one weight and fine gold, which is called aurum obryzum, of another, and so of all the metals.

Citizen: By what has been said it seems that as in fountains so in minerals there are found differences in weight yet gold, wherever it is found, is always heavier than any other metal even though the species may be found to vary with a certain latitude, and this is true of other metals also.

Orator: But couldn't the characteristic or proportion of the value of metals be found out, by the characteristic or proportion of their weights?

Citizen: Lead is the closest to gold in weight, but not in perfection; therefore, we must consider one weight only, but every kind of weight; for if one looks at the weight of the heat of fusion of gold and lead; he finds that lead comes not as near to gold as other metals do. And if one looks to the weight of the heat in the melting of iron, he finds that iron comes closer to gold than any other metal, even though the heaviness of iron does not come so close. Therefore, we must look at all of the weights and not the weight of heaviness only, and so we find that silver is next to gold.

Orator: Vitruvius says that in speaking of the natural heaviness of gold, it alone sinks in quicksilver even though other metals of greater weight and greater bulk float.

Citizen: Quicksilver is naturally conjugible to all the metals because of something which it has in common with them; but it more readily clings and adheres to gold, as that which is imperfect to its own most perfect nature. For this cause, the Alchemists strive to tame quicksilver in the fire until it not only jumps from the fire itself but clings to all other metals to which it is joined. And not only to this extent but until it also compacts them all into the weight of gold and colors them with a fixed permanent color while their own fluxion and moisture still remain.

Orator: But do you think that through these means they can fulfill their purpose?

Citizen: Precision is always hard to see, but the balance will show how much they accomplish; without the balance nothing is certain. For through the judgment of the fire and the balance the truth of this question must be resolved.

Orator: Couldn't all precious stones be weighed in the same manner?

Citizen: No doubt of it, they might all be one by the same device, for a diamond has no weight in respect to the magnitude of lead as does neither a sapphire. And by this diversity, the habitude of proportion of lead to either weight may be known and, therefore, it was very good to have these weights written down, by the way of a static experiment with their differences known of these originals, that if there were any sophistication done with Beryl or colored crystal, they might be known and found.

Orator: Yes, and furthermore, there being one weight of a stone in air, another in water, and another in oil, it is good to have these diversities that without any habitude to lead or any third thing, the difference of the weights might be known.

Citizen: That is very true.

Orator: Tell me, do you have any device through which the virtues of stones may be weighed?

Citizen: I think the virtue of the lodestone might be weighed, if putting some iron on one scale, and a lodestone on the other, until the balance became even, then taking away the lodestone and putting something else of the same weight on that scale, then by holding the lodestone over the iron so that the scale would begin to rise; by reason of the lodestone's attraction to the iron. Now by taking weight off of the other scale until equilibrium is again achieved, I believe that the weight of what was taken out of the contrary scale would be proportional to the weight of the virtue of power of the lodestone. And in a similar manner, the virtue of a diamond may be found since they say it hinders the attraction of the lodestone to the iron, and so other virtues of other stones could be found always considering the greatness of the bodies because in a greater body there is a greater power and virtue.

Orator: Couldn't a workman also use these means to determine the amount of mercury and sulphur contained in every metal?

Citizen: Certainly he could determine such things by the concord and difference of weights; also the elements of quicksilver, by the diversity of its weight in air, water, and oil compared to oil, water, and ashes of the same greatness weighed against it; and similarly with sulphur. Through these methods man may come to a true conjecture of the elements of all metals and stones and the weights of those elements.

Orator: This is fine, but couldn't the same be done with woods, herbs, flesh, living creatures and humans?

Citizen: I believe it could be done in all things, for in weighing a piece of wood and then burning it thoroughly and thus weighing its ashes it is known how much water is in the wood, for there is nothing that has a heavy weight but water and earth. It is known, moreover, by the various weights of wood in air, water, and oil how much water in the wood is heavier or lighter than clean spring water, and so how much air is in it. Thus by the various weights of the ashes the amount of fire in them and the elements may be even more closely determined, though precision is always unattainable. And as I have so described for wood so it can also be done with herbs, flesh and other things.

Orator: There is a saying that there is no pure element; how is this proved by the balance?

Citizen: If a man should put a hundred weight of earth into a great earthen pot, then taking some herbs and seeds, weigh them, and plant or sow them in that pot, then let them grow there until they weigh one hundred weight, he would find the earth very little diminished when he weighed it again. From this he may gather that all the herbs received their weight from water. Therefore, the waters being impregnated in the earth attracted a terrestreity, and by the operation of the Sun was condensed into the herb. If these herbs are then burned to ashes, couldn't one guess by the diversity of all the weights how much more earth was found than one hundred weight and then conclude that the water brought all of it? For the elements are convertible one into another by parts as we see by placing a glass of water in snow and watching the air condense into water and flow into the glass. So we find by experience that some water is turned into stones, some into ice, and there is in some fountains a hardening and petrifying power which it is reported turns things put into them into stone. It is reported, there is a certain water fountain found in Hungary which through the power of the virtue which is in it turns iron into copper, by such powers and virtues it is evident that the waters are not purely elementary but elemented, and so it would be very nice to have weights of all these waters of such various virtues that by the diversity of these weights in air and oil one might come nearer to a value of their virtues.

Orator: Couldn't one also do it with the soil?

Citizen: Yes, even with the soil, because one soil is fertile, another barren; in one there are found stones and minerals and not in another; therefore, for the searching into the secrets of nature it would be very helpful to know the various weights of the soil, in water, air, and oil; so that by the difference of weights of wines, waxes, oils, gums, alums, onions, leeks, garlics, and all such things, I think that the virtues that are different in them might in some manner be determined, and we might give a close estimate of the weight of the whole earth: for the circumference and the diameter are both known from which may be gotten the capacity and the contents and the number of miles, therefore numbering even one solid inch of earth, the weight of the whole capacity may be easily determined.

Orator: These things could hardly be written in one huge volume.

Citizen: Experimental knowledge requires many volumes, for the more there are the easier we may arrive at answers in experiments from the knowledge contained in them.

Orator: Perhaps in time a man may even determine the weight of air.

Citizen: If any man would put a great deal of hard packed dry wool in one pan of a balance and stones to counterbalance it in the other, he would then find by experience that when the air condenses the weight of the wool would increase; and when the air becomes arid, it would decrease; and by these differences he might weigh the air and might give predictions of the change of the times and weather. So if any man should desire to know the various strength of the sun in different climates, he should take and weigh a thousand grains, either of wheat or barley from the most fertile field of the one and the other, by the difference of the weights, he might determine the various powers of the sun, for if the number and field be similarly fruitful in any place, the difference has to be in the sun. So you may also determine the different powers of the sun in the mountains and the valleys, and also the same when it is rising and setting.

Orator: Couldn't a man by letting a stone fall from a high tower and during the time of fall let water run out of a narrow hole into a basin; and then by weighing the water that had run out and then doing the same with wood of the same size, determine the weight of the air by the difference of the weights of the water, wood and stone?

Citizen: If a man should do this in different towers of equal height and at different times, he might come near to a likely estimate. But he could determine the weight of air sooner by different figures or shapes of things of equal heaviness. For if I would drop one pound of lead which was round in shape from a high tower and weigh the water that ran out of the hour glass in that time, and then do the same with an equal weight of lead which was broad; I might by the different weights of the waters, determine the weight of the air. For we know from experience that birds are more still when they spread their wings because they take up more air; just as also something which is heavy will sink faster in water if it is round than if it is square. And possibly the air may yet be more easily weighed: as if equal bellows were equally filled, in different times and places, for by the motion of those equal bellows, and the measurement of these motions by dripping water through an hour glass of equal height during the time of motion and by comparing the weights of the waters, the weight of air might easily be known. For the proportion of the two waters will be the same as the proportion of the air in the two bellows. But the best way of all is to take an empty glass full of air, suppose the glass weighs just a pound, then filling the hole with wax, put it under water, then if a one pound weight exactly will hold it under water, then you could say that the air in the glass is of the lightness of two pounds. So in this method one may know the proportion of the lightness of one air to another in different places, times, and regions. One can also weigh smoke and wind by using a bellows: for by pressing out the air from a bellows and filling it with smoke which you can weigh the same as for the air, you can then determine whether smoke or air is lighter and by how much. And so also can you do it with wind. And you may also by the motion of the smoke while so many drops of water distill in the hour glass and the motion of fire during the distilling of so many drops determine the lightness of fire, above smoke or air.

Citizen: And it can be done with a piece of lead, made in the shape of a crescent such that one end is heavier than the other, and on the light end fasten an apple or some other light thing. When such an instrument is thrown into water the heavier end will reach the bottom first, then having reached the bottom the apple is freed and will again return to the surface, provided you first have the knowledge of how long the lead will be sinking, and the apple is rising in a water of a known depth; for then by the difference of the weights of the water, or sand of the hour glass, from the time the lead was thrown in and the apple's return in various waters, you may find what you are looking for.

Orator: I believe that the depth of the water may be searched both by this and by other means. But tell me, can it not also be guessed at, by the way ships do it at sea?

Citizen: How do you say?

Orator: By throwing an apple as far as one can out from the prow or fore part of the ship and then letting the water run from the hour glass until the ship comes up to the apple and comparing the weight of the water at one time with the weight of it at another time.

Citizen: It can be done that way and also by shooting an arrow from a cross bow and weighing the water when the ship comes up to the arrow.

Orator: The knowledge of the strength of the bows and other engines, it seems, are proportional to the water which flowed out of the hour glass, from the time when the shaft is shot upwards and returns again to the earth, provided that in various engines the shafts are always equal.

Citizen: Not only the strength of the bows and engines but of the winds also, the flying of the birds, the running of men and beasts and whatever is similar may be determined by the static experiments and the running of water from an hour glass.

Orator: How may the strength of a man be known by this method?

Citizen: Using a pair of even scales let a man hold on to one of them and in the other put as much weight as he can lift until the balance is even: (it will be more exact if the man has something to hold his feet against) then take the weight of that which he has lifted and deduct it from the weight of the man himself, the remainder being proportional to his strength.

Orator: Couldn't the breath of a man also be weighed?

Citizen: The weight of man is different when he draws in a breath and when he breathes out; and it is also different while he is living and while he is dead. This is true of all living things. Therefore, it would be good to have these differences noted in various living things, various men, and of various ages of men, so that one might determine the weight of the vital spirits.

Orator: Couldn't man determine the heat and cold, and the dryness and moisture of the weather?

Citizen: Certainly, for if in frosty weather you would note the weight of the water before and after it is frozen you shall find it different: since ice floats in water we know it to be lighter than water: and therefore, according to the intensity of the cold, there is a greater difference of the weight; or if you would weigh green wood and after a time find the difference in weight you would know the excess of heat and cold, moisture and drought.

Orator: Couldn't the time of day be also weighed?

Citizen: If you would let the water run out of an hour glass from sunrise of one day and let it run until the sunrise of the next day, and then let it run for another day beginning at sunrise, by the proportion of water that has run on this day to that which ran out on the first day, you may determine the hour and time of day.

Orator: From this could he also determine the time of the year?

Citizen: Yes, if for an entire year you would run water through an hour glass every day from sunrise to sunset and observe the weight, you may give a close guess by the balance at any time, to the day of the month and the hour of the day, although on shorter days the difference will be less certain than on others.

Orator: I see that by this invention one may determine even the motion of the heavenly bodies, as Nimrod is said to have done, and Hipparchus to have written.

Citizen: What you say is true, though in this case there is a great need for an explanation: for if any man noting a fixed star in the Meridian line, would gather and note the water running from an hour glass, until the return of the same star to the same place and do the same for the sun from its rising until its rising again on the next day, he might find the motion of the sun to the east by the change of the decrease of the water's weight, of the star's motion from the meridian line to its return to the same place, respectively, to the motion of the sun from its rising to its rising; for it is determined by the difference of weight in comparison to the weight as a whole if the motion is in order to the equinoctial circle, not to the Zodiac, which is not described upon the poles of the world, but its own. So if any man would determine how much the sun was moved in fifteen minutes in relation to the same star, he might do it in the same manner, different distance of the sun's rising respectively to the place of that star on the meridian line. As for example, if today the distance of the place of that star, in the line from the sun's rising is found in some proportion by the hour glass, and fifteen minutes later it is found in another proportion, by the difference of those proportions the motion might be proved, so it is always in the equinoctial.

Orator: May the motion in the Zodiac be also found in this manner?

Citizen: Certainly, by the motion of the sun from noon to noon, and from the East to the East, and from the East to the West; for by these differences the declination of the Zodiac from the equinoctial might be reached.

Orator: And what may be done concerning the variety of the motion, which is said to be caused by the Eccentric?

Citizen: That also may be determined, when in a year you shall find the inequality of the Zodiac, in equal days: for the sun moves in the summertime from the equinoctial, and does not return to the equinoctial again in the same number of days in winter, for in winter it returns sooner; for it would not be found to have spent the same number of days in going from Libra to Aries as from Aries to Libra. By this difference one would get the eccentric, or little circle of the spica, by the difference of the motion.

Orator: And what about the size of the sun's body?

Citizen: By the weight of the water that runs in the hour glass, in the equinoctial, from the beginning of the rising of the sun until it is far above the horizon, in the position of the water of the star's revolution, is known the size of the sun's body. But one may also determine the size of the sun's body by the eclipses of the sun.

Orator: How?

Citizen: First we would determine the motion of the moon as we have of the sun. Then by the eclipse and its motion through the shadow of the earth, we determine the size of the moon in proportion to the different shadow of the earth, by which we conclude the average proportion to be the proportion of the moon's size to that of the earth. Then by the motion of the moon, and the eclipse of the sun, we determine the sun's distance from the earth and its size; and although it be a subtle way of determining, it is still conjecture.

Orator: From what you have already said, it seems that all the differences of motions, and eclipses of the sun and moon, yes the progresses of all the planets, their stations, retrogradations, directions, and eccentricities may be determined by the same means, that of the hour glass.

Citizen: You may do it yourself, if you work at collecting the differences.

Orator: What do you think of the judgments of the stars?

Citizen: I think that by the variety of the weights of the water, in several years, and certain other differences in the weights of woods, herbs, and grain, one may guess at the future plenty or scarcity of corn, better and quicker by experiments of the past, than by the motion of the stars. For if in March, there is such a proportion of weight found in water, air and woods, then fruitfulness of the earth will follow, or barrenness, or at best mediocrity. The same for wars, pestilence, and all other ordinary things. And this is the basis through which in these second causes we hunt after the judgment of the stars. Since by the increase or decrease of marrow in living creatures, fishes, and sea crabs, in trees and rushes, we seek to determine the age of the moon; and by the tides of the sea, its place in the heavens.

Orator: I have heard that the Egyptians used to predict the disposition of the year by the plentiful or scarce overflowing of the Nile.

Citizen: There is no country where one could not find some similar means of prediction; as by the fatness of fishes and creeping things, in the beginning of winter we say that there will be a long and cold winter for which nature has provided its living creatures.

Orator: What do you think of questions asked Astrologers; couldn't this device determine an equal answer for them all?

Citizen: Although not an equal one, I think (because you shall consider me a mere layman in all respects) some answer may be made in this way. But how an answer may be given of all things that are asked would require a great deal of inquiry. The way that this can be done cannot be written up in books; but by the weight of the question; for the curiosity of the inquirer seems to be caused by the foresight of the future event, though he himself may not see from where the motion comes, as someone who feels something in his eye which he does not see asks someone else if there he sees what is hurting him.

Orator: I think that you mean, as in the wheel of Pythagoras, by the various combinations of the name of the asker, his mother, the hour of the day and the light of the moon, there is a way taught of giving the answers: or as a prophet makes judgments from lots or by casual reading of Sibylline Books, or by the Psalter; or from buildings or geometric figures, or by the chattering of birds, or the bending of the flame of a fire, or the relation of a third man, or any other casual occurrence that intervenes.

Citizen: There are certain individuals who have correctly sought to give answers, by conferences which they have had with the inquirer, in making him tell some news of the disposition of this country, for the impulsive spirit has to make itself known in long discourse. For if the inquirer is inclined to talk of sad things, so shall it be; if it is a glad and merry discussion then so, also, will the event be. But I imagine conjectures might be formed according to the face, garments, motion of the eyes, form of words; and of weights looking upon the lot of those things which I ask the inquirer again and again to bring to me; yet the more valuable conjectures come from him to whom some truer thing fell without premeditation, in whom a certain spirit seemed to speak. Nevertheless, in this matter, I neither think that this art is possible, nor that he who has it can communicate his judgment, nor that a wise man should use such a means.

Orator: What you say is very good, for St. Augustine reports that he had in his time a certain drunken companion, who would read men's minds, discover thieves, and show other secret things, in a strange manner; and yet he was at the same time a light vain fellow, and no wise man.

Citizen: I know that I myself have foretold many things as the spirit gave it to me, and at the same time was utterly ignorant of the cause. Finally I seemed to see, that it was unlawful for a serious man to speak without cause, and since then I have held my peace.

Orator: Enough said about the motions of the stars, now add something of music.

Citizen: The experiments of balance are most profitable to music. For by the differences of weights of two bells that sound a tone, it is known in what proportion of harmony the tones consist. The proportion of a Diapason, Diapente, and Diatessaron as well as all other harmonies is known by the weight of pipes, and of waters that fill the pipes, and likewise that by the weight of hammers which strike upon an anvil harmonies arise, and by the weight of drops which drop from a rock into a pond and make different sounds, and of pipes and all other musical instruments; the reason is best and most precisely reached by the balance.

Orator: Is it the same in voices and songs?

Citizen: Yes, generally all harmonic agreements are best found out by weights. Yes, the weight of a thing is properly the harmonic proportion, arising from the varying combination of various things. Also, the friendships and enmities of living creatures, and of men of the same species, and whatever else is weighed by harmonic agreement and by contrary dissonances. So the health of a man is weighed by harmony, and sickness by that which is contrary to harmony, and in the same manner, lightness and heaviness, prudence and simplicity, and many other such things, if you notice diligently.

Orator: What do you think about geometry?

Citizen: I think the nearest proportions of the circle, and the square, and all other things which belong to the difference of the capacity of figures, may be better proved by weights than in any other manner. For if you would make a vessel fashioned like a column of a known diameter and height and another cube-shaped of the same diameter and height, and then fill them both with water, by the difference of the weights you will get the proportion of the square to the circle. And in this manner you may also surmise to the squaring of the circle, and whatever else you may like to know about this. And if you would take two equal plates, shaping one into a circular column and the other into a cube and fill both with water you shall know by the differing weight of the water, the different capacity of a circle and a square of the same circumference. And having many such equal plates you may find the differences of capacities in a triangle, a five cornered, a six cornered vessel, etc. Again by using weights you may determine the capacities of vessels of any shape whatever, and to instruments of measuring and weighing, how balances are made, how a one pound weight can lift up a thousand by its distance from the center, and the various descents either straight or angled, and how all the exact instruments of ships and other engines ought to be made. For these reasons I think that this knowledge of weights is very profitable, for anything concerning geometry. You may also, if you wish, and are curious enough, determine the number of hairs, leaves, grains, sands, or of anything else in a bushel, if you put a small quantity in the balance, and taking the weight and number of them afterwards weigh the whole. For by the proportion of the one weight to the other you may know the proportion of one number to another.

Orator: You have now explained the reasons why you wished the weights of things were taken by the balance and orderly written down. It is very likely that such a book would be very profitable; important individuals could be brought together and their knowledge of various areas could be collected into one system. This would greatly facilitate a deeper knowledge of things yet hidden from us. As for me, I will never cease in promoting this everywhere.

Citizen: If you love me, be diligent in it, and so goodby.